CHURCH, WORSHIP AND HISTORY

CATHOLIC SYSTEMATIC THEOLOGY

DANIEL C. HAUSER

CHURCH, WORSHIP AND HISTORY

CATHOLIC SYSTEMATIC THEOLOGY

DANIEL C. HAUSER

Catholic Scholars Press
San Francisco - London - Bethesda
1997

Library of Congress Cataloging-in-Publication Data

Hauser, Daniel C., 1954-
    Church, worship, and history : Catholic systematic theology /
    Daniel C. Hauser.
        p. cm.
    Includes bibliographical references and index.
    ISBN 1-57309-032-8 (pbk : alk. paper). -- ISBN 1-57309-033-6
    (cloth : alk. paper)
    1. History (Theology)--History of doctrines--20th century.
    2. Liturgics--History--20th century. 3. Lord's Supper-
    -History--20th century. 4. Catholic Church--Doctrines-
    -History--20th century. I. Title.
    BR115.H5H45   1996
    231.7'6--dc20   96-31392
                                                                 CIP

Editorial Inquiries:
International Scholars Publications
7831 Woodmont Avenue, #345
Bethesda, MD 20814

To order: (800) 55-PUBLISH

Table of Contents

Acknowledgments

As any book, this work is only part of one's intellectual journey, a journey shared by others. The book is not perfect, yet I believe it makes some serious contributions to the questions that are raised by systematic theology, especially ecclesiology and sacramentology. My family members, my wife Lori and children Meagan, Alyssa, Sarah and Tom have supported me through the many hours of research and writing that the book has taken. The ever-present encouragement of my parents Bernard and Elaine Hauser has certainly been a factor in the completion of this work. My colleagues, such as John Hittinger, Kevin McMahon, Fr. Joseph Lienhard, S.J., Fr. Joseph Murphy, S.J. and Fr. George Berthold have been steadfast in their support of my work over the years. In addition, my colleagues at the College of St. Francis; Karen Kietzman, Jeff Chamberlain, Aurelie Hagstrom and Marcia Marzec have continued to support my work in and out of season. I would also gratefully acknowledge the assistance of the College of St.Francis, whose President, Dr. James Doppke, has made numerous efforts to support this project. Finally, I would like to thank Fr. Donald Keefe, S.J. for his continued support of my efforts to do theology. Over the years his intellectual insight and friendship, and not least of all prayers, have sustained me in my work on this project. As a student of Fr. Keefe, this book is in many ways a tribute to his dedication to the service of the Church. His systematic theology entitled, *Covenantal Theology: The Eucharistic Order of History,* provides much of the intellectual inspiration for this book. In effect, his work is much more comprehensive and learned than this writing. This work attempt to "unpack" some of the central points of his theology. The extent of my debt to him cannot be measured.

Introduction

Scandalized by their confessional divisions and imitating the recent efforts of Catholic-Anglican dialogue, Lutherans and Catholics today are profiting from the ecumenical shift of Vatican II. "To be sure, the first phase of post-Vatican II ecumenism frequently was theologically superficial and contributed to a climate of relativistic indifference to normative truth."[1] These early ecumenical efforts reflected an implicit theological pluralism which failed to understand the relationship of Church teaching and theology.[2] Attempts were made to unify the confession in a minimalistic and external manner that failed to resolve the deeper doctrinal differences. "To explain all these contradictions as misunderstandings seems to me like a form of rationalistic arrogance which cannot do any justice to the impassioned struggle of those men as well as the importance of the realities in question."[3] According to this approach to ecumenism, the Reformation often ends up being some kind of mistake or a misunderstanding. The "new ecumenism" does not focus upon the externals of the confessional differences, but is concerned with the very theological issues that lie at the heart of these differences.[4]

The "new ecumenism" begins with the wisdom of the Delphic oracle, "Know thyself." It rests on the belief that each Christian confession must first decide as to the central tenets of its understanding of the Christian faith before any fruitful dialogue with

---

[1] Richard J. Neuhaus, "Ecumenism and Authentic Renewel: A Response to Paul Johnson on Papal Strategy," *Catholicism in Crisis*, Dec. 1984, p. 10.

[2] Joseph Cardinal Ratzinger, "Luther and the Unity of the Churches: an interview with Joseph Cardinal Ratzinger," *Communio*, Fall 1984, pp. 214ff.

[3] Ratzinger, "Luther and the Unity of the Churches," p. 214. Also see Gerhard Ebeling, *Word of God and Tradition*, trans. S.H. Hooke (Philadelphia: Fortress Press, 1968), pp. 89ff. "Underneath the diversity and doctrinal differences we encounter extraordinarily deep-rooted and active differences in mode of thought, in the understanding of reality, and in speech whose existence seems to militate against any possibility of understanding." (p. 89)

[4] Neuhaus, "Ecumenism and Authentic Renewel," p. 9.

2

another confession can take place. So, the first step is for Lutherans to become more Lutheran, Roman Catholics more Roman Catholic Orthodox more Orthodox. Only in this way will reunion be rooted in the Christian truth which alone can be the basis for real unity, and not simply the result of cultural forces that overwhelm and distort traditional confessional beliefs.[5]

While we must recognize the fundamental agreements that offer the hope for future unity, we also must not blind ourselves to the continuing confessional differences. The demands of this "new ecumenism pose a most difficult task, but it is a task that must be undertaken with the zeal of a reformer. Ecumenical efforts must always begin with the past, attempting to reclaim those truths that are embodied in past theological dispute. Nevertheless, ecumenism needs to break through the old confessional reproaches to find new means of dealing with confessional materials and new bases for dialogue. Today, perhaps more than ever, any attempt to achieve a real unity requires "new steps."[6]

This work intends to contribute to this project. It will show that the confessional divisions are the result of different understandings of the historicity of faith. That is, the divisions between religious confessions are governed by different conceptions of the manner in which God is present to his people in fallen creation. These variations in the theology of history reflect different interpretations of the revelation and the meaning of that revelation for the faith today. Therefore, by

---

[5]Karl Lehmann, " The Focus of Discussion Today: Luther and the Unity of Churches," *Communio*, Fall 1984, pp. 196ff. Lehmann points out that one of the difficulties of ecumenical discussion is that from a Roman Catholic perspective it is hard to identify the "true" Lutheranism. His lack of systematic approach, combined with the dominance of his own spirit and religious development, makes it difficult to pin down the exact nature of Lutheranism. This is also a problem in Lutheranism from the very beginning. See Joseph Lortz, *The Reformation in Germany*, trans. Ronald Walls (New York: Herder and Herder, 1968).
    For further discussion of the problems that this represents for ecumenical discussion see Ratzinger, "Luther and the Unity of the Churches," pp. 215ff; and *The Ratzinger Report*, ed. Vittorio Messori, trans. Salvator Attanasio and Graham Harrison (San Francisco: Ignatius Press, 1985), p. 155. Also see Ebeling, *Word of God and Tradition*, p. 37. Here Ebeling points out that one of the difficult tasks of ecumenism is the need to arrive at some agreement as to what constitutes the essential unity of the churches.
[6]Ratzinger, "Luther and the Unity of the Churches," p. 214.

discovering the theology of history operative in a given confession, the essential differences between the religious confessions will be made more evident

Gerhard Ebeling supports the thesis that the Christian confessions are most profoundly divided on the question of the historicity of the Christ-event and the historicity of faith in the present. The central question dividing the Christian confessions is concerned with the ability of fallen creation to mediate the grace of Christ in the present stage of the process of salvation. Since the Christian faith has the source of its life in the revelation of Christ, "What is essential for the existence of the Church is that its proclamation and faith have constant reference to the historical event which constitutes the origin of the Church not only in the historical sense but, simultaneously, in the sense that it is the basis of the Church's existence today."[7] Ebeling continues:

> Its connection with history is an essential element in the nature of the Church. As the Church of Jesus Christ it stands or falls by its once-for-all origin which, as eschatological revelational activity of God in history, stands out as superior to all subsequent Church history. The Church continues to exist in history in virtue of its witness to this once-for-all revelation event, and its interpretation of it as continuing in our contemporary history in the present. The significance which the Person of Jesus Christ and the Holy Scriptures possess for the Church, and which is summed up in the epithet applied to the Church in the Creed, "Apostolic", is fundamental for the 's own and inalienable connection with history. Since the relation of the Church to its origin is absolutely decisive for its existence in the world today, the problem of the relation between the Church and history clearly ranks as the main problem for any attempt to describe the Confessional churches and the Confessional questions in general.[8]

---

[7]Gerhard Ebeling, *The Problem of Historicity*, trans. Grover Foley (Philadelphia: Fortress Press, 1967), p. 84.

[8]Ebeling, *Word of God and Tradition*, pp. 38-39.

4

Christians are in agreement that time takes its meaning from the revelation of God in the Christ-event, but they are divided as to how this relationship is to be understood; i.e., as to their interpretation of history and the corresponding understanding of the nature of the faith.

During the present aeon, the time of the Church, the center of Christian life is its worship, wherein the believer encounters the Christ who is the goal and source of his life. In liturgy, the Christian participates in the central event of salvation history, the full revelation of Christ, and comes to participate in the definitive revelation of the truth that alone sets one free. Consequently, any theology of history, any interpretation of the meaning of temporal existence, must begin with reflection on worship.[9] The hypothesis upon which this work is based is as follows: history is the result of a free interpretation of time and this interpretation, as communal, is liturgical.[10]

---

[9]For an example of this type of reasoning see Hans-Georg Gadamer, *Truth and Method* (New York: Crossroads, 1982) and "Hermeneutics as a Theoretical and Practical Task," ed., Frederick G. Lawrence (Cambridge, MA: M.I.T. Press, 1981), pp. 118ff. With the Reformation the interpretation of Scripture is elevated to the center of religious worship. The later hermeneutical focus of philosophy reflects this theological shift. History is the result of a liturgical interpretation of time. For a parallel significant work within Roman Catholic theology see Donald Keefe, S.J., *Covenantal Theology: The Eucharistic Order of History* (Lanham, MD: University Press of America, 1991). "The intelligible unity of the *ecclesial* affirmation of the faith, while credal and possessed of an intelligibly communicable and factually communicated content, is fundamentally liturgical; it is historically concrete rather than abstract, and is incapable of reduction to an idea or an abstract method, for the criterion of the faith, its formal object, is the revelatory presence of the risen Christ to his Church, not a theological method which might presume to a criticism of the Church's faith. As Worship, the liturgical utterance of the Catholic faith is the appropriation of the Revelation, of the Christ. Thus it is the expression of a commitment at once personal and communal to the freedom of the truth of the Revelation Who is received in the Church and to the freedom of the reality which is uttered in and by the faith of the Church in the risen Christ: i.e., to the truth of the good creation that is good because it is created in Christ." (pp. xi-xii)

[10]Gerhard Ebeling, *Word and Faith*, trans. J. W. Leitch (Philadelphia: Fortress Press, 1963), pp. 32ff. The meaning of time is judged by its relationship to the Christ-event, the center and norm of all history. Different theologies of history reflect different understandings of the relationship of the present to the revelation. Within Protestant theology of this century this focus has found articulation in the debate over the historicity of the faith. For a summary and analysis of this debate see James M. Robinson and John B. Cobb, eds. *The New Hermeneutics* (New York: Harper & Row, Publishers, 1964) and *Theology as History* (New York: Harper & Row, 1967). Also see James M. Robinson, *The New Quest for the Historical Jesus* (Philadelphia;

At the heart of this hypothesis is the presupposition that religious worship is fundamental to human life. "Man's world is an ordered world of meaning, but the organizing principle is interpreted as a revelation which comes from sources outside ordinary life. It is this source which is given (revealed) and (it) defines any further possibility of man's existence."[11] Worship is the *a priori* by which a religious people encounters reality - being itself, the divine - drawing man into the truth of existence, thereby disclosing the meaning of life. "That which is created through this meeting is nothing less than all reality which the community or assembly needs in order to live. This includes the natural, historical and the spiritual realities among which, of course, the ancients did not distinguish."[12] Since worship cannot be other than the locus of one's understanding of existence, where the truth of existence is given and appropriated, an analysis of the structure of worship cannot but yield important insights into the nature of the religious beliefs proper to a given religious or confessional tradition.[13]

Fortress Press, 1964). For a Roman Catholic discussion of this same issue see Donald Keefe, *Covenantal Theology.*

[11]Charles H. Long, *Alpha*, foreward Alan W. Watts (Toronto: Collier Books, 1963), p. 11.

[12]Sigmund Mowinkel, *Religion and Cult*, trans. J.F.X. Sheehan (Milwaukee: Marquette University Press, 1981), p. 108. Also see Joachim Wach, *The Comparative Study of Religions*, intro. Joseph M. Kitagawa (New York: Columbia Paperback, 1958), pp. 97ff. Gerhard Ebeling, *Word and Faith*, pp. 197, 199. In primitive religions the world takes its meaning from its participation in the cosmogony, the original act of creation, always a divine act. See Mircea Eliade, *The Myth of the Eternal Return*, trans. Willard R. Trask (New York: Pantheon Books, 1949); and Wach, *The Comparative Study of Religions*, p. 84. Wach points out that in these cosmogonies "a purpose is envisioned and thus the ultimate destiny of the universe will be conceived in terms of the relationship which the idea of the origin implies." In their worship these primitive peoples participate in the cosmogonic act, ordering and giving meaning to their life. That worship orders existence is also true for Judaism. It is in the cult, the historical locus of the covenantal unity between God and His people, that Israel finds the meaning of existence, a meaning that distinguishes Israel from all other primitive peoples. For the Jews worship links them to the process of salvation history, a process given in the historical, and therefore free, revelation of God to his people. See Gerhard von Rad, *Old Testament Theology*, vol. I, trans. D.M.G. Stalker (New York: Harper & Row, Publishers, 1965), p. 104.

[13]Mowinkel, *Religion and Cult*, pp. 172-173. "If the goal of worship is to impart holiness and strength to the life of society, then it follows that it includes the insight or knowledge which are necessary for society's existence. The rules and the forms of worship are insight in the most

Within the Christian tradition, the center of Church life is the Eucharistic worship. In the Eucharist, the believer participates in the New Covenant, the decisive event of all history wherin one encounters the Lord of history.

> In the New Testament context of the period following Easter this connection of the present with the events of the decisive period now past gains a special significance in worship because here the actual Christ-event, the death and resurrection of Jesus, is made present in the Lord's Supper.[14]

It is from this liturgical encounter that the Christian churches receive their life. In fact, the Eucharist can be said to be the cause of the Church, for this liturgical action gives meaning and identity to Christian existence. Consequently, to better understand the Christian faith it is necessary to understand the eucharistic worship. It is from this conviction that Gerhard Ebeling works out his theology.

According to Ebeling, what is at stake in the relationship between worship and the Christ-event is the historicity of the Christian faith.

> The central theological importance of this question becomes clear when we recognize that it is concerned with the actual realization of the once-for-all revelation of God in Jesus Christ in its relation to the origin of the Churchas the event upon which the very existence of the Church as such depends. It is here that the question of the relation of the Church to history is presented in its sharpest form. It is over the idea of the actual realization of the historical once-for-all

---

fundamental reality." A similar view is found in Eric Voegelin's work, *Order and History*, vol. I (Baton Rouge: Lousiana State University Press, 1956), pp. 2ff. According to Voegelin, the order of society is based on an approximation of the truth and its embodiment in the society.

[14]Oscar Cullmann, *Salvation in History* (New York: Harper & Row, Publishers, 1965), p. 184. As to the continued significance of the Eucharist to the life of the Christian Churches see "Catholic-Lutheran Statement on the Eucharist," *Origins*, Jan. 1979, vol. 8; no. 30, p. 468. Also see the debate concerning the sacrifice of the Mass, Paul Empie and T. Austin Murphy, eds., *Lutherans and Catholics in Dialogue I-III* (Minneaplois: Augsburg Press, 1965).

revelation event that the different churches are divided. It is therefore understandable that the meaning of the Eucharist should be a central feature of the discussion between the churches. Here the question of the actual realization of the revelation event assumes its most acute form. The answer to it affects the very existence of the Church in the world; it is decisive for its influence upon world history and the dialogue with world history.[15]

For Ebeling, the question of the historicity of the faith is of unique importance for the existence of the Church, and insight into this question requires an examination of the worship of the Church.

Since the Reformation the interpretation of the Eucharistic worship is a matter of inter-confessional dispute. Ebeling understands this dispute to be the result of different interpretations given to the relationship between the Eucharist and the Christ-event. "The revolution which the Reformation produced in the complex of questions just sketched is so tremendous that it could be said: the antithesis between Catholicism and Protestantism rests on the different understandings of the present actualization of the historical (once-for-all-ness) of revelation."[16] This division is not only to be found between Roman Catholics and Protestants; it is also to be found within Protestantism. Nevertheless, the primary division resulting from the different interpretations of the actual presence of Christ in the present time is in the split within Christianity between those who emphasize the liturgy of the sacrament and those who emphasize the liturgy of the word.

> While, according to Protestant doctrine, the whole
> Gospel is contained in the Word itself, and Gospel is

---

[15]Ebeling, *Word of God and Tradition*, p. 39.

[16]Ebeling, *Word and Faith*, p. 35. Also see Joseph Lortz, *The Reformation in Germany*, p. 260. "All baptized persons, that is, still formed a unity. Together with the real presence of our Lord in the Lord's Supper, this is the point at which a new sacramental fellowship in Christ may one day be able to restore the unity of the Church."

8

> essentially the spoken Word; according to Catholic doctrine the advent of grace in its real and full meaning is bound up with the sacraments. In the Protestant view *sola verba* is the decisive word; but this in no way excludes the sacraments in the Protestant understanding of them; on the contrary, it includes them in so far as they are only another form of the Word; the distinctive promise which they offer is none other than that of the Word itself. . . . In the Catholic view, on the other hand, the decisive word is *solo sacramento*. Of course this does not exclude the Word. It has an indispensable function for the action of grace, yet only preparatory, introductory, and following. Real grace in the full meaning of the word, justifying grace and sanctifying grace, is exclusively imparted sacramentally, a fact which only emphasizes the sole exception that, in case of need, an expressed wish for the sacrament (*votum sacramenti*) may suffice. [17]

These seemingly external differences signify a deeper division between the confessions on the manner in which they view revelation, and how they view the very nature of the historicity of the faith.

Despite the doubts of many as to whether the interpretation of the liturgical symbols as *sola verba* and *solo sacramento* remains a viable approach to confessional questions, it cannot but be significant if the Eucharist is understood to be the cause and source of the life of the Church. Through an examination of the two forms of

---

[17]Ebeling, *The Word of God and Tradition*, pp. 211-212. Also see Ebeling, *Word and Faith*, pp. 34ff. It should be noted that there are objections to Ebeling's conceptual division between the liturgy of the sacraments and the liturgy of the word. Yet contemporary scholarship that rejects this approach has not found other ground for a discussion of the issues that this division so richly articulates. The result is usually the reduction of one to the other. In most instances they argue that the event-character of the proclaimed word is identical to the event character of the sacrament. See Michael Lawler, *Symbol and Sacrament: A Contemporary Sacramental Theology* (New York: Paulist Press, 1987). Here his tendency is to reduce all sacramental theology to hermeneutics, thereby accepting the nominalist view of history, a temptation common to all Christian theology since long before the Reformation. See the introduction to Donald Keefe's *Covenantal Theology*. As a result the Catholic interpretation of the operation of the sacraments *ex opere operato* is sacrificed. See Karl Lehman, 'The Focus of the Discussion Today," pp. 169ff. For a Roman Catholic assessment of Luther's understanding of the sacraments *opus opertum* see Lortz, *The Reformation in Germany*, pp. 449-450; and Vinzenz Pfnur, "Beyond an Old Polemic," *Origins*, January 1979, vol. 8; no. 30.

worshipand their implicit understandings of the historicity of the faith the present study intends to clarify and help resolve some of the issues found in contemporary ecumenical dialogue. This examination will explore the confessional divisions between Roman Catholic and Protestant understandings of the Eucharist, between the emphasis on the liturgy of the sacrament and the emphasis on the liturgy of the Word, and the effect of these interpretations on contemporary Protestant and Roman Catholic theology.

Part I: Protestant Theology and the Liturgy of the Word

The question of the relationship of faith and history is one which continues to dominate modern Protestant theology. Theological discussions concerning the historical Jesus, the "old hermeneutics" of Bultmann, the new hermeneutics, the salvation history theologies and liberation theologies are all representative of this problem. One might even say that the question of the faith and history debate dominates all theology since the Reformation, and especially since Schleiermacher[18].[19]

In this section of the book a number of Protestant theologies will be examined to determine whether those who interpret the Eucharistic symbols in terms of the primacy of the liturgy of the word share a common understanding of the relationship that exists between faith and history. The selected theologians represent a range of contemporary Protestant theological perspectives usually characterized by their division into the new hermeneutic and salvation history theologies.[20]

The theology of the "new hermeneutic" is based on the Reformation principle of *sola fide, sola scriptura*. Just as the truth of the faith and the meaning of reality is given in the word of God and conveyed the proclamation of that word. Language is not a later addition, but from the very beginning all reality is given in language.[21] Theology then must be hermeneutics.

---

[19]Wilhelm Pauke, *From Luther to Tillich* (New York: Harper & Row Publishers, 1984).

[20]James M. Robinson, "Revelation as History," in *Theology as History*, ed. by James M. Robinson and John B. Cobb, Jr. (New York: Harper & Row, Publishers, 1967), pp 1ff. In addition to the distinction between the new hermeneutics and salvation history theologies, I would further distinguish salvation history theology from the theology of praxis.

[21]As an example of this approach to reality see Hans-Georg Gadamer, *Truth and Method* (New York: Crossroads, 1982), p. 350. In his philosophy language is the medium in which reality is given. This approach has its liturgical roots in the reformation and the nominalism that holds that the word of God alone mediates all truth, *sola fide, sola verba*.

In Ebeling's "new heremeutics," the result of his interpretation of the eucharistic symbols in terms of the primacy of the liturgy of the word, reveals an understanding of the relationship of faith and history which reflects this interpretation. That is, the historicity of the faith is informed by this worship, a faith centered on the personal encounter of the believer with the preached word of God. It will also be noted that this interpretation of the liturgy results in certain difficulties, at least in Ebeling's theology, concerning the historicity of the faith.

Another representative of the new hermeneutics, Ernst Fuchs,understands theolgy to be an extension of the work of demythologizing begun earlier in the century by Bultmann.[22] According to this hermeneutic all attempts to "objectify" the revelation are mythical and distort the subject matter of faith "These objectifying tendencies in mythological language overshadow the understanding of existence as 'eschatological' (i.e., as having no certainty in `objective' reality, whether of history or nature), an understanding which seeks to express itself through this terminology."[23] The new hermeneutic, rather than attempting to base faith on "facts," works toward a more appropriate form of expressing the faith. According to Achtemeier, "The first century conceptuality must be replaced by a modern conceptuality which will better display the understanding of existence implied in the New Testament writings."[24] The new hermeneutic arrives at its understanding of existence through its emphasis on the event character of language. It is in the event of language that the believer encounters that

---

[22]Ernst Fuchs, "What is a Language-event?," *Studies of the Historical Jesus*, trans. Andrew Scobie (Naperville, IL: Alec Allenson, Inc., 1964), pp 210-211. Also see, Osborn, "A New Hermeneutic?," pp 400-411.

[23]Paul Achtemeier, "How Adequate is the New Hermeneutic?," *Theology Today*, Vol 21:No 1, April 1966, pp 448-457.

[24]Ibid., p. 103.

which is of ultimate significance for his life. The proclaimed word of God brings our very being into question, it calls us to a decision, it brings us to faith.[25]

The salvation history theologies of Oscar Cullmann and Jürgen Moltmann, on the other hand, stress that faith is grounded in and dependent upon historical realities. Rather than understanding language as the basis of faith, these theologians maintain that history is the bearer of all reality.[26]

The relationship between revelation and history, between faith and historical mediation, will be examined in the above mentioned theolgies in their articulation of the historicity of the faith. In this way, an attempt will be made to discover the range of understandings of the relationship of faith to history among theologies which presuppose Christian worship interpreted in terms of the liturgy of the word.

---

[25]Ibid., pp 104,106. Also see James M. Robinson, "Hermeneutics Since Barth," *The New Hermeneutics*, eds. James M. Robinson and John B. Cobb, Jr. (New York: Harper & Row, Publishers, 1964), pp 1-77.

[26]Robinson, "Revelation as Word and History," pp. 26ff.

Chapter I: Ebeling and the Historicity of the Faith

The theological question that dominates the work of Gerhard Ebeling is the problem of the relationship of Church and history. On the one hand, according to Ebeling, Christianity is a historical phenomenon grounded in the revelation of God in history. On the other hand, he believes that today we are separated from those events which form the basis for the faith and are thereby distanced from these normative events. Also, since those events that form the basis of the faith are historical, the meaning of these events is subject to the changes and limits of temporal existence.[27] Consequently, the difficulty for theology is to explain how these past events, which define and sustain faith, become the source for the living faith in the present. To answer this question Ebeling utilizes what he considers to be the Reformation understanding of the relationship of faith and history.

In the broadest terms, Ebeling understands the real meaning and nature of the Christian faith to be located somewhere between two extremes: between the Roman Catholic belief which tends to identify the Body of Christ with the Church in the world, and those docetic enthusiasms of certain Christians who completely separate the true Church of Christ from any empirical reality.[28] As a representative of the "true" Reformation understanding of the faith, Ebeling believes himself to have avoided these unsatisfactory alternatives. He understands the Reformation solution to the question of the historicity of the faith, and the consequent historical nature of the Church, to be derived from a theology which centers on the proclamation of the historical revelation. The faithful receive the faith through the proclamation of the word of God. The Gospel's proclamation of the promise of salvation given in the liturgical life of the

---

[27]He accepts the modern historicist premise that all understanding is limited to a particular historical period, a specific intellectual horizon. As that horizon changes the truth about human existence changes and needs to be reinterpreted. There appears to be nothing normative or "objective" in the historical realm.

[28]Ebeling, *The Word of God and History*, 23ff.

16

Church informs the life of faith, and the historicity of that faith reflects the historicity of the proclamation.[29] Ebeling claims, then, that the locus of the redemptive activity of Christ is to be found in the worship of the Church: especially in the Eucharist as a proclamation event.

A. Worship, language and proclamation

In his effort to articulate the relationship between the confessional differences and the historicity of the faith, Ebeling distinguishes between two fundamentally different interpretations of the Eucharistic symbols. The first upholds the primacy of the liturgy of the sacrament. The other holds the primacy of the liturgy of the word.[30]

---

[29]Ibid., p. 26. Ebeling understands history to me more than simple chronology, a sequence of events (Histories). It is meaningful history (Geschichte).

[30]Ebeling, *Word and Faith*, p. 34ff. "Das Christentum steht und fällt mit der Bindung an seinem einmalig historischen Ursprung. Das Besagt zunächst: Das Christentum ist eine geschechtliche Grüsse. Es kommt aus einer bestimmten historischen Vergangenheit her und steht darum in historischer Relation zu dieser Vergangenheit. Aber der Satz, daß das Christentum steht historischen und fällt mit der Bindung an seinem einmaligen historischen Ursprung, besagt viel mehr als dies. Er enthält eine im Vergleich zu allen übringen geschechtlichen Ersheinungen paradoxe Behauptung. Er besagt nämlich nicht nur, daß der historische Ursprung des Christentum die Eigenart eines primum movens am Anfang eines geschichtlichen Entwicklungsprozesses habe, sondern schreibt diesem historischen ursprung für die gesamte geschichtliche Ersheinung des Christentums schlechtlin eine für allemal bleibende, normative, absolute Bedeutung zu. Das heißt: Dem historischen Ursprung des Christentums wird Offenbarungscharakter zugesprochen. Er ist damit Reklativität und Vergänglichkeit alles geschichtlichen Geschehens entzogen. Er bildet einem für allemal umgrenzten, vor den übringen Geschichtsphanomenen ausgezeichneten Bereich, -ein Urteil, das in der Festlegung des Kanons heiliger Schriften zum Ausdruck kommt. Die Tragweite dessen wird allerdings erst deutlich, wenn das, was als Offenbarung angespochen wird, näher umgeschrieben ist. Als Offenbarung gilt nicht so sehr - ich drüke mich bewußt unscharf aus, um der Männigfaltigkeit des Offenbarungsverständnisses, wie es uns in der Geschichte des Christentum entgegentritt, Raum zu geben - oder wenigstens nicht in erster Linie die Heilige Schrift. Denn als Offenbarung gilt nicht so sehr wenigstens nicht in erster Linie die Enthälung und Mitteilung allgemeiner zeitlos Warhheit. Offenbarung ist vielmehr primär und eigentlich ein bestimmtes, nämlich des in der Heiligen Schrift, bezeugte Geschehen und heir widerum in noch engerer Umgrenzung und in absoluter Besonderheit die Erscheinung Jesus Christi." Gerhard Ebeling, *Wort und Glaube* (Tübingen: J.C.B. Mohr, 1960), pp. 13-15. Also see *Word of God and Tradition*, trans. S. H. Hooke (Philadelphia: Fortress Press, 1968), p. 35.

These interpretations reflect essentially different views of history which, in his view, are what really separate the Roman Catholic and Protestant confessions.

Ebeling understands the difficulty of the Roman Catholic view of the Eucharist to be its sacramental emphasis: the real actualization of the event of revelation takes place primarily in the sacraments. In particular, the actualization *par excellence* takes place in the sacrifice of the Mass, where one finds a direct correlation between the grace given in the Christ-event and the presence of Christ in the Church.

> The Roman Catholic conception of the Church provides an unambiguous starting point for the definition of the essential nature of Church history. The identification of the Church with the mystical Body of Christ on the one hand, and with the historically verifiable Roman Catholic Church on the other, makes the history of the Church the direct continuation of the Incarnation and therefore of the history of Jesus Christ. In this way both the theological and the historical character of Church history remain free from ambiguity. The sanctity and unity attached to the Church belong also to its history in time.[31]

According to Ebeling, this interpretation of the historicity of the faith is problematic. Roman Catholic ecclesiology ends with the identification of revelation and its external historical form,[32] an identification unacceptable to Ebeling. The identification of the incarnate Christ with the Church fails to distinguish between the Kingdom of God and our present condition in Fallen creation.

In opposition to the Roman Catholic emphasis on the sacraments, Ebeling begins his theology with the Reformation principle that salvation is by faith alone. *Sola fide*, in its positive sense, is a statement of the first commandment - it affirms the

---

[31]Ebeling, *The Word of God and Tradition*, pp. 22-23.

[32]Ebeling, *Word and Faith*, pp. 33ff, 256ff. Ebeling points to the claims of papal infallibility as evidence of this error, the identification of divine power with it earthly mediation. Also see,

18

absolute sovereignty of God against all attempts at reducing the faith to human control. In addition, according to Ebeling, the *sola fide* principle of the Reformation functions as an anti-clerical and anti-sacramental bias.[33] It rejects works as salvific in themselves, placing the emphasis on the one sacrifice of Christ through which all are to be saved: there are no guarantees of salvation in history, except one's relationship to Christ.[34] Faith, then, is a participation in the promise given to Christ and to us through Scripture.

The proclamation of the word of God is the only link between the faith of the believer and the events upon which that faith rests. All other attempts at assurances must be forsaken.

> Revelation and the present are separated from each other in such a way that only one bridge remains: the Word alone - and indeed, lest any misunderstanding should arise, the Word interpreted as salvation, *sola gratia, sola fide*. All other bridges have been broken up. The whole system of Catholicism has thereby collapsed.[35]

Ebeling, *The Word of God and Tradition*, p. 22; and *The Problem of Historicity*, trans. Grover Foley (Philadelphia: Fortress Press, 1967), p. 89.

[33]Ibid., pp. 33ff. Also see Gerhard Ebeling, *Introduction to a Theological Theory of Language*, trans. R.A. Wilson (Philadelphia: Fortress Press, 1973), p. 39; and *Luther: An Introduction to His Thought*, trans. R. A. Wilson (Philadelphia: Fortress Press, 1970), pp. 249ff.

[34]Ibid., pp. 36, 204, 237, 295.

[35]Ibid., p. 36. The Reformation emphasis upon Scripture reflects the collapse of all other authorities.
It should be noted at this point that there is a difficulty as to the use of the term "word of God." Ebeling understands both the proclamation and the Christ-event as linguistic events. In his writing he fails to distinguish the two because they are like events, both linguistics. [Remember, for Ebeling all of reality is given in language.] In the present study I will distinguish between the proclamation of the Church and the events being proclaimed. In the text, the Word as the Christ-event is always capitalized, the word as proclaimed or preached word, or the proclamation of the word of God is in small case. Ebeling would not accept such a distinction, but I make it in order to clarify the relationship of the faith with the events at the source of the faith.

Taking as its basis that the Christian faith comes into existence by the power of the spoken word, the revelation of Christ is understood to be a linguistic event.[36]

> We could also formulate it in this way: the scriptural principle of the Reformation surrenders the unity of the Church to the hermeneutical problem and stakes the unity of the Church on the risk of existing without the security provided by a broadened concept of tradition; this is existence solely by virtue of the Church's link with the original testimony, a link which now is made extremely dependent upon the task of interpretation of this original witness.[37]

Scripture alone, as the source upon which the faith rests, is the sole locus of the encounter with the Savior, Jesus Christ. The promise of Christ given in Scripture, a linguistic event, is the source of the faith.[38]

Ebeling, following the line of thought in Luther's theology, begins with the Reformation principle that the preaching of the gospel is of primary function of the Christian faith. In this preaching, the law/gospel tension surfaces as the locus of the Protestant discussion of the nature of faith and the problem of the historicity of that faith.[39] The gospel provides a new view of reality which breaks through the bonds of the law and illumines the believers. Consequently, the gospel is not simply any word, but the gospel of Christ which brings to expression what it empowers, the salvation of Christ.[40]

---

[36]Gerhard Ebeling, "Word of God and Hermeneutics," *The New Hermeneutics*, ed. James M. Robinson and John B. Cobb, Jr. (New York: Harper & Row, Publishers, 1964), p. 78.

[37]Ebeling, *The Problem of Historicity*, p. 87. Also see Gerhard Ebeling, *The Nature of Faith*, trans. Ronald G. Smith (Philadelphia: Fortress Press, 1967), p. 24.

[38]Ebeling, *The Word of God and Tradition*, pp. 127ff. *Sola Scriptura* is the final affirmation of the position *ipse verba*, that the Holy Scriptures are the sole source of their own interpretations.

[39]Ibid., pp. 38, 67, 113, 117, 198.

[40]Ebeling, *Word and Faith*, p. 409.

20

The emphasis on the proclamation of the word of God is a direct result of the *sola fide* principle of the Reformation. *Sola fide* corresponds to *solus Christus*, witnessing to Christ as the unique source of salvation. Faith as the encounter of man with God is an "event" in which a new grace is present in the world. A "new creation" takes place as the believer is born into the life of Christ and defined by what comes to expression in Christ. According to the principle of *sola fide*, the act of faith is the sole means to salvation. In our response to this offer of grace, the act of faith occurs and is informed by the Christ-event from which it is derived.[41] If one wishes, then, to understand the historicity of the Christian faith, one must seek to examine the nature of this faith encounter.

According to Ebeling, by means of faith Christ is actualized in the life of the believer. "But the actualization of revelation, understood as the self-actualization of Christ, takes place in each individual case through the word - *sola fide, sola gratia.*"[42] This proclamation and coming to faith is a dynamic process that functions differently from the event character of the *ex opere operato* emphasis within Roman Catholicsacramental theology. Rather, faith is always intimately linked to the acceptance of the word by the believer. The proclamation, in both the preaching and hearing, constitutes the dynamic event of faith, wherein salvation becomes operative in the life of the believer. And this proclamation, which evokes faith in Jesus with the promise of salvation, is always a personal encounter.

> For the essence of personal encounter lies in the sphere of the word - whereby the word is not only the thing that demands faith but also the thing that evokes it. Faith can be directed only to the person who awakens faith. Not everyone of course can be believed, but only the person who corresponds to what he promises, who stands by his word, whose word does not disappoint, on whose word one can depend, whose word, or rather

---

[41]Ibid., 295.

[42]Ibid., 36.

who himself through his word can be the ground of faith.[43]

Faith, as a personal encounter, is always the offer of salvation *pro me*, demanding a response to a proclamation through which the source of human salvation, the grace and promise of Christ, is given.

Within the believer the exact point at which this personal response takes place is the individual conscience. This makes the conscience the locus of the contact between God and the world. Ebeling writes,

> It is true that our talk of God aims solely at the inmost being, the conscience. But precisely what happens in the inmost part has the outmost effect. The nature of man's inmost being, his conscience, is grasped only when it is clearly realized that here it is not a case of man in the abstract, separated from the world, and of his then necessarily likewise abstract relation to God; rather, the conscience is, as we said already, the place where God and the world meet.[44]

The conscience is the center of man's coming to faith the point at which belief stands or falls, viz., where one chooses belief or unbelief. As the inmost being of man, where

---

[43]Ibid., p. 209. As Ebeling describes it, salvation *pro me* is antagonistic of the Roman Catholic interpretation of the sacraments. The Catholic understands the sacramental presence to be *ex opere operato*, that is, the realization of the Christ-event takes place through the power of Christ apart from the faith of the believer. According to Ebeling, it fails to consider the appropriation of the grace of the sacrament by the believer. Protestantism, on the other hand, begins with the question of appropriation, believing it to be a constitutive part of the sacramental event.

Catholics might respond that such an understanding of sacraments might result from a failure to distinguish between the *res et sacramentum* and the *res tantum*. Consequently, such a theology would be unable to recognize the sacramental character of the Church

[44]Ibid., p. 360.

God and the world come together, the conscience is, to Ebeling the core of faith as it is manifest concretely in history.

In this theology, Christ is made present to his people through the preaching of the Church, a word-event, *solo verbo*, in which the dynamic character of the faith is revealed. Through the faith, the believer is brought in contact with those events which constitute not only the chronological origin of the Church, but which also provide the source for the act of faith in the present.[45] The same event is the historical cause of faith, as well as the cause of faith in the life of the believer in the present; i.e., the Christ-event, the source, goal and measure of all life. It is this event which is the heart of the proclamationa proclamation that engages the believers in their consciences, eliciting the act of faith.

This phenomenological approach to the faith immediately appears to pose two particular problems. First, despite the centrality and uniqueness of the Christ-event, this revelatory event appears to be indistinguishable from the rest of fallen history, not only in the particular event itself, but also in its consequences, for sin remains and the revelation appears to be subject to the ambiguities of fallen creation.[46] Since there is no "evidence" that this historical life is definitive or unique, the act of faith is reduced to a private event in the hearts of men, with no public corallary. Only in the light of faith can the revelation, as historical, be understood as the normative event of all history.[47] But such an understanding of faith leads to the dilemma that faith is only supported by certain historical events that can be understood as important by the very faith that they claim to support.

This leads to a second concern about the nature of faith as described by Ebeling. That is, how can the Christian, with his modern historical consciousness, still

---

[45] Ebeling, *The Problem of Historicity*, p. 84.

[46] Ibid., p. 74.

[47] Ibid., p. 74. Also see Ebeling, *Word and Faith*, p. 295

retain contact with and receive the benefits of this normative event, the Christ-event, a past event, which Christians claim to be the decisive event of the Christian faith? Such an understanding of the faith lacks any public realization or any temporal continuity with the source of the life of faith, thereby isolating the present from the events that Ebeling claims to be the source of the faith.

This problem, the relationship of the Christian to the source of his faith, is finally the problem of the historicity of religion. It is the problem of whether, in Christ, the fullness of the Trinitarian Godhead can enter into the fragmented, limited created order. This problem needs to be addressed from two perspectives: one, from the point of view of modern historical consciousness; second, from the point of view of fallen creation, a creation *simul justice et peccator*. In both cases the ability of creation to mediate the grace of the redemptive activity of Christ is thought to be compromised. In the first instance by temporality, in the latter instance by sin.

If one accepts the premise of modern historical consciousness, all things are the product of a particular historical period and are subject to change. The historicist premise is that there are no perennial questions, that truth is the product of the times or culture, and as the times change, the truth of the past is no longer binding on the present. Ebeling accepts this modern historicist analysis of time and the faith. He says, "There can be no *theologia perrenis*, and even the historical reality of the church is necessarily subjected to continuous change."[48] So one must ask in what manner the events of the revelation of Christ can in any sense be definitive?

Likewise, the historicist position concludes to a view of fallen creation as described by *simul justice et peccator*. In both cases history cannot be thought to mediate the full redemptive activity of Christ. Nevertheless, they differ as to the reasons why such a mediation is no longer possible. According to the historicist premise, the problem is not sin; rather, the problem is the ability of contingent temporal existence to mediate the fullness of the divine. In such a framework, history is always

---

[48]Ibid., p. 27.

24

incomplete, fragmented by the change and flux resulting from materiality. Redemption or fullness of grace cannot be found within that limited, contingent existence. It can only be found in an escape from history or at the end of history.[49] On the other hand, the view of fallen creation represented by *simul justice et peccator* likewise sees the world as fragmented, not by materiality *per se* but by sin. As a result, fallen creation is not able to mediate the fullness of the Christ-event.

If one accepts either one or both of these premises, it is difficult to see how a past historical event can be the basis for a truly living faith. This means one must raise the question again about the relationship of our present faith to the truth revealed in the life of Christ. Can the Christ-event have any significance for us and for our salvation? In answer to this problem, Ebeling holds that it is the proclamation of the Gospel message which is the connection between the present faith of the believer and the absolute revelation of God in his Son. "The only thing that can lead us out of historical difficulty is the view of history which takes its bearing on the word-event and consequently on the linguisticality of reality."[50] Ebeling develops this observation into a theological theory of language, his solution to the problem of the historicity of the faith posed by historicism and the ambiguity of fallen creation.

B. Proclamation and a theological theory of language

Ebeling uses modern philosophies of language as the foundation for his own theological theory of language. Since all reality is given in language, language is the

---

[49]Mircea Eliade, *The Myth of the Eternal Return*, trans. W.R. Trask (New York, Pantheon Books, 1949). Also see C.T. McIntire, *God History and Historians* (New York: Oxford University Press, 1977). The philosophical works that give a historicist accounting of the Christian faith are numerous. Perhaps one of the best is Spinoza's *Theologico-Politcal Treatise* where he separates true religion from any revelatory events. Others who share his definition or "redefinition" of Christianity are Hobbes, *The Leviathan* and Locke, *A Letter Concerning Toleration*. For those who give transhistorical solution for the dilemmas of history see the writings of Rousseau, Marx and Hegel.

[50]Ebeling, *Word and Faith*, p. 295.

necessary means to understanding.[51] All human experience is linguistic in nature and in language we encounter reality in all its dimensions. Not only does language make the encounter with the world possible, but language creates the horizon in which it is possible to come to some understanding of the world. The world is not first given to us and then later language is added to it; rather, the original experience of reality is given in language.[52] To use language is to be drawn into the world view that language creates.[53]

The real function and power of language is to bring to articulation those dimensions of the world which seek expression but are hidden in the confusion and darkness of our experience of the world. Language brings order and meaning to human life in the world.[54]

One important facet of language's power is its capability to make present the past and the future, the meaning of which is often hidden amid the ambiguities of fallen creation.

> The presence of the hidden indicates what the decisive
> function and power of language consists of. The
> function of language, therefore, is seen in a particularly

---

[51]Ebeling, *Introduction to a Theological Theory of Language*, pp.158-159. For a brief analysis of modern hermeneutics and its historical development see James M. Robinson, *The New Hermeneutics* (New York: Harper & Row, Publishers, 1964), pp. 1-77.

[52]Ibid., pp. 102ff. This replaces the old sign theory of language, that a word is attached to the thing it represents. Also see Robinson, *The New Hermeneutics*, pp. 6ff. "Rather than language being a secondary distorting objectification of meaning that must be removed to free the meaning behind the language, the language of the text is regarded positively as an interpretative proclamation of that meaning and hence as our indispensible access to it." The conclusion is that subject matter which is interpreted into our historical and finite language makes possible our understanding of the finite and historic world. The roots of this modern nominalism lie in the theology of William of Ockham and later traces of it are found in the Reformation, See Heiko Oberman, *Harvest of Medieval Theology* (Cambridge: Harvard University Press, 1963). For an example of its contemporary form see Hans Gadamer, *Truth and Method*.

[53]Ebeling, *The Problem of Historicity*, pp. 15ff. Learning a foreign language is a simple example.

[54] Ebeling, *Introduction to a Theological Theory of Language*, p. 126.

26

> impressive way in its power of transcending the present
> moment. It is able to make present what no longer
> exists and what does not yet exist.[55]

Just as important is the idea that language is also the basis upon which we shape reality
by encountering all that is other.

> Thus making present the past and the future and the
> bringing to light what is hidden are the characteristic
> tasks of language. To describe the function of
> language as that of a sign is not sufficient to describe
> this relationship to its subject. Rather, language brings
> about an encounter with the subject itself. One can
> describe the direction of the movement which leads to
> this either by saying that language brings the hearer to
> the thing, or that it brings the thing to him.[56]

Language creates the horizon in which men are able to enter into community, making a
personal encounter with another possible,[57] and fully mediating man's encounter with
the divine.

The fact that all being is given in language also means that when God comes to
expression he does so in words.[58] Revelation as word-event is not simply a word
about God's action in the world, but the Word of God. "For with God word and deed
are one: his speaking is the way of his acting."[59] In this theology, the word of God is a
"happening word" which reaches its fullest expression in the Incarnation. Ebeling

---

[55]Ibid., p. 54; and pp. 101, 174.

[56]Ibid., p. 102.

[57]Ibid., p. 91.

[58]Ebeling, *Word and Faith*, pp. 359ff.

[59]Ebeling, *The Nature of Faith*, p. 90, and *Word and Faith*, p. 332.

describes John 1:14 to mean, the "word became event in a sense so complete that being word and being man became one."[60]

> Thus everything now comes to this, that knowledge of God is knowing God as a Person. This, however, cannot be presented on its own, but only in the context of the doctrine of the Word of God. The doctrine of the Word of God is at heart nothing else than the doctrine of God as Person."[61]

Given in this Word is the revelation of God himself.

C. Faith as language-event

Just as all reality is given in language, so too is man's existence: our life is a language-event. "His (man's) existence is, rightly understood, a word-event which has its origin in the word of God and, in response to that word, makes openings by a right and salutary use of words. Therein man is the image of God."[62] The precise purpose of this proclamation is for man to encounter the source of all reality, the salvation given in the cross of Christ, which calls him to authentic life before God.

This proclamation has a special character, for unlike the language of man, which is subject to the ambiguities of history, the word of God stands as the norm by which man is able to come to faith.

---

[60]Ebeling, "The Word of God and Hermeneutic, p. 101. The question becomes whether such an understanding of the relationship of the Incarnate word and proclaimed word is adequate. In the tradition, the identification of the two lead to lead to monophysitism, or other monadic reductions of the divinity and humanity of Christ, as Luther and other reformers were accused of after the Reformation.

[61]Ebeling, *Word and Faith*, p. 352.

[62]Ibid., p. 327.

But the concept, the "word of God," properly understood, provides the most striking expression for what happens to man from the side of God, that is to say, for the way in which God deals with man. For with God word and deed are one: his speaking is the way of his acting. We must be prepared, in matters of the language of faith, to win free of the traditionalism which clings to formulas without understanding them and without making the responsible effort to realize them. If we refuse to do this, the really important thing, faith itself, is abandoned in favor of certain ideas of faith which we think cannot be given up. Now the concept of the Word of God holds the key position in the relation of faith and language. If we found it necessary to regard talking about the Word of God as unreal, and strictly speaking inappropriate mode of speech, then the whole Christian way of speaking of faith would be called into question. For the nature of Christian faith depends upon God himself speaking in the Word.[63]

Language is not simply equated with a written word distant or secondary to the faith of the believer; rather, it would be more precise to say that preaching is man's only access to the Christ-event, an event which is not simply the dissemination of ideas or concepts about God, but an engagement, an invitation to partake linguistically in the grace of Christ.

Notably, in Ebeling's theology there is a continuity and a tension between the Incarnation, which itself is a language event, and the preached word of God. "For this turning to man is God's humanity. His word which is directed to man is as such a human word. There is no trace of a difference."[64] Yet it is God Himself who is given in that word.

---

[63]Ebeling, *The Nature of Faith*, p. 90.

[64]Ibid., p. 92.

The revelation and the believer's response in faith is an encounter in the realm of language. The message of the Gospel becomes clear in its historical expression and demands a response from man. At this point the word-event has a normative character, where the true meaning of all words is found, and consequently of salvation. "For it is the Word which in the last analysis makes history. Where God enters history, the arch stretches from what is said to what the Word has as its goal. There life is lived in memory and expectation, between past and future."[65] History, then, becomes time interpreted in the light of this linguistic event, the preaching of God's word bringing to historical expression the full meaning of history in the reality of the Christ-event.

It has already been noted that when God comes to expression he does so in a word which discloses the reality of man in the world.[66] In the word-event, man is called to the fullness of existence: man is called to faith. As part of this process, the word of God, not as logic but in its historical function as proclamation, brings all of man's self-assurances about his existence into question and awaits an answer.[67] This description of the act of proclamation bringing reflects the influence of the *sola fide* emphasis of the Reformation.[68] It points to the sinfulness of man and forces the believer to see through the fallaciousness of any human guarantees of salvation and to admit his impotence as he stands before God. "It negates our nature, which has fallen prey to illusion; but this is the way the word of God affirms our being and makes it true."[69] It destroys all idolatry makes man aware that faith is the only means to salvation.

---

[65]Ibid., p. 94.

[66]Ebeling, *Word and Faith*, pp. 359ff.

[67]Ibid., p. 352.

[68]Ibid., pp. 351, 211ff.

[69]Ebeling, *Introduction to a Theological Theory of Language*, p. 17. In the past, hermeneutics meant a process whereby a subject came to interpret an object, resulting in understanding. The system out of which Ebeling is working, influenced by the existentialism of

The only reason why there is any talk of faith here at all
is, that the man in question has no confidence
whatsoever in himself, but is so to speak thrown
entirely off himself on the ground over which he has no
command yet which is itself endowed with infinite
power to command. Where faith is spoken of in these
stories, it is always a case of men who have grounds for
despair - which is the same as to say that the ground
of their existence is shattered - and who now (it
remains to see how), without their situation in itself
changing in any way, find ground for faith. It is
because, and only because, it is here *eo ipso* implicitly a
question of being thrown upon God, that it can be a
question of faith in that absolute sense - not of an
uncertain idea or an impotent wish, but a faith whose
certainty and power are the certainty and power of
God himself. For that reason these statements about
faith would be completely meaningless, if they were not
understood as referring to God, i.e. in such a way that
faith can exist only as a relation to God.[70]

In the dynamics of this encounter, the words that "draw us into concord and peace with
God" become the basis for justification "which is none other than the belief in creation
and the hope of the resurrection," a faith based on the miraculous power of God.[71]

In the proclamation of the word of God we encounter that which calls us to
salvation (God, the ground of existence) and to a faith which man experiences and lives
in words.[72] It is here alone that the life of the believer becomes fully grounded. In the

---

Heidegger, understands the subject matter to place the subject into question. For an analysis see
Robinson, *The New Hermeneutics*, pp. 23ff.

[70]Ebeling, *Word and Faith*, p. 233. Also see pp. 211ff, 239, 240.

[71]Ebeling, *Introduction to a Theological Theory of Language*, p. 17.

[72]Ebeling, *The Nature of Faith*, pp. 87-88, and an *Introduction to a Theological Theory of
Language*, p. 30.

act of faith man is freed to seek and find (and even become) the answer, which is proclaimed to him.

D. The proclamation of the word and the Church

Inasmuch as faith comes into existence by means of the power of the proclaimed word, it is this proclamation that is the source of the faith of the church, the People of God. The church exists "in virtue of and for the sake of the word of God" and the life of the Church reflects this worship, the liturgy of the word.[73] According to Ebeling, the word proclaimed in the church is the word of God, a word that informs the life of the church and its worship.[74]

> The word of God has absolute priority and superiority over the church as the thing that calls it to life and maintains it in life, as the constitutive ground of its existence. The church does not exist on its own alongside the word of God, but its existence has in the strict sense its true source in the word of God, so that in virtue of the fact that its existence has its source in the word of God its *actio* is nothing but *passio in quo nihil statuere, ordinare facere, sed tantum statui ordinari, fieri habet.* The *verbum dei* is *creato ecclesiae,* the *ecclesia* is *creatura verba dei.* This passivity of the church on the ground of the *actio* of the word of God does not by any means merely belong to the past as a once-for-all event by which the church is founded, but it is and remains constitutive of the being of the church in the sense of a *creatio continua.*[75]

---

[73]Ebeling, *Luther,* pp. 266-267.

[74]Ebeling, *Word and Faith,* pp. 318ff.

[75]Ibid., p. 169. Robinson, *The New Hermeneutics,* p.58. "Theologically speaking, proclamation is such a language event in which the Body of Christ is constituted; assembled. The Church as assembly takes place in the language event of proclamation. Here the distinctive Protestant definition of the Church in terms of the preaching of the Word has been restated in terms of the new hermeneutic's understanding of language."

32

In the proclamation of the incarnate Word of God the salvation of Christ is mediated to all times. By the power of this linguistic event, the salvation of Christ, absent under the conditions of fallen creation, is given as promise, a promise that is given to the church as the source of its life.[76] But ultimately ecclesial life is grounded in the individual acts of faith of the believer. One might say that the church's faith is simply the sum of individual acts of faith.

According to Ebeling, the historicity of the faith is grounded in the individual act of faith, the act of a particular human living in time and space.[77] This identification of the historicity of Christianity with the historicity of the individual believer is based on an inherent tension. On the one hand, Ebeling insists that man is unable to ground his own existence, so that the very nature of faith transcends the historical life of any particular man: human beings cannot give final and absolute meaning to their lives. In particular, it is the eschatological dimension of the faith that transcends the limits of human life in fallen creation, not yet available to man in the world. On the other hand, Ebeling insists that the faith is grounded in man, as believer, as he stands in a particular situation in the world. It is this tension, the tension between the present ambiguous faith of man and the future fullness, that remains at the center of the life of faith. Within this dynamic tension the conscience becomes the locus of the revelation of the promise, but a promise that points beyond itself to a future eschatological realization.

Ebeling describes this eschatological tension in the two inseparable dimensions of faith, the call of God and the response of man. Such proclamations as interpretations, that is, the making of the word accessible to the present, are directed to the believer's situation in space and time. Faith is never a one-time event, but a process in which one is continually called in each moment of one's life to respond to the

---

[76]Ibid., pp. 327ff.

[77]Ibid., p. 419. Human life is always lived in a linguistic horizon. This, according to Ebeling, is "concrete" in the broadest sense.

33

redemption of Christ.[78] The faith event appears then to be the source of continuity in the Church, for it is where the unity of God and man is realized in space and time. But in a real sense this is not a continuous process since each proclamation is new and each response is new. These acts of faith each manifest isolated moments in the relationship between man and God. They are acts that take place in the conscience, but lack a verifiable continuity and public historicity, both of which are characteristic of historical events. There is no doubt that such acts are real, transforming the life of the believer. Nevertheless, the question of the concrete continuity of faith still remains to be solved.

Part of the problem that Ebeling faces reflects the fact that in Protestant Christianity there is no definitive proclamation or response (except for Christ) to God's offer of grace in history. Both preaching and faith, as historical, are subject to the vicissitudes and fragmentation of a fallen creation. Consequently, outside the full unity of God and man realized in Christ, this faith event can never be definitive, even in its own limited situation, because the work of interpretation is never finished, no complete human response to the word of God is possible.[79] It only has limited, qualified significance and can never be definitive under the present sinful creation; i.e., it cannot be salvific.

The tension between the definitive revelation of God given in the Christ-event and its imperfect proclamation in the present is explained by Ebeling:

> The word of God, being at the same time both a historical and an eschatological event, is the sole basis of the continuity and unity of Church history; it does not, however, guarantee the permanence of any kind of organization, institution, religious group or system. It is not the word of God which, in the history of the Church is subject to change and movement - Jesus

---

[78]Ebeling, *The Problem of Historicity*, pp. 11, 15.

[79]Ibid., p. 14. "Not only does the translation remain imperfect with respect to the original text, always lagging behind the original, but every translation also remains part of the historical past, since every living language is involved in change." (p. 22)

34

> Christ is the same yesterday, today and forever - but
> the interpretation of this same word of God in all the
> heights and depths of the world and human existence.[80]

Consequently, man's only experience of the divine in the world is limited to that which is mediated through the partial, ambiguous proclamation of the word of God. It is discontinuous with its full manifestation, where the completeness of the revelation is given in the past Christ-event and in a future into which the full reality of Christ will return.

The nature of this mediation by means of proclamation becomes even more complex and ambiguous when one looks again to the function that Scripture performs in Ebeling's theology. According to Ebeling, a constitutive part of the living word of God is its proclamation. This is not simply a repetition of Biblical texts, but it is a personal address to the hearer that calls the hearer to a decision.[81] Scripture, as a written word and as a word belonging to the past, is not itself the word of God. It becomes the word of God only when it is proclaimed in the present.[82]

> *Sola Scriptura* is the necessary result of such an
> interpretation, since it is only in Scripture that Christ is
> to be found. But his presence in the Scriptures must
> not be thought of as competing with his presence in the
> word as preached, in the sacraments, and in the
> Church. Both these aspects of Christ's presence are
> inseparable; but the direction is irreversible; only the
> Christ to whom Scripture bears witness is the present
> Christ, and the word alone is the way of his presence,
> and only through faith. Thus Christ as the *verbum
> promissionis*, and therefore as *verbum fidei*, is the
> substance of Scripture. Since this manner of making

---

[80]Ebeling, *The word of God and Tradition*, p. 31.

[81]Ebeling, *Word and Faith*, pp. 36ff.

[82]Ebeling, *The Problem of Historicity*, pp. 14-15. Here is further evidence of the historicism in his theology. It finally divides all that is past from the present.

> his presence known in the word corresponds to his nature, the Church is and continues to be solely dependent on Scripture as the source from which she can and must continually draw afresh the contemporary proclamation of the word of God.[83]

The witness of the apostles, as found in the New Testament, is the basis for our proclamation today. Yet the possiblity of such a proclamation is questionable, for the Church's own historicity relativizes the witness of each age. Consequently, one must ask, is not even the witness of the apostles relativized by its historical context and thereby sacrificed as the norm for the preaching of the word of God? "Even the earliest community was not only in continuity with Jesus, but in divergence from him, it was not merely an understanding community, but also a misunderstanding one."[84] As a fragmented witness in the fallen world, the witness to Christ (the proclamation) like all things in history, stands in both continuity and discontinuity with the Christ-event. As such, though, the value of such a witness always remains ambiguous.

Ebeling holds that the Christ-event remains normative for the life of Christian faith, but on account of his historicist assumptions about time, he creates the problem of how to determine the exact nature of this "normative event."[85] If one understands the historical as being subject to the ambiguity of the vicissitudes of space and time, there is a sense in which there can be no normative dimension of any historical event, even that of Christ. Temporal existence is limited and thereby fragments reality. History, as simple chronology, relativizes the significance of each particular event to a certain temporal period.

---

[83] Ebeling, *The Word of God and Tradition*, pp. 135-136.

[84] Ibid., p. 149. By continuing along this line, Ebeling calls into doubt the canon of Scripture. According to him, it cannot be turned into and authoritative basis for the faith.

[85] Ebeling, *Word and Faith*, p. 32.

Certain problems occur when one tries to reconcile this understanding of history with traditional ideas of the Incarnation, the full revelation of God in history. Ebeling accepts the normative nature of the revelation given in Christ, yet he holds to a theory of history which appears to prohibit such a revelation. If the only solution would be to say that the normative character of the Christ-event is eschatological, revealed at the end of time, then one must ask about the value of the life, death and resurrection of Christ for the life of faith.

The ramifications of this problem are many, but the most important one poses a question about the possibility of faith in the present. For, if the mediation of the Christ-event takes place through the ambiguous proclamation of the Christ-event, then it is difficult to discern how the conscience can have historical access to the Christ-event.

> By definition conscience calls with a measure of certainty; but existentially, as a matter of fact, it does not speak with so certain a word that it can actually bring forth a response in freedom, history and truth. Existentially the call of conscience is at the same time a call for a saving act of God, for God himself. If man is to be saved, God must act so that man can become certain about and have faith in the word of conscience as the word of God. Man's separation in the uncertainty from his conscience must be viewed then as his separation from God; and when God establishes man's conscience in certainty and freedom, he reconciles man with himself.[86]

Faith, as based upon an always partial proclamation of the word of God under the present conditions of historical existence, cannot be defined as a direct historical human encounter with the fullness of the divine. The conscience, the point of encounter between God and man, must either transcend time and space or simply be only an ambiguous historical access to the revelation of Christ.

---

[86]Robert Osborn, "A New Hermeneutic?" Interpretation, October 1966, Vol. 19-20, p. 407.

Of course it is ambiguous, as all events are. But it is noteworthy that faith today, as always, appears as an event. For this reason the relation between faith and history is perhaps different, even radically different from what is commonly supposed. We must first note something that is both simple and basic; faith comes to us out of history, and it takes us into its history. Even what we are doing here is a participation in the history of faith. For faith is not some kind of innate truth of reason, which we may come upon of ourselves and which we can recall as we please. Nor is it a purely inward happening which concerns us solely in our private existence. Rather, faith comes into being as the consequence of the witness of faith. And it depends for its nourishment on the constantly renewed witness, the word of faith. That is to say, it comes into being, and continues in being, when it is handed on, in tradition. However manifold the effects and consequences of faith, its primal and real expression consists in its holding to the fact that it is faith. That is, it holds by the place of its origin, it confesses its origin, it declares that it is bound once for all to this its origin, in a simple once-for-all decision in the way that only birth and death, of all that may happen in history, are simply once for all.[87]

Ebeling is here insisting that faith is a decisive event for man. Yet at the same time, in that all of human history is ambiguous, lacking actual public or historical expression in the present. It becomes difficult to determine the exact nature of this "faith event."

E. The historicity of the faith and the liturgy of the word.

In Ebeling's theology, the events of faith and the events of revelation are unlike other events in human history. There is a certain disjunction within the temporal realm,

---

[87]Ebeling, *The Nature of Faith*, pp. 24-25.

38

since the full meaning of these revelatory events is not accessible to man outside the context of faith.[88] Still, Ebeling insists that like all events in time, the faith affects the whole person and not simply some private, personal dimension. "Its reality is obviously of the nature of an event, which effects a total transformation, and yet never becomes a possession, but remains an event - the justification of the sinner which lasts as long as the sinner lives."[89] "It ought rather to be clear that faith is an event, but not, as is so often said, a spiritual event taking place in the inwardness of the believing subject, but an event taking place in relation between the existing person and that which is outside himself, namely, God."[90] Even though the act of faith is an external event that has its source outside of each man, the act is definitive of the believer's life, the basis upon which the true meaning of reality becomes intelligible. This faith relationship, then, is not something added to man's autonomous existence in the world, rather, it is this relationship which is the ground of the reality of the very existence of the believer and his world.[91]

Ebeling explains that the central dynamism of this faith is the tension between belief and unbelief. "The decisive thing in the event of faith is indeed its arising, that is, the turning from unbelief to faith. And this must always determine anything else that we have to say about faith."[92] This is a struggle, a struggle for faith and true existence, that finds its locus in the conscience, affecting the whole of man's existence and giving it new meaning.[93] Since it affects the whole person, the act of faith cannot be reduced to any momentary decision or any one dimension of human life. Also, as a temporal

---

[88]Ebeling, *The Problem of Historicity*, p. 74.

[89]Ebeling, *The Nature of Faith*, p. 127.

[90]Ibid., pp 164-165.

[91]Ebeling, *Word and Faith*, pp 297ff. Also see Ebeling, *The Nature of the Faith*, pp 168-169.

[92]Ebeling, *The Nature of the Faith*, pp 165-166.

[93]Ibid., pp 168-169.

act, faith must have a "public" dimension. But this description of the dynamics of faith again raises the question of the historicity of the faith, an activity whose locus is the conscience. It is precisely on this point that one finds a certain amount of ambiguity in Ebeling's theology.

Ebeling does insist that faith is not an isolated event, but has continuity, since in the act of faith one enters into the dynamic struggle between belief and unbelief which permeates the existence of each individual Christian. In a moment of personal decision, the individual enters into this struggle for faith which makes the Christian's view of the world intelligible.

On the other hand, the continuity of the worship of the Church is linked to the preaching of the Gospel, where the individual is brought into this struggle between belief and unbelief. Despite the fact that this periodic preaching is public, it lacks the continuity by which history is constituted. "The communication of the word of God is not a continuous process, but is only given in the constantly renewed interpretation of Holy Scripture. This interpretation is not to be separated from its relation to the actual assembly of those who hear it, and as hearers fulfill it. Herein lies the genuine historical character of the word of God."[94] In preaching, the promise of salvation is given to each individual, placing him in a new relationship to God which depends solely on God, who manifests himself in the preaching of the Church. But the hearing of the word is itself only partial and has no demonstrable unity. According to Ebeling, the faith event is not so much anchored in spatio-temporal existence, as fragmented by it. Yet, the faith needs to be ever renewed in the believer's response to the proclamation of the word of God.[95]

---

[94]Ebeling, *The Problem of Historicity*, p. 15.

[95]This dilemma over the historical mediation of the grace of Christ in fallen creation takes us to the central problem of all theology. In one sense most Christians would agree that Ebeling is correct when he states that no one act of faith is ever final and definitive of the human life of faith. All of our acts, our responses, to the grace of God are limited by the ambiguities of fallen creation therefore the final act of salvation rests upon the power of God to save us. On the other hand, one might debate the issue as to whether the fullness of the grace of Christ is "actually"

40

This understanding of the nature of faith has implications for the Church and its relationship to history. If the faith event, is the sole point in which God and man are united in the present, it is this faith which provides the continuity in the Church. "[T]he unity of the church is a present reality at every moment, just as truly as this origin of the church, as a genuine, believing relationship to Jesus Christ, is a present reality and a present basis of the church's existence (although this admittedly remains a hidden reality whose hiddenness must be attested at every moment, because it is revealed to faith alone)."[96] In this theology, the Church has no integrity apart from the lives of the believers, for it is in their lives that the act of faith - the unity of God and man - has its locus.

Despite the inability of the fallen creation to mediate the fullness of Christ, Ebeling still holds the Church to be historical. Its historical character rests on the preaching of God's word. "The fact still holds good that from the moment of the Church's birth in the Easter event, it has entered into history, and exists in history by virtue of the witness of Jesus Christ fulfilled in the interpretation of Holy Scripture which means in the first place the Old Testament."[97] This witness forms the basis for the preaching of the Church.

> Altogether this means that man exists authentically as he lives in history, in a movement from word to word. We have also stated that faith opens up to man the meaning and truth of his present situation, or rather, that faith is meaningful experience in the present situation. Conscience is the concept which holds these two meanings of the "word" together and which ties them to the present situation.[98]

present here and now, or is it only present as "promise," something to come at the end. This appears to be the vital question at the heart of any serious theology.

[96]Ibid., p. 97.

[97]Ebeling, *The Word of God and Tradition*, p. 27.

[98]Osborne, "A New Hermeneutic?," p. 406.

In the event of preaching the relationship between God and man finds its focus.[99] Still, Ebeling affirms time and again that this preaching is fragmented and ambiguous as is all human existence. It is a faith that is discontinuous with the past and future and, as fallen, cannot be historical in any concrete sense.

But this creates a problem if historicity is understood to be constituted by a public expression and public continuity. Since in Ebeling's theology the real continuity of the Church resides in the non-observable acceptance of each individual believer of the promise of the salvation accomplished in Christ, the Church lacks this public continuity. We may agree with Ebeling that "The Church has never existed, not even in primitive Christianity, as a demonstrable and undisputed unity."[100] But it is exactly the insistance that such a unity is "historical," a unity incapable of a reliable communal or public expression, that is problematic.

A Roman Catholic may refer to the Church as the sacrament of the Kingdom. This means the Church, acting like a sacrament, stands in continuity with the incarnation, the historical presence of Christ, continuing to mediate the fullness of redemption offered in Christ. The burden, then, of Catholic theology is to show the nature of the historical continuity of faith with the Christ-event, and the consequent burden of articulating a supporting ecclesiology and theology of history. This door is closed to Ebeling: he must solve the problem of the unity of history not by a sacramentology, but by a theology of the preached word of God.

In his theology, Ebeling holds that the word is proclaimed in the world, yet it is independent of any historical manifestation in the Church. "And to confuse the *vera unitas ecclesiae* with the organizational unity of an ecclesiastical body inevitably leads to a false view of the true unity of the church, because precisely then non-essential marks are elevated into essential marks of unity and consequently to essential marks of

---

[99]Ebeling, *The Word of God and Tradition*, p. 29.

[100]Ibid., p. 95.

42

the Church."[101] The Church's true unity and continuity lie in the discrete acts of faith, possessing no temporal continuity, wherein the believer encounters the source of his faith. Any attempt to confuse this faith with structures or to elevate what is non-essential to the rank of essential leads destroys the faith, leading the faithful astray. Such a condemnation of idolatry reflects the truths behind the *sola fide* principle of the Reformation, where the true faith cannot be mediated in and by fallen creation. As a result, a kind of vacuum exists in the midst of fallen history and the fullness of the faith; its unity and continuity are only given in the eschaton.

Such an understanding of faith leads to the difficulties related to Ebeling's understanding of the historicity of the faith. On the one hand, Ebeling points to the "internal" continuity of faith, but this lacks any concrete public expression. On the other hand, Ebeling holds that the proclamation of the word of God is the source of continuity, but he also admits that this preaching is fragmented and momentary. One must either define historicity in the light of a personal existential decision for the life of faith, leaving one to guess at the meaning of revelation and history, or one must seek to look for ways of linking the faith experience and spatio-temporal existence.

F. Summary: Faith and history

The key to unravelling the problem of the historicity of faith is in Ebeling's Christology. The historicity of the faith is determined by the manner in which the once-for-all event of Christ is said to be present in time.[102] Yet Ebeling nowhere locates the unambiguous representation of the Christ-event in the present since all that remains in time are the fragmented and ambiguous acts of faith, which may affect our life profoundly, but as partial these actions cannot definitively determine the question of our salvation. This conclusion begins with a certain understanding of creation as fallen,

---

[101]Ebeling, *Word and Faith*, p. 182.

[102]Ibid., p. 35.

and thereby ambiguous. Ebeling is well aware of this problem and he attempts to solve it by emphasizing the eschatological character of faith.

According to Ebeling, the faith is never given completely in experience, but awaits the future.

> We have at all times something that is not an object of experience, and therefore not completely given in the finished sense of the perfect tense. This aspect of eluding experience is positively characterized as the quality of being still to come, being future, having to be awaited . . . . For the ground of the fact that God encounters us only in word is, that his encounter has purely the character of promise.[103]

The word of God is simply the promise of a future presence of the fullness of Christ, a fullness not present now, except as promise. The direction of faith is toward the future, toward that which fulfills faith.[104]

The liturgy of the word, as based on the promise of the word of God, gives life to the Church. And just as the revelation of God will come again in the future, so too the Church's destiny is linked to that future. It is an eschatological Church, which as inviolable does not exist in the world.[105] Consequently, there can be neither historical unity or continuity, nor can there be a Christian confession which is infallible. The Christian must be viewed as moving toward the Kingdom of God, a kingdom not of this world,[106] since the finite world offers no definitive presence of the redemption of God. "The holy and eschatological people of God" look beyond the fallen world.[107]

---

[103]Ebeling, *Word and Faith*, p. 413.

[104]Ibid., pp. 171, 240.

[105]Ebeling, *The Word of God and Tradition*, pp. 52-53.

[106]Ebeling, *Word and Faith*, p. 170.

[107]Ebeling, *The Problem of Historicity*, p. 100.

44

"It is in one's relationship to Jesus Christ, that is, in faith, that the eschatological act of God takes place. Here Jesus is present, the dominion of the world has come to an end, the eternal life becomes real in the midst of time."[108] "In the present living union with Jesus Christ the believer becomes contemporary with the whole history of the Church and enters into the communion of saints, which transcends not only space but time."[109] "If the eschatological act of God takes place in our relationship to Jesus Christ, this relationship apparently cannot be historical, to the extent that historicity involves change."[110]

In these statements one sees clearly the dichotomy which plagues the theology of Ebeling. On the one hand he states that the living Christ is "contemporary" with the Church, and on the other, Christ is said to be present in a history which does not change. It would seem that he tends to reinterpret history not in terms of the present significance of time and space, but in the light of the eschatological event, an end into which the meaning of every present fades. The eschatological faith, rather than submerge man in the world, tends to submerge man in the non-historical reality of Christ, accessible only at the end. The reality of Christ since the resurrection transcends time and space. It must be asked if this is really an historical faith.

The key to Ebeling's theology of history rests in his emphasis on the mediation of the Christ-event through the proclamation of the word of God. It is here alone, in the liturgy of the word, that the promise of salvation is given to man. History, as it

---

[108]Ibid., p. 100.

[109]Ebeling, *The Word of God and Tradition*, p. 30.

[110]Ebeling, *The Problem of Historicity*, p. 100.

reflects this interpretation of the Eucharistic symbols, itself remains ambiguous and unredemptive. Redemption is either future, transcending space and time, or quite simply is outside space and time.

Chapter II: Ernst Fuchs - The Meaning of History

Like Ebeling, Ernst Fuchs begins his theology by proposing the need for a new interpretation of the traditional language of the faith. He presupposes that the modern world is remote from the origins of Christianity; consequently there is the need to interpret the traditional language of faith so that modern man can have access to the definitive revelation of God in Jesus Christ. The problem of the faith, then, becomes a linguistic problem, ultimately of interpreting the New Testament proclamation. Fuchs tries to solve this problem with what he describes as a theology of the word.[111]

A. Language and faith

Fuchs assumes that the liturgy, as all reality, is mediated by language. It is through language that all of being expresses itself.[112]

> [T]he question arises: is there reality without language? One must answer no. The common opinion that reality is constituted before being seen or perceived proves to be a half truth. There is no seeing or perceiving without understanding. But there is no understanding without the active possibility of language. Language does not consist of only the audible expression of meaning content. Nor is language necessarily speech. Rather, language is primarily a showing or a permitting to be seen, a signifying in an active meaning.[113]

---

[111]Ernest Fuchs, *Hermeneutik* (Tubingen: J.C.B. Mohr, 1970), pp 91ff.

[112]Ibid., pp 126ff.

[113]Ibid., p. 131. This quotation was translated into English by Joseph Weber, "Language-event and Christian Faith,"*Theology Today*, 1965, Vol. 21:No. 1, pp 450ff. James M. Robinson points to the evidence of the influence of Heidegger here. See "Hermeneutics Since Barth," in *The New Hermeneutics*, eds James Robinson and John B, Cobb, Jr., (New York: Harper and Row, Publishers, 1967) p. 49. Also see Achtemeier, "How Adequate is the New Hermeneutics?," *Theology Today* , April 1966, Vol. 23; No. 1, pp 101ff. He points out that Fuchs assumes that that which comes to expression in language always clarifies. There appears to be a simply univocal relationship between language and reality, a questionable assumption. Achtemeier

48

Language gives us the horizon in which we live, expressing reality (Wirklichkeit) and giving us access to that which constitutes reality. Language is not something external to human nature, a secondary addition, a mere conceptualization; rather, language is a mode of encounter in which humanity confronts itself and that which is other.[114] Language seeks an answer, the answer being man himself. "Man exists therefore between call and answer. He is called by language, and he answers by language and thus man is essentially 'linguistic' in his existence."[115] Likewise, since Being confronts man in language, it is only in language that man can understand reality. The question of the nature of the faith, sacraments and history, then, must be understood in terms of the historicity of language.[116] It is in human language that the reality of God is mediated.[117]

Fuchs often points to the linguistic character of reality which finds one of its expressions in human language. He finds this human expression in language an important starting point for understanding the faith.[118] Faith is an encounter with God, an encounter with the revelation of the unfathomable fullness of God. According to Fuchs this encounter has no particular external form, nor can it be conceptualized, for whenever the revelation is said to coincide with its "symbol" (the identity of sign and signified) revelation becomes reduced to an object. Against such attempts to confine

---

himself points out that "Since language and reality do not overlap, it must be possible for language to give distorted expression to reality, and thus hide, or obscure it." (p. 118)

[114]Ibid., p. 97.

[115]Achtemeier, "How Adequate a New Hermeneutic?," p. 108.

[116]Weber, "Language-event and Christian Faith," pp 451ff. "Hence language appears to be critical responding to the 'call' of being which comes through language. Being is that which calls man to become what he should be. Being is that primal relationship to which existence points. This relationship is possible on the basis of language, but the ground of language is Being, which calls through language." (pp 451-452)

[117]Ibid., pp 126ff.

[118]Ibid., p. 113.

the presence of God to a certain location, object or concept, Fuchs understands linguistic mediation as a relationship that frees God's activity from any human reductionism. All attempts to objectify the free activity of God distort the truly free nature of the faith which understands faith as a dialogue, a personal encounter between God and man. Such temporal mediations tend to objectify this revelation of God and must be avoided.[119]

To guard against all such objectifications, Fuchs asserts that the call of God comes to us from a distance; outside the sphere of human worldly power.[120] The call of God, the source of faith, comes to us as word. "Faith is a speech-event, an event which comes from and leads to speech."[121] It is the pure response on the part of man to the question posed to him by the revelation of God in Jesus Christ.[122]

Within this theology, the significance of the incarnation of Christ is to bring to expression the fullness of the revelation of God. The revelation of God in Jesus Christ is rooted in Jesus' consciousness of God's presence in his time and his identification of the presence of God with his own presence.[123] In his Christology, Fuchs does not speak of the relationship of Jesus to the Father in the traditional Nicene manner.

---

[119]Fuchs, *Hermeneutik*, p. 122.

[120]Fuchs, "Die sakramentale Einheit von Wort und Tät," *Zeitschrift fur Theologie und Kirche,* 1971, Vol 1:No 2, p. 222.

[121]Robert Osborn, "A New Hermeneutic?," *Interpretation*, Oct. 1966, Vol. 20, p. 401. Osborn is quoting Fuchs, *Zur Frage nach dem historichen Jesu,* (Tubingen: J.C.B. Mohr, 1960), p. 379.
Both Fuchs and Ebeling share the problems of a theology beginning with the hermeneutical principle that all of reality is given in language. As a result he fails to distinguish between the Christ-event and the proclamation. Since both are "language-events" this lead sto confusion in their theology an for the reader.

[122]Faith as a language-event stands in tension with the efforts to root all faith in historical events. It understands such efforts as objectifications and therefore distortions of the faith. See Achtemeier, "How Adequate is the New Hermeneutics?" p. 110; and Weber, "Language-evet and Christian Faith," p. 455. For this reason Fuchs rejects the problem of the historical Jesus which he understands to be an attempt to objectify the faith.

[123]Gerald B. O"Collins, S.J., "Reality as Language: Ernst Fuchs' theology of revelation," *Theological Studies*, 1967, Vol 28, p 78.

50

Rather, he understands the relationship of Christ to the Father to be a linguistic event understood in terms of the linguisticality of reality where God reveals himself to us in His Word, Jesus Christ.[124]

Despite the fact that the revelation comes from outside of "this World," it is precisely this revelation in Christ that is the source of our faith. The revelation in Christ is the locus of the proclamation of the word, the center at which the believer encounters the source of faith. In this encounter, Jesus demands that the hearer make a decision to echo the response of Christ to the call of the Father.[125] "All that Jesus could do was to grasp the 'time' of the rule of God in a new way; i.e., he could attempt to make the time of the rule of God his own."[126] Our "faith in Jesus," then, is not simply a belief in doctrine about him. Rather, our faith is a response to the decision, one of perfect obedience to the Father, which took place in Jesus and is now offered to us through His Word. God acts for us in Jesus, where the fullness of the act of faith is revealed as the repetition of Jesus' decision for God.[127]

Here, what is of primary importance for the life of faith are not the events of Jesus' life, but the word character of the Christ-event. Faith is not grounded in what "happened" to Jesus, rather what is decisive is the proclamation "by" and "about" Jesus.

> For faith, reflected for example in discipleship, arose as
> the result of his preaching. So his preaching may

[124]Ernst Fuchs, "Sola Fide, *Zeitschrift fur Theologie und Kirche*, 1976, Vol 73: No 3, pp 311ff.

[125]Ernst Fuchs, "The Quest of the Historical Jesus," in *Studies of the Historical Jesus*, trans Andrew Scobie (Naperville, IL: Alec R. Allenson, Inc., 1969), p. 22.

[126]Ibid., p. 23.

[127]Ibid., pp. 28ff. According to Fuchs, the resurrection is the acclamation of those who make the decision as Christ. Just as Christ chose to be obedient to the Father, obedient unto death, so too.all beleivers participate in the same decision. The acclamation of the resurrection is not the reaction to the bodily resurrection of Christ, but the product of the faith of those who share in the obedience of Christ. Also see Ernst Fuchs, "Jesus and Faith," *Studies of the Historical Jesus*, trans Andrew Scobie (Naperville, IL: Alec R. Allenson, Inc., 1964), p. 63 and Weber, "Language-event and Christian Faith," p. 454.

reflect basic experiences of faith as well... what is decisive is not in the first place the content, but that Jesus spoke at all. Only then too we come to grips with the content of his preaching.[128]

Both the decisive character of the event (the call of God) and our access to the event are linguistic. "The new factor lies purely in the event of a proclamation of this kind, and therefore in its unconditional nature: Jesus' word applied unreservedly to whoever accepts it."[129]

The encounter of man and God creates a new situation in which the believer is called to respond ever anew. Faith is simply a response, or a series of responses, to the proclaimed word of God: that our being (Dasein) should be totally dependent upon God.[130] "If faith, because of its decision, is termed the representative of Jesus, preaching is now revealed as the new representative of God. God comes to us in his question to us, as in Jesus so through the preaching about Jesus."[131]

B. Proclamation, sacraments and the liturgy of the Word

According to Fuchs, revelation, which is the source of faith, is not against time, but in time; taking place in the full historical situation.[132] Like Ebeling, Fuchs understands that one can best understand this mediation through an examination of the

[128]Ernst Fuchs, "The New Testament and the Hermeneutical Problem," *The New Hermeneutic*, eds. James M. Robinson and John B. Cobb, Jr. (New York: Harper & Row, Publishers, 1964), p. 123.

[129]Ernst Fuchs, "Jesus' Understanding of Time," *Studies of the Historical Jesus*, trans. Andrew Scobie (Naperville, IL: Alec R. Allenson, Inc., 1964), p. 141.

[130]Fuchs, "The Quest for the Historical Jesus," p. 30.

[131]Ibid., p. 30.

[132]Fuchs, *Hermeneutik*, pp 94-95.

worship of the Church.[133] This worship is understood in terms of the proclamation of the word of God.[134] In continuity with the Reformation, Fuchs defines the sacraments in terms of the liturgy of the word. "Hence I can describe the 'sacramental' happening as the hermeneutical principle of faith."[135] The sacraments are understood to be an eschatological gathering of the People of God, whose unity is both caused by and nourished by the word of God, its unifying principle.[136]

Following Luther, Fuchs understands that the sacraments are not works, because the power of the sacraments belongs solely to God.[137] The purpose of the sacraments is to increase faith - participation in the life of God. They bring about a unity between the believer and God, a unity not the result of any human program, but the result of a participation in the eschatological Kingdom of God through the proclamation of the word of God.[138] In faith, one leaves behind the profane world, where deceit, error and untruth dominate and fragment reality. One moves beyond the illusion of this worldly unity, to a "real" unity given in the promise of the word.[139]

In his description of the Lord's Supper, Fuchs equates the presence of the Lord in the sacrament with his presence at the final coming. It is not the Lord himself that is present in a localized manner, rather, the sacraments of the Church are the word and promise of this Lordship. It is in this promise, the promise of Lordship, that unity

---

[133]Fuchs, "Die sakramentale Einheit von Wort und Tät," pp. 219ff. "Diese Geschichte is deshalb ein sakramentale Vorgang weil da wie in der Szene Fuss waschung Wort und Tät zu jener Einheit zuasammengefuhrt sind, in welcher das Wort durch die Tät eingelast wird wie das Wort als das Tät hervorscheint, ja selber Tät ist." (p. 210)

[134]Robinson, "Hermeneutics Since Barth," p. 55.

[135]Fuchs, "What is a Language-event?" p. 210.

[136]Fuchs, "Die sakramentale Einheit von Wort und Tät," p. 220.

[137]Fuchs, "Sola Fide," p. 309.

[138]Fuchs, "Die sakramentale Einheit von Wort und Tät," pp 213-214.

[139]Ibid., p. 213.

53

resides.[140] The unity of the Church consists of an eschatological unity in the Spirit in which all things are made anew and all become one in Christ (Gal. 3:26-28).[141]

What is at stake in the sacraments is the same thing that takes place in every act of faith, without distinction. The sacraments have no particular intrinsic primacy; they are simply one among several forms of the proclamation. Through the proclamation of the word of God, the believer comes to share in the future fulfillment of Christ, a fulfillment not simply an ideal, but extremely practical and concrete. In the sacraments, as in all forms of proclamation, the believer partakes in the events which are of ultimate significance for his life. Sacramental worship is an event of word and deed by means of which the believer's world is transformed to a life in Christ.[142]

C. Faith and history

At the heart of this theology is the postulate that faith is a decision to believe. It is essentially the "hearing" of the proclamation, a hearing that demands a response and that evokes faith in the believer.[143] The proclamation is a call, as for Abraham, to an "all or nothing" decision, to accept or reject God, the most fundamental dynamic of human existence.[144] Faith is a choice between the flesh (self-affirmation) and the spirit (self-surrender), the decision to put on a "new Man."[145] The one to whom this call is addressed, the believer, is the focal point through whom God enters the world.

---

[140]Ibid., p. 215.

[141]Ibid., pp 215-216.

[142]Ibid., pp 218ff.

[143]Ernst Fuchs, "Translation and Proclamation," *Studies of the Historical Jesus*, trans. Andrew Scobie (Naperville, IL: Alec R. Allenson, Inc., 1964), p. 197.

[144]Fuchs, "Sola Fide," p. 307.

[145]Fuchs, "Translation and Proclamation," pp 202-203.

54

Like Ebeling, Fuchs views the conscience as the focal point of the decision and therefore the key to understanding the historicity of the faith. "The struggle with the world does not become easier or more abstract but more earnest and concrete when it is fought out in the conscience."[146] In the conscience man is confronted with the nothingness of the world and the possibilities of faith.[147] In the conscience, the struggle with fallen creation takes place, ever seeking to be established by God in certainty and freedom.[148] It seeks that which can ground its existence in an absolute manner, but unfortunately in the present such a unity is hindered by sin. However, in the proclamation of the Word the battle for faith and freedom occurs, for it is in language that the truth of the revelation of God is proclaimed. Man's conscience is a response to the proclamation of the word of God. In this decision history comes to have meaning.

It should be remembered that history is time interpreted in the light of that which is decisive for life; i.e., that which is considered to be of ultimate significance for the existence of man. Accordingly, for the Christian, history should be understood in terms of the decision for faith, because it is in that decision that man encounters the ground of his existence. Yet faith is not to be understood as some objective reality, an objective knowledge in the possession of man, rather it is an event which demands the response of man to the proclamation of the promise of salvation. And, as simply eschatological, this faith-event lacks full public historical expression. It is faith founded upon the promise of an eschatological fullness.

In this faith the believer decides to turn from the nothingness of fallen existence. But such a turning requires the preaching of the Gospel, since it is the only context wherein freedom for salvation is possible. Without this freedom man is held captive by the ambiguities and divisions within the fallen creation. (An example of this

---

[146]Ernst Fuchs, "Language of Faith," *Studies of the Historical Jesus*, trans. Andrew Scobie (Naperville, IL: Alec R. Allenson, inc., 1964), pp 70,71.

[147]Ibid., p. 70.

[148]Osborn, "A New Hermeneutic?, p. 407.

is the separation of word and deed.) "If God's will is to call to salvation in the present, there can be no more explicit obedience in the present than that the call should be heard and accepted. But the calling gives freedom."[149] Since a person is called by the preaching of the word of God, that person now stands in a new relationship to everything. The present moment is more than simply a moment of transition to the future, it is the moment in which man as a believer participates in the future redemption.[150] All time now stands in the light of the moment of decision. This is the center of all possible historical meaning.

Since man's relationship with God is dependent on his access to the source of his faith through language, "God is nowhere closer to us than in the word. Therefore we will be closest to him as soon as everything depends on the word."[151] Since all faith is dependent upon the word and the word is dependent upon God, faith is understood to be a gift.[152] Fuchs affirms this by his emphasis on the non-objective character of faith. He says, "The question of how faith arises remains hidden. That it arises through public preaching is no satisfactory answer, it only pushes the question further back."[153] Faith avoids all human attempts to control it. Faith, *sola fide*, finds its sole source in the will of God.

According to Fuchs, one of the major tensions that occurs on account of this hidden character of the faith is the tension between the docetic negation of the significance of all that is visible and the danger of false objectification of the faith. For

[149]Fuchs, "Jesus' Understanding of Time," p. 144.

[150]Ibid., p. 144.

[151]Ernst Fuchs, "Language in the New Testament," *Studies in the Historical Jesus*, trans. Andrew Scobie (Naperville, IL: Alec R. Allenson, Inc., 1964), p. 82.

[152]Fuchs, "Sola Fide," p. 307.

[153]Ernst Fuchs, *Glaube und Erfahrung, in Gesammelte Aufsatze*, vol. III (Tubingen: J.B.C. Mohr, 1965), p. 29. Translation by Gerald B. O'Collins, "Reality as Language," p. 81.

56

Fuchs, the latter is the greater danger and his theology reflects an attempt to avoid it.[154] In the human conscience one finds the struggle for faith between the visible and the real, which calls for the internal transformation of man.[155] *Sola fide* calls for a real human appropriation of this faith, and guards against any external assurances of justification. Contrary to "external works," it is the faith alone that saves. Works can make no claim on the word (Rom. 3:21-31).[156]

The decision between faith and works is another form of the decision for or against God. The answer of faith is the answer which recognizes the sinfulness of the world and that salvation rests solely on the power of God.[157] From this perspective, all works are non-salvific; they are not definitive of one's ultimate destiny. They remain tied to the ambiguous, fragmentary and restrictive efforts of a fallen world.[158] Faith remains simply the giving over of oneself to God's love in free self-surrender.[159]

"According to the experience of St. Paul, he who accepts Jesus as Lord has thereby himself become lord over anxiety, and indeed over that terrible anxiety in face of God, from which nothing can give security, least of all works."[160] Like St. Paul, Fuch holds that faith is a matter of the heart. Since faith takes place in the conscience, in the heart, in the moment of decision, it is not visible or public. Such an understanding of faith avoids the real danger of objectifying the faith, whether it be a

---

[154]Fuchs, "Language in the New Testament," p. 79.

[155]Fuchs, "Jesus and Faith," p. 53.

[156]Fuchs, "Die sakramentale Einheit von Wort und Tat," p. 217.

[157]Fuchs, "Sola Fide," p. 307.

[158]Ibid., p. 307. Also see O'Collins, "Revelation as Language," p. 81.

[159]Fuchs, *Hermeneutik*, p. 123.

[160]Fuchs, "The Quest for the Historical Jesus," p. 17.

mythological objectification or an overemphasis on the historical facts of Jesus' life.[161] Nevertheless, despite Fuchs' concern about reifying faith, he lacks an equal concern about the tendency to dehistoricize or spiritualize the faith. As a result, the meaning of the historicity of the faith that is implicit in this theology is difficult to determine.

D. Procalmation, history and eschatology

The word of God frees us to love in the present by continuing to proclaim the power of God, the future redemption given in Christ. "[T]he hearer [is] no longer dependent on Jesus' actual conduct, because the declared kindness of God in the acts of the proclamation continues, at least as an act of the proclamation."[162] "The rule of God really consists of the fact that Jesus' word finds faith in the future."[163] The power of the word, then, is to make present the future, a future which governs the present.

In the proclamation the final act of the Christ-event is promised to the believer and directs the present. The future, then, is not something simply to be awaited. It is the horizon of the power of God that stands outside the present and calls the believer to a free decision for faith in Christ in the present. Faith is the call to believe in the promise of a future salvation, a promise which affects and transforms the present. This means that history, or the interpretation of time, must be understood in terms of this call: a call rooted in the future coming of Christ, a call which is not visible under the present conditions of fallen history.

---

[161]Fuchs, "Language in the New Testament," pp 79-80. Achtemeier, "How Adequate is the New Hermeneutic?," pp 114-115. Also see Ernest Fuchs, "The Reflection which is Imposed on Theology," *Studies of the Historical Jesus*, trans. Andrew Scobie (Naperville, IL: Alec R. Allenson, Inc., 1964). "For we do not come nearer to Jesus through having a word of the historical Jesus preached; what should be preached is that Jesus' word demands faith." (p. 38)

[162]Fuchs, "The Reflection which is Imposed on Theology," p. 38.

[163]Ibid., p. 38.

58

This call is personal, not public, and it becomes the decisive act of faith in the struggle of man. The present time is a time of decision which is controlled by the promise of the eschaton. Only in the encounter with the promise of the future fullness of Christ is the historical ambiguity overcome.[164] Yet, it is in the believer, as he stands in the world, that the event of faith takes place.

It should again be noted that the act of faith is not visible because faith is based upon a certain understanding of the revelation which places it outside of fallen history. It is a revelation that is not perceptible today in any unambiguous external fashion.[165] What are perceptible today are the results of the individual coming to faith. The proclamation of the Gospel creates a time of love, but this never fully coincides with our present earthly situation. It has its own time. "Jesus' understanding of time is of this kind. It can be reached only in his word, because his word was a word of love. Therefore, his time was also independent from every other time."[166] In the believer, love and faith create time and history because they create a new world for man apart from our present divided existence.[167] The time of faith is a new mode of existence in love, not mere chronological change.[168]

> Therefore love does not dispense with perceptibility; instead it provides the very greatest perceptibility, because it sees made manifest in Jesus what love always makes manifest: the event of its word. It knows: all that is mine is yours. It is its joy to distinguish between God and man, because everything

---

[164]Fuchs, "Jesus' Understanding of Time," pp 112ff.

[165]In that faith mirrors the revelation which "causes" the faith, Fuchs holds that faith as based on the invisible must itself be non-visible. Here he attacks thrologians like Cullmann and Pannenberg who contend that faith is based on observable data. See Robinson, "Hermeneutics since Barth," p. 159.

[166]Fuchs, "Jesus' Understanding of Time," p. 159.

[167]Fuchs, "Die sakramentale Einheit von Wort und Tät," p. 220.

[168]Fuchs, "Jesus' Understanding of Time," p. 126.

has its time - God, and therefore also man in the world.[169]

Faith becomes perceptible when it causes the person to act, to state, to live according to a standard other than that of the fallen world, as in the time of Jesus when his disciples came to see in the actions of Christ the love of God at work.[170] For the Christian, history must be understood as the history of love, for it is from this life of love that all time takes its meaning.

E. Summary: Fuch's understanding of the historicity of the faith

If history is an interpretation of time in the light of that which is of greatest importance for one's life, then for Fuchs, as for Ebeling, time must be interpreted in light of the Christ-event, which is a word-event.[171] But for history to be understood in its fullness, it must be interpreted in the light of that unambiguous event which fulfills history. Time and events must be interpreted in the light of the salvation of Christ, which is nowhere present to man except as promise.

> There are certainly events which can be fixed by dating. But what they `signify as historical (geschichtliche) events cannot be definitely fixed. We must therefore say that an historical event will be recognizable for what it is - in fact, as historical - only in the future.

---

[169]Ibid., p. 166.

[170]Ernst Fuchs, "Theology of the New Testament and the Historical Jesus," *Studies of the Historical Jesus*, trans. Andrew Scobie (Naperville, IL: Alec R. Allenson, Inc., 1964), p. 172.

[171]Fuchs, "The Reflection which is Imposed on Theology," p. 44. History cannot be understood as having meaning if it is purely a causal relationship. In such a deterministic relationship there is no freedom, only fate and death. Only a free history, a history based on the freedom of faith, the freedom of the proclamation of the word of God, can there be the basis of a meaningful history.

60

> Then we can also say that the future of an historical
> event belongs to the event.[172]

It is only in the event of faith that the believer encounters the fullness of creation, a fullness that is simply future. Consequently, history becomes an event of faith, for it is only in faith that the present can be understood in the light of future fulfillment. In one sense faith causes history, for it is only in faith that this definitive future is now present. But paradoxically, the event of faith is understood as the end of history, where faith destroys the tension that once constituted our life. The tension remains only in the fact that man still exists in time. Yet in faith, one transcends the present fallen history, breaking the tension between the old man and the "new man," the past and the future.[173]

> It is a struggle for the lordship of Jesus Christ in the
> world. It is a struggle for time, and it takes place in
> time, in the sphere of freedom from sin and death
> which is spiritually effective and therefore spreads out
> into the world.[174]

During this time of struggle, there is no fullness of redemption in the present. All that constitutes the fallen, visible world is incomplete.[175]

According to Fuchs, then, history becomes an event of faith which finds its locus in the human conscience.

> It remains the case that this event of God's kindness
> announces itself within the history which is to be

---

[172]Ibid., p. 39.

[173]Ernst Fuchs, "What is Interpreted in the Exegesis of the New Testament," *Studies of the Historical Jesus*, trans. Andrew Scobie (Naperville, IL: Alec R. Allenson, Inc., 1964), pp 94ff

[174]Fuchs, "Jesus and Faith," pp 54-55.

[175]Ibid., p. 55.

> understood. But according to the verdict of faith, history is only properly understood when it is drawn into the light of God's kindness. The event of faith is itself also causally linked with history. For faith considers itself to be the response to Jesus'proclamation. But in faith the event turns to what happens between God himself and man himself[176]

The act of faith is a dynamic relationship which preserves human freedom and therefore history. The power of God is not simply a power that "causes" faith, like a physical occurrence. Rather, it is in the light of the promise of the future that freedom for faith is now possible.

To better understand the nature of this struggle of faith, which is constitutive of the historicity of the faith, it would be helpful to return to Fuchs' discussion of the point of decision. It has been shown that faith is considered to be a language-event which reflects Fuchs' presuppositions about the linguisticality of reality. Human existence, as well as all of reality, finds its historicity in language.[177] Therefore, history must be interpreted in terms of the word, for in the proclamation of the word of God, man is called to a decision for faith. Consequently, personal being is historical in that it always converges on the moment of decision for ourselves and our being in the world.[178] This is the focal point of all history, because it is only in the individual that faith enters the ambiguity of fallen creation. The community of faith is not essential to the act of faith. It is in the decision alone that faith is possible.

> History must be content with the fact that the word of faith is handed on, even though history resists this with catastrophes. What matters now is the course of the word in history; i.e., the question, which word makes

---

[176]Fuchs, "The Reflection which is Imposed on Theology," pp 41-42.

[177]Fuchs, "What is a Language-event?," p. 211. Also see Robinson, "Hermeneutics since Barth," p. 55.

[178]Fuchs, "The Essence of the Language-event and Christology," p. 217.

> its way past the catastrophes of history. This is the word which, within history, admits only faith; the word therefore, which is distinguished only by being able to continue, to be transmitted without perishing in history.[179]

The understanding of history that is at work here is one which seems to bring together the varied points of Fuchs' theology of history. It is first of all to be noted that the word is in history, but not subject to the corrupting effects of history. In this sense it is really the end of history. The word opens man to the future, the promise of the fullness of salvation which overcomes "history." Secondly, this means that history, as we see it now, is judged by the word to be partial.[180] The word exposes the inadequacy and sinfulness of the historical order. And man, called by the word, is the point of tension between these two "realities."

> One of the consequences of faith is that it makes the believer glad. But another of the consequences is that faith must always be disappointed, for otherwise the transcendence of its object - God's coming, God's power and intervention - would be reduced to the this-worldly sphere of the controllable, and faith would thereby be destroyed by itself.[181]

---

[179]Fuchs, "What is Interpreted in the Exegesis of the New Testament?," p. 101.

[180]Fuchs sees history as a fallen history which stands over and against the word. The word condemns this history and breaks its power, but only by means of the decision for faith. It is in this decision that the Kingdom of loveis realized - through of course the power of God - in the world. But there is no full realization here and now. see Fuchs, "Die sakramentale Einheit von Wort und Tat," p. 217, and "Language in the New Testament," p. 71. The fullness of resurrection, the forgiveness of sins is not given in this world. It is given only as promise.

[181]Fuchs, "What is Interpreted in the Exegesis of the New Testament?," p. 100.

63

One of the difficulties with Fuch's interpretation of history is the problem of continuity.[182] Faith in the present is always in crisis and must continually renew itself. This presupposes that the call of faith, given in the proclamation of the word of God, demands a decision, and that that decision is momentary.[183] "Faith therefore continually requires renewal, in order to go into the future with the present, that is, in order to remain present faith. Faith, therefore, continually requires the word which calls to faith."[184] Faith takes place in these momentary experiences of call and decision that link present and future fulfillment. If there is continuity in history (history as time interpreted in terms of the faith of the believer), this continuity rests on the proclamation and interpretation of the word of God. "Such persistence in faith is, in fact, only possible if Jesus' word remains operative subsequent to his death."[185]

The promise of future fullness is given in the proclamation of the word, in the faith of the Church under the present condition of fallen creation.[186] It is in the light of this future fullness that man, in faith, can learn to love and take responsibility for his history within history.[187] This love actualizes itself in the individual decision for faith, but it still remains partial in fallen history. Real history becomes the history of love whose reality is revealed now in the proclamation of the word, but which is present

---

[182] This is the point upon which the "Heilsgeschichte" theologies criticize Fuchs and Ebeling.

[183] Fuchs, *Hermeneutik*, pp 91-111.

[184] Ernst Fuchs, "The Essence of the Language-event and Christology," *Studies of the Historical Jesus*, trans. Andrew Scobie (Naperville, IL: Alec R. Allenson, Inc., 1964), pp 218-219.

[185] Fuchs, "The Reflection which is Imposed on Theology Today." p. 43. Also see Weber, "Language-event and Christian Faith." p. 457. Weber argues that there is no continuity in Fuch's understanding of history. There is only an eternal present which in some fashion stands outside of history.

[186] Fuchs, *Hermeneutik*, pp. 113-114.

[187] Ibid., pp 114-115.

64

only as promise, as future.[188] A history of this kind has no continuity in the present, for in our present temporal existence, faith is only realized ambiguously in the fragmented everydayness of fallen human existence.

In an even more radical fashion, the possibility of faith itself becomes a problem. If all is fallen, fragmented and ambiguous, then there can be no discernable, binding, unambiguous doctrinal or moral expression of the life of faith. This results in an interpretation of the preaching of the word of God whose unity and reality are not historical, but eschatological, for as Fuchs points out, the new life of love stands against our present fragmented existence.

One finds here, as in the case of Ebeling, that Fuchs, as a representative of those who interpret the Eucharist in terms of the primacy of the liturgy of the word, is unable to locate any unambiguous presence of Christ under the conditions of fallen history. The "norm," the fullness of salvation revealed in Christ, is now given only in the future. This position, like Ebeling's, tends to minimalize the historicity of the faith, for the world as fallen is unable to mediate the salvation of Christ in any unambiguous and publicly available manner.

---

[188]Fuchs, "Die sakramentale Einheit von Wort und Tät," pp. 218-220. The sacramental word as promise grounds faith in a personal decision. This act lacks a visible verifiability that reflects a particular view of history as fallen and ambiguous. In its public form, faith reamins at best a work of kindness or a confession of faith. But these always remain fragmented.

Chapter III: Cullmann and the Meaning of History

Perhaps more than any other contemporary Protestant theologian, Oscar Cullmann is concerned with the question of history. His preoccupation with the questions raised by theology about history can in one sense be understood as a reaction against a European mileu then dominated by what he calls "existentialist theology," whose membership ranges from the older hermeneutics of Bultmann to the "new hermeneutics" of Ebeling and Fuchs.[189] Cullmann understands such theologies to always dehistoricize the faith, an approach unacceptable to him.[190] He describes this "dehistoricization" as a fundamental relativizing of the events of the revelation themselves so that they have no normative meaning for the life of the faith; the individual act of faith is all that matters.

Despite all his efforts to prove the inadequacy of the theology of existentialist theology, Cullmann is struggling with the same question: what is the essence of the New Testament faith? At stake in the answer is the nature of faith and the meaning of material and temporal existence for that faith; i.e., the meaning of history.

A. Salvation history as the foundation of the faith

Unlike advocates of "existentialist theology," Cullmann asserts that the fundamental theme of the New Testament is the unfolding of "salvation history" (Heilsgeschichte); i.e., the New Testament revelation is the revelation of the plan of God unfolding in temporal events. The existentialist theologians, on the other hand, insist that salvation history was a convention of the early Christian communities used to

---

[189]These "existentialist theologies" are those theologians, who following Bultmann, place the center of the faith in the individual existential decision for God. See Robinson, *The New Hermeneutics* and Cullmann, *Salvation in History*.

[190]Oscar Cullmann, *Salvation in History*, Sidney G. Somers (New York: Harper & Row, Publishers, 1967), pp 20, 21, 146; and *Christ and Time*, trans. Floyd V. Filson (Philadelphia: Westminster Press, 1964).

66

alleviate the tension caused by the delay of the second coming of Christ. Therefore salvation history was not part of the original message of Jesus. Instead, they insist that the real message of Jesus is the word-event in which the believer by means of the proclamation of the Gospel comes to self-understanding of his true existence.[191] Any attempt to objectify the faith, even by anchoring the faith in the revelation of God in history, is a false attempt to ground faith. For someone like Bultmann, salvation history is a mythical, external structure imposed on the word which prevents the true encounter of faith, an event that calls the individual believer to faith in the innermost structure of his being.

Cullmann attacks the existentialist theology for distorting the biblical message by imposing foreign and, in some cases, antithetical philosophical principles upon it.[192] On account of the philosophical presuppositions that underlie their work, the existentialist theologians are not faithful to the revelation, explaining away what Cullmann understands to be distinctive of the Christian faith.

The problem with existentialist theologian is that they reject the significance of the historical nature of revelation because they understand faith to take place in an "eternal now," a concept which not only eradicates all boundaries between stages in salvation history, but which undermines the meaning of history itself. "If Jesus' teaching must really be interpreted existentially, then every saving event is a punctual present as an encounter with the 'wholly other,' and only that. It is no longer a present bound to salvation history."[193] As understood by existentialist theology, faith, a punctual present, has no real historical continuity, for faith is simply a momentary

---

[191]Cullmann, *Salvation in History*, pp 11, 20, 46, 49; *Christ and Time*, pp 5-6. According to Bultmann salvation history is the faulty solution of "early Catholicism." Salvation history becomes a substitute for the existential decision for faith. Bultmann rejects salvation history just as he rejects the classical formulations of the faith. Both are external, distorting the original meaning of the revelation. See *Salvation in History*, pp 22ff.

[192]Cullmann, *Christ and Time*, pp 11-12.

[193]Cullmann, *Salvation in History*, p. 169.

encounter with God. Consequently, salvation becomes a discontinuous series of points, abstract and unrelated. There can be no overall meaning to history, because these theologies maintain that what is essential to an understanding of time is not the external sequence of events, but the self-understanding of the believer in the light of the decision for faith. But for Cullmann this existential theology, in its caution against any assurances for faith, has destroyed what is essential to the faith.

Cullmann asserts that salvation history is not simply a secondary addition to the original proclamation of the Church. Rather, he understands this revelation history (as redemptive history) to be the heart of the New Testament message, and to deny the centrality of salvation history is truly to undercut the basis of the faith.[194]

> The rejection of the Christian faith, in so far as it takes place on account of the conception of salvation as effected by revelation in history, rests upon a more correct grasp of what is essential and central than does the preaching of a Christianity that is deprived of its life nerve, that is, of the 'offense' of the redemptive history . . . For it simply is not true that one can give up this entire redemptive history of the New Testament with a perfectly free conscience and yet hold fast to the Christian faith.[195]

Such a methodological approach would leave the faith rootless and unhistorical.

Both Cullmann and the existentialist theologians agree that the New Testament faith is based on a continual and direct relationship to Christ. But it is precisely on the question of what this faith means that Cullmann and the existentialist theologians part company. In the end, Cullmann is forced to reject existential theology, because it reduces salvation history to myth. Salvation history becomes for them an impediment that needs to be removed before one can understand the Scriptures. They claim the

---

[194]Ibid., p. 27.

[195]Ibid., p. 27 and 28. According to Cullmann, this salvation history is already present in the early creeds of the New Testament. *Christ and Time*, pp. 22ff.

68

need to demythologize the New Testament. But Cullman claims that such an effort also dehistoricizes the faith, in substance denying the possibility of the historical mediation of the divine: i.e., fallen creation cannot mediate the full grace of Christ.[196] In this existentialist scheme, salvation history is understood to be the history of sin and death that cannot mediate salvation.[197] It is opaque to the Christ-event which alone awaits us at the end of time.[198]

Cullmann understands the essence of the New Testament faith to be the unfolding of the plan of salvation. From the very first, the New Testament does not speculate on the nature of God's eternal being. Rather, it begins with God's self-revelation in his own activity. "The whole content of the New Testament (and of the Old as well) is God's acting, not his being."[199] "God's self-revelation in his activity, not his eternal being, provides the basis from which all questions about things other than his doings are answered."[200] The existential theologians like the early gnostics, try to eliminate salvation history, underestimating the significance of the historical event in favor of the kerygma.[201] In these gnostic interpretations of the New Testament, faith becomes participation in the eternal truth which stands beyond the confines of time and space.

---

[196]Cullmann, *Christ and Time*, pp. 28ff and *Salvation in History*, pp. 20, 21, 139, 146.

[197]Cullmann, *Salvation in History*, p. 52.

[198]Ibid., p. 21.

[199]Ibid., p. 277; Also pp. 27, 117. Gerhard von Rad, *Old Testament Theology*, vol II, trans. D.M.G. Stalker (New York: Harper & Row, Publishers, 1965), p. 368. He speaks clearly of the notion of salvation history in the Old Testament. Also see von Rad, *God at Work in Israel*, trans. John Marks (Nashville,TN: Abingdon Press, 1974), pp 112, 154.

[200]Cullmann, *Christ and Time*, p. 11.

[201]Cullmann, *Salvation in History*, pp 90-91. "However, the history of dogma teaches us that the decisive debate of the ancient Church consisted in its successful resistance against the gnostic attempt to eliminate the salvation history of the Bible by philosophical interpretation." (p. 23) This is exactly what Cullmann understands existential theologians to be doing.

But the center of the biblical teaching is an explicit rejection of the gnostic view of the faith. Both the Old and New Testaments understand revelation as a temporal process.[202] Time is not cyclic; rather, it is the context in which God reveals himself, moving from the Old to fulfillment in the New.[203]

> The acceptance of the Old Testament in the New is exceedingly important if it means that Christian faith is a faith in a divine salvation happening consisting in a sequence of events especially chosen by God, taking place within an historical framework. This indicates that Christian faith, like Jewish faith, was distinguished from all other religions of the time by this salvation-historical orientation.[204]

Salvation history is a process in which the past is not denied by the present revelation of God, but is interpreted ever anew. In historical events there is a continuity and unity that is made intelligible by the revelation.

The Bible affirms the historical dimension of tthe faith by rejecting the gnostic tendency to subordinate history to myth or metaphysical speculation. Cullmann puts it most succinctly when he says that history is not subordinate to myth, but that myth is subordinate to history (unlike the gnostic speculation which tends to absorb the historical into the archetype).

> The Old Testament historicized myths by firmly attaching them to Israel's history. In this, the New Testament went still further by subjecting all myths more rigidly to one event in history - the death of Jesus and the events connected with it which immediately followed. The myths are placed at the service of the

---

[202] Cullmann, *Christ and Time*, pp 52ff.

[203] Cullmann, *Salvation in History*, pp. 85, 244.

[204] Ibid., p. 25.

> salvation-historical perspective at whose mid-point
> stands an historically controllable event.[205]

The New Testament historicizes the faith by drawing all things into a continuity with the events of salvation history.

The New Testament faith is essentially a participation in the process of salvation, which has a definite historical locus in the Incarnation. From this center of all history, Christians of all time are united to participate in the process of salvation. Since the Incarnation, the event in which the infinite and eternal God enters into human history, it is now possible to partake of salvation in time and space. In the Christ-event, the beginning and the end of time, the significance of each historical moment, is revealed in Christ. Still, the authority of Christ awaits a final stage in the Church.

Cullmann likens this process of salvation history to a war in which the decisive battle has been won (the Christ-event) and the imminent end is not yet attained.[206] This does not mean that time has come to an end, but it does mean that the future final victory of salvation will take place in time.

> It would be contrary to the meaning that is contained in
> this word if from it one were to conclude that there is a
> timelessness in the realization of our salvation. It is not
> the attainment of our salvation that is elevated above
> time; on the contrary, this attainment is completely
> bound to stages in time: divine foreordination - Christ's
> atoning death - the final glorification.[207]

---

[205]Ibid., p. 139. In this scheme the historical revelation of God is part of the very essence of his revelation. it is only in the light of these historical events that all things are made intelligible. Even the cosmic events are summed up in the historical process. In the New Testament, even the future, the eschaton, must be interpreted in the light of these events. *Salvation in History*, pp 82, 271; also see pp 94, 128, 141, 313; and Cullmann, "The Tradition," *Early Church*, ed. A.J.B. Higgins (London: SCM Press, LTD, 1956), p. 84.

[206]Cullmann, *Christ and Time*, p. 84.

[207]Ibid., p. 70.

Neither the past nor the future is denied. Hope in the future is supported by the past and like the past is embedded in temporality. The decisive battle has been won in the central event of time, an event from which all things take their meaning.[208]

According to Cullmann, this understanding of the Christ-event is the scandal of Christianity, yet it is this understanding of revelation which is of central importance for dealing with the question of the historicity of the faith and it has many significant implications for theology.

This approach to revelation establishes biblical history, a Christocentric history, as the norm of all history. "This . . . view, however, makes the claim that, upon the basis of the slender Christ-line of the Biblical history, it is entitled to render a final judgement even on facts of general history and on the contemporary course of events at any period."[209] Such a view of salvation history prevents any possible separation of the sacred and the profane, the religious and the secular, into two mutually exclusive realms. Religious truth, as historical and therefore public, is accessible to all and cannot be reduced to personal opinion.

> Here the close connection between Christian revelation and history comes to light, and here in the final analysis lies the "offense" of the Primitive Christian view of time and history, not only for the historian, but for all "modern" thinking, including theological thinking; the offense is that God reveals himself in a special way and effects "salvation" in a final way within a narrowly limited but continuing process.[210]

This makes all of theology, in essence, an examination of this process of salvation in biblical history.[211]

---

[208]Ibid., pp. 68, 85, 86.

[209]Ibid., p. 20.

[210]Ibid., p. 23.

[211]Ibid., p. 23.

72

B. Faith, salvation history and worship

It was noted that the existentialist theologies tend to minimalize the significance of the external dimension of the faith and maximize the emphasis on the individual decision for faith as a response to the proclamation of the word of God. Cullmann insists that faith is not faith in faith, but that true Christian faith rests on the revelation of God to us in history.[212] Here Cullmann is attempting to give faith a basis outside the existential, subjective encounter with the divine in the human conscience which he believes results in the dehistoricizing of the faith. He fights relativizing the historical character of the Christian revelation; i.e., in particular, Cullmann claims, they relativize the historicity of the Christ-event, the source of Christian life. Nevertheless, like the existentialist theologians who he considers to be his opponents, Cullmann considers faith to be rooted in a personal decision which cannot be based solely on historical "facts." But he insists that the historical revelation of God in events in time is necessary for the realization of the full Christian faith.[213] "It is essential to faith as it is found in the New Testament, and as it is asked of its readers, that it be related to events not instigated by the readers, nor by the readers' faith; events having taken place apart from their faith - *pro nobis*, but *extra nos*."[214] By emphasizing this "event character" of the faith, Cullmann attempts to guard against any conception of salvation which rests on a purely a-historical subjective basis.

It should be noted that Cullmann argues against the accusation of trying to secure faith in the empirical facts of history by pointing out that salvation history is ambiguous to man in history. For humanity experiences temporality both as a history

---

[212]Cullmann, *Salvation in History*, p. 324.

[213]Ibid., p. 70.

[214]Ibid., p. 119. One needs the personal response of the believer.

73

of disaster as well as salvation.[215] No one can be totally certain of the meaning of events in the present. The difference between man amid the ambiguities of history and the believer is that the believer, through grace, can begin to understand the plan of God as he sees it unfold in his actions in history.

In the Christ-event, the believer is called through the proclamation of the word of God to align himself with the events of salvation history.[216] This is the act of faith.

> It is constitutive of salvation history that the revelatory process is incorporated in it. For this reason, the first witnesses' faith is at the same time a decision in faith for their own alignment with a series of connected events. They see a divine extension of a saving work begun long before them in the fact that a new revelation has been imparted to them. They have the same self-consciousness of being instruments of the divine plan of salvation in so far as they must proclaim it.[217]

This act of faith leads to a truly new self-understanding, because here it is possible to put oneself at the disposal of that historical reality which alone can fulfill human life (save).[218]

> If one does makes a decision anchored in salvation history, it is not left floating in the air. It is only through salvation history that decision takes on the very concrete character that existentialism demands, and ceases being simply decision for decision. Decision for Christ is not vague decision for what is not at my disposal, for desecularization, for the 'wholly other.' Decision for Christ places me into a very definite

---

[215]Ibid., p. 116. On the question of the ambiguity of history and error in the Church see *Salvation in History*, pp. 86ff.

[216]Ibid., p. 70.

[217]Ibid., p. 116; also see pp. 54, 118, 120, 267.

[218]Ibid., p. 121.

74

context which is conditioned by salvation history past and future.[219]

Only in the context of salvation history does our life of faith have a definitive meaning.

Correspondingly, the very nature of God is to reveal himself in his word, but this word is not simply a linguistic event; it is an action.[220] "It is utterly impossible to make a chronological distinction between word and event in God himself."[221] Action and the event are inseparable. There is always a reciprocity between the present event and the traditional kerygma. "Word and event are not separable in the mind of God himself, and, accordingly in the biblical view, the Word is an event, and conversely the event is a Word."[222] Because of this relationship, it is possible to speak of the Christ-event as the Word become flesh in the Incarnation of the innermost revelation of God in history. But from a human point of view, the event always has primacy.[223]

> Primitive Christian theology treats this fact with unreserved earnestness; it makes the offensive assertion that the climax and central point of all revelation is the fact that the self-revealing God, that is, his Word, his Logos, once entered so completely into history that this unique entrance can be designated by dates just as can every other historical event; under the emperor Augustus (Luke 2:1); under the emperor Tiberius (Luke 3:1).[224]

---

[219]Ibid., p. 330.

[220]It is precisely on this point that Cullmann differs from Ebeling and Fuchs. For them reality is given in language, while for Cullmann, all reality is given in action, in the revelation of God. Words articulate this activity in a "secondary" fashion. The Incarnation, Cross and the Resurrection have primacy; consequently they are more central to faith than proclamation.

[221]Cullmann, *Salvation in History*, p. 136.

[222]Ibid., p. 97.

[223]Ibid., p. 136.

[224]Cullmann, *Christ and Time*, p. 24.

The scandal lies in the fact that it is this one concrete historical event, among the many that constitute "secular" history, that is the definitive revelation of God, the norm by which all revelation and time is to be judged.[225] It is this historical event which the early Church understands to be the cornerstone of the Christian faith.[226]

In its worship, the People of God participate in this revelation in Christ, the central event of the life of the Church.

> In the New Testament context of the period following Easter this connection of the present with the events of the decisive period now past gains a special significance in worship because here the central Christ-event, the death and resurrection of Jesus, is made present in the Lord's Supper. In addition, in the same situation of worship, the connection with the future is indicated since the 'breaking of the bread' is an anticipation of the Messianic meal and therefore of a final union with Christ. Thus in early Christian worship the whole fullness of the 'already' is made manifest. But even here the end is only anticipated.[227]

From its very beginnings, Christian life was formed by the Eucharistic worship. This worship not only structured Christian social life, but informed the nature of Christian faith.

The goal of worship is to build up the body of Christ by bringing the believer into contact with the life of Christ and the history of salvation.[228] The Church comes into existence because in worship a certain perception of reality informs the faith of the

---

[225]Such a revelation undercuts all docetic tendencies of the early Church. See Cullmann, *Christ and Time*, pp. 55ff.

[226]The early creeds attempt to articulate this process, Cullmann, *Christ and Time*, pp. 24ff.

[227]Cullmann, *Salvation in History*, p. 184.

Church, uniting believers in a common faith. Consequently, the historicity of the Church reflects the historicity of the worship of the Church. In Cullmann's theology, the historicity of the worship of the Church reflects the community of believers' faith formed by tension between the present realization of the Christ-event and its future consummation. The same tension between history and eschaton can be found in Cullmann's eucharistic theology.

For Cullmann, the scriptures belong to this central Christ-event, concretizing this mid-point and guarding against any distortions of the faith during the present age.[229] By means of this normative proclamation, the Holy Spirit is present to the Church and builds up the life of faith.[230] Worship proclaims to the believers the whole process of salvation and calls them to that history.[231]

> Here in a direct way the past and future of salvation history become present, and nowhere does the central role attached to salvation history appear more evident than in this highly significant fact that the whole worship of the Christian Church, like Jewish worship, is orientated towards salvation history.[232]

The worship of the Church incorporates the believers into the process of salvation history, uniting them with a past that announces the consummation in the future.[233]

---

[228] Oscar Cullmann, *Early Christian Worship*, trans. A. Stewart Todd and James B. Torrence (London: SCM Press, LTD, 1966), pp. 38, 57.

[229] Cullmann, *Christ and Time*, p. 171. This is the meaning of the formation of the cannon. The very act shows a recognition of the uniqueness of the apostolic period. See pp. 171ff ; and "The Traditin," pp. 89ff.

[230] Cullmann, "The Tradition," p. 80.

[231] Cullmann, *Early Christian Worship*, p. 26.

[232] Cullmann, *Salvation in History*, p. 313.

[233] Ibid., pp. 313ff. Unlike Fuchs and Ebeling, who minimalize the significance of salvation history, Cullmann emphasizes the fact that the sacraments only have meaning in salvation

The Eucharistic symbols are understood as proclamations, as forms of the liturgy of the word.

As all worship, to separate the sacraments from salvation history would be to destroy the historicity of the sacracraments. According to Cullmann, the sacraments bring us into a relationship with the risen Christ. From the very beginning, Christians understood the breaking of the bread in the light of the appearance of the risen Christ at table with his disciples.[234] In this interpretation of the Eucharist, the emphasis is shifted away from the deeds of the historical Jesus to the encounter of the resurrected Christ in the Supper, including away from the cross and towards the presence of the resurrected Christ. Cullmann argues that today, this emphasis on the Eucharist as a fellowship meal with the Risen Christ is lost and abberent interpretations occur. For instance, the Roman Catholic interpretation of the Eucharist is that "Christ's presence is bound up exclusively with the elements, and the occasion is no longer an actual meal, while in the early community Christ is thought of as sitting at the table with his own and sharing the meal."[235] The emphasis has shifted from eating with Christ to the eating of Christ.[236]

Despite the fact that there is no historical presence of Christ in the Church which presently corresponds to the full historicity of the Christ-event, Cullmann tries to hold together the worship of the Church and the fullness of the Christ-event by emphasizing the role of the Spirit. He insists upon the presence of the Risen Christ in the Lord's Supper by the power of the Spirit. Nevertheless, the question that remains is one concerning the exact nature of the historical character of this presence.

The problem that Cullmann is dealing with in this instance is much the same as the one Luther struggles with in his discussion of the nature of Christ's presence in the

---

history. (pp. 255ff) On the other hand he contests that the Catholics too readily identify the sacraments and salvation history.

[234]Cullmann, *Early Christian Worship*, pp. 30ff.

[235]Ibid., p. 19.

[236]Ibid., pp. 13ff.

Lord's Supper. Cullmann insists that the Eucharistic presence is a real presence, but refuses to assign an event character to the sacramental actions, such as those implicit in the terms "sacrifice" or "transubstantiation" as used by Roman Catholics to describe the Mass. Instead, by referring to it as a "spiritual" communion with the Risen Christ, Cullmann appears to de-emphasize the historical character of the Eucharist; i.e., a communion with Christ that is not antecedent to the present faith of the believer. The Church, as the Body of Christ, is identified with the now risen Christ, an eschatological identification which makes vacuous the historicity of the Church as it now exists in the world.

By approaching the question of real presence in this way, Cullmann asserts an eschatological significance to history. He argues that the encounter in the Eucharist of the Church with its Lord is an eschatological meal in which the Church encounters the Risen Lord in its worship just as the Risen Lord ate with his disciples after the resurrection. The Risen Lord "appears" to his disciples in response to their prayer, maranatha.

> In the Maranatha prayer . . . we come right down to the specifically Christian element in the early liturgical prayer, an element which connects closely with the fact that the day of the Christian service of worship is the day of Christ's resurrection. On this day Christ appeared at a meal with his disciples. So now he ought to appear again, in the Christian celebration of the Meal, since, "where two or three are gathered together in my name, then am I in the midst of them" (Matt. 18:20).[237]

According to Cullmann there is no evidence of sacrifice in these early Christian practices.[238] The risen Christ is present by the power of the Spirit as on the day of

---

[237]Ibid., p. 13.

[238]Ibid., pp. 13, 18. According to Ebeling this is a later addition, playing no part in the early liturgical formulations.

great joy when the believer remembers the when Jesus, after the resurrection, appeared to his disciples at a meal.

C. Worship, the Spirit and the Church

The Church as an eschatological community lives by healing power of the Spirit present in the fallen world. In its worship, the Church is given the promise of the final salvation of the world by God.

> In the primitive Christian worship this anticipation becomes visibly apparent. For the essence of the primitive Christian worship by no means consists only in preaching and reading of the Scripture in accordance with the synagogue pattern; rather, the specifically Christian feature in the primitive Christian assemblies manifests itself in its clear goal, the building up of the body of Christ. Christ's resurrection body is to gain a definite form in the congregation. Therefore the high point of every primitive Christian service of worship is the solemn meal in which Christ is present with his people.[239]

The Lord's Supper, the locus of our encounter with Christ, plays a central role in the "causing" of the Church. The Church is an eschatological community, whose life foreshadows that final triumph of God.[240] In the Eucharist the eschatological fullness of Christ, not yet completed due to sin, is "given" to the believer.

Cullmann insists upon a presence of Christ in the Lord's Supper, which he understands to exceed the "real presence" of the linguistic analysis given by Ebeling and Fuchs. Short of the Roman Catholic interpretation of the Mass which views it as a "representation" of the one sacrifice of Christ, Cullmann describes the Eucharistic

---

[239]Cullmann, *Christ and Time*, p. 73.

[240]Ibid., p. 155.

presence of Christ as the presence of the Risen Christ. But like Ebeling and Fuchs, Cullmann understands the essential nature of this presence to be that of a "promise" which is directed toward a future fullness, not yet actualized under the conditions of fallen history. A consequence of this understanding of the Eucharist is the refusal of any historical, spatial, temporal, public mediation of the presence of Christ. Cullmann insists that the reign of God is now present, but the question that must be answered here bears upon the nature of this presence, given that it is a presence that reflects the ambiguity of a particular understanding of fallen creation and its inability to mediate grace.

In his discussion of this problem, Cullmann likens the sacramental presence to the miracles of Jesus. "The sacraments occupy the same position in the Church as the miracles in the ministry of Jesus, for they, too, are miracles of the Holy Spirit. . . . But within the body of Christ which became the Church when the Holy Spirit was poured forth on the day of Pentecost, the miracles of the Spirit are identified more and more with the efficacy of Baptism and the Lord's Supper."[241] It is the 'spiritual body' of Christ, and through participation in it in worthy enjoyment of the Lord's Supper the believer already appropriates the fruits of the Holy Spirit, even in the area of his earthly life. (I Cor. 11:30)"[242] The sacraments of the Church mediate an eschatological fullness given by the Holy Spirit.

One should be careful not to automatically expect that Cullmann's understanding of the Church dehistoricizes the faith simply because he labels it the "spiritual" body of Christ. But there is evidence in his theology that leads one to believe that the fullness of the Christ-event, whose historicity was so concrete as to be available to secular history, is nowhere actual in the Church or sacraments. The Church in the interim, between the end of the apostolic age and the final

---

[241]Oscar Cullmann, "The Proleptic Deliverence of the Body according to the New Testament," *The Early Church*, ed. A.J.B. Higgins (London: SCM Press, LTD, 1956), p. 170.

[242]Cullmann, *Christ and Time*, pp. 154-155.

consummation, is filled with ambiguity. And although the Risen Christ is present to his Church through the sacraments, it appears that this presence is never fully realized in such a way as to permit us a full offer of grace from God. The first evidence of this is that the presence of the Risen Christ lacks the "physicality" of the Christ-event.[243] It cannot be denied that the Spirit is already transforming the world. The question is - where in the present is the fullness of this Christ-event to be encountered? Is our time and space devoid of an encounter with the fullness of the incarnate one? If so, then does not Cullmann, even though he stresses the historical foundation of faith, become guilty of the same dehistoricizing of the faith of which he has accused the existentialist theologians?

In response to such questions Cullmann insists upon an "actual" presence of Christ in the Eucharist, but not a material presence. "It is the body of the Risen Christ which is present in the Lord's Supper. He raises us up to life here and now and therein lies the promise of our resurrection."[244] Christ, the bread of life, comes indeed from heaven, but when he descends to earth he now chooses for himself the humblest mode of appearance in his historical incarnation in the Church.[245] "Christ remains still the revelation in his person, no longer in historical incarnation, but in the Church and indeed here in the sacrament of the Lord's Supper, where he is not 'materially' present but actually present."[246] The separation of the person of Christ from the historical incarnate Christ leads to a disjunction in his theology that is problematic. This presupposes that Christ is not actually corporeally present to his Church and that the

---

[243]Ibid., p. 236. This statement is made in the context of his discussion of baptism, although it appears to be applicable here.

[244]Cullmann, *Early Christian Worship*, p. 97.

[245]Ibid., p. 97.

[246]Ibid., p. 98.

corporeal identity of the Church is a different corporeality from that of the incarnate Lord.[247]

At this point, the key issue in the question of the historicity of the faith becomes clearly tied to the problem of "presence" in the worship of the Church. The difficulty in determining the nature of this "real presence" can perhaps be stated best this way: for the presence, the encounter with Christ, must be an event in order to be historical. But such historical events require a public expression and a physical continuity with the Christ-event. If this public character is lost and this continuity is sacrificed, then is not the historicity of the worship of the Church and faith also sacrificed?

D. The historicity of the faith

Perhaps Cullmann's central insight is that the Christ-event is not the revelation of some abstract truth, but the full revelation of God himself in Christ which gives meaning to all reality. "The event of the word-made-flesh contains within itself the entire salvation history that came before and that comes afterwards; but it also aligns itself with this history."[248] Because time is the arena in which salvation is worked out, time has meaning in relation to this event.[249]

> In the first place, salvation is bound to a continuous time process which embraces past, present and future. Revelation and salvation take place along the course of an ascending time line. Here the strictly straight line conception of time in the New Testament must be

---

[247]According to Cullmann, the word and sacrament perform the same function. Both claim the same historicity. One cannot distinguish between what the word does and what the Lord's Supper does. Cullmann, *Early Christian Worship*, pp. 26ff. The two are bound togethr from the start, just as word and deed are bound together. The Spirit is given in the same way in the sacraments and in the proclamation of the gospel.

[248]Cullmann, *Salvation in History*, p. 100.

[249]Ibid., pp. 82, 86, 99, 231, 250, 294; and *Christ and Time*, pp. 21, 24, 25, 90, 91, 105, 113.

> defined as over against the Greek cyclical conception and over against all metaphysics in which salvation is always available in the "beyond," and we must show how according to the Primitive Christian view revelation and salvation actually "occur" in a connected manner during the continuous time process.[250]

In the second place, "it is characteristic of this estimate of time as the scene of redemptive history that all points of this redemptive line are related to the one historical fact at the midpoint, a fact which precisely in its unrepeatable character, which marks all historical events, is decisive for salvation. This fact is the death and resurrection of Jesus Christ."[251] This Christian interpretation of time does not understand time to be mere chronology, nor is time understood in terms of its origin or end, but real time is significant time, time measured and evaluated in the light of the Christ-event.[252]

The biblical notion of time as expressed in the New Testament is not a rationalism imposed on history by the autonomous human reason; rather, the New Testament understands temporal existence to have an intrinsic intelligibility, a meaning, given in the redemptive actions of God.[253] As a matter of fact, the biblical accounts are "stumbling blocks" to any rationalizing efforts. "Because the realization of the divine plan of salvation is bound to such time points or *kairos* chosen by God, therefore it is a redemptive history. Not all fragments of ongoing time constitute redemptive history in

---

[250]Cullmann, *Christ and Time*, p. 32. According to Cullmann, the New Testament understands all revelation to take place in the temporal process. Even eternity is temporal. That is, it is not an escape from time, but it is considered to be endless time (pp. 62ff). This is not simply a mythical or metaphysical addition; rather, for Cullmann this is an essential dimension of the New Testaemnt message.

[251]Ibid., pp. 32-33.

[252]Ibid., pp. 58, 76ff. "Our system, however, does not proceed from an initial point, but from a center; it takes as its mid-point and event which is open to historical investigation and can be chronologically fixed, if not with complete accuracy, at least within the space of a few years. This event is the birth of Jesus Christ of Nazareth. Thence proceed in the opposite direction two enumerations, one forward, the other backward, 'after Christ,' 'before Christ.'" (p. 17)

[253]Cullmann, *Christ and Time*, p. 39.

the narrower sense, but rather these specific points, these *kairoi*, singled out from time as a whole."[254] Such *kairoi* remain outside the realm of secular history, only discernable by faith.[255]

Cullmann distinguishes in the revelation two inseparable elements; the events of salvation history and their interpretation.[256] There is a circular relationship in which the events give rise to interpretation and the interpretation allows the believer to see the significance of the event in the light of the fullness of salvation history.[257] "In these passages is meant the present, *kairos*, whose significance in the entire plan of salvation is known to the believer upon the basis of past *kairoi*, that is, the death and resurrection of Christ."[258] This sequence of *kairoi*, which includes both event and interpretation presents a coherent whole which Cullmann calls salvation history.

It is this sequence of *kairoi*, this line of the redemptive acts of God, which provides the continuity in salvation history. It has its origin in man's need for redemption and finds its conclusion in the "new creation."[259] At times the continuity of this salvation history is difficult to discern; i.e., salvation history appears to be a sequence of disconnected events. "I have emphasized from the beginning that the salvation-historical faith is definitely not faith in an 'unbroken' causal connection, but faith in a connection revealed only by God, resting upon a completely incalculable

---

[254]Ibid., pp. 39-40.

[255]Ibid., p. 40. Cullmann points out the need for prophecy in order to arrive at he proper understanding of these *Kairoi*. (pp. 89ff).

[256]Cullmann, *Salvation in History*, pp. 148ff. "Revelation takes place in both event and interpretation." (p. 149)

[257]Ibid., pp. 89ff.

[258]Cullmann, *Christ and Time*, p. 42.

[259]Cullmann, *Salvation in History*, pp. 161, 264-265. Salvation history is necessary because of sin.

selection of individual events. Therefore the question may even be raised whether one may properly use the expression 'salvation history'."[260]

> The events constituting salvation history indeed run in chronological sequence as do those of history. But whereas events of history unfold as a general chronological, historical sequence without interruption, and the record of them is set down accordingly without any gaps, it is essential to biblical salvation history that it shows "gaps" which are quite remarkable from an historical standpoint, and which unfold entirely by leaps. Isolated events appear differentiated and sorted out of the total historical process, historically speaking, in an arbitrary way. Nevertheless, a connection exists between them.[261]

Cullmann insists that history is a free redemptive history initiated by God, not reducible to a cause-effect sequence, nor to human logic. The continuity in salvation history, which Cullmann insists upon, exists by means of the power of the Spirit.

In spite of the presence of the Spirit in creation, sin remains, continually resisting God's plan of salvation. The result is that until the second coming of Christ, the plan of salvation history is not clearly seen, for in the "fallen" world, there is no unambiguous mediation of Christ apart from the Incarnation.[262] There are only the individual *kairoi*, God breaking periodically into time.[263]

---

[260]Ibid., pp. 55. The process of salvation history is understood in terms of the idea of election. The chosen people (Israel) is reduced to a faithful remnant, then to Christ (through Mary to one), and from Christ the Church again goes out into the world to save all (one to many). This is the order of the process of salvation history as revealed in Christ.

[261]Ibid., pp. 153-154.

[262]Cullmann, *Christ and Time*, pp. 39, 40, 90ff, 115; and *Salvation in History*, pp. 55, 98, 124, 153.

[263]The events are interpreted in the light of other revelations. This is a free process, a process in which a sequence of empirically unrelated events are brought together to form salvation history.

One might ask at this point whether Cullmann can be accused of the same error of which he accuses the existentialist theologians, of reducing salvation history to a point in time, an eternal now.[264] In opposition to this Cullmann asserts that history is a sequence, or a larger context, in which all revelation and acts of faith must be set. The question is, how does this provide a continuity that permeates all of history and is available now in the time of the Church? If it is a non-historical continuity which locates faith in pure interiority, then Cullmann is guilty of the same punctual notion of history of which he accuses his opponents. (All revelation will be a moment of ineffable insight or encounter with God and can have no public expression or discernible continuity. There are simply moments of encounter with either the trans-historical Christ or the eschatological Christ - the Christ now seated at the right hand of the Father, or the Christ who is to come.) If, on the other hand, as Cullmann insists, this salvation history is truly in time and has continuity, then he must be able to locate this presence in time and space.

E. The Church and history

The life of the Church, like the Lord's Supper, has its source in her participation in the life of Christ, the full revelation of God in the concrete facticity of the created order. And, the historicity of the Church mirrors the historicity of the revelation of Christ, the very source of the Church's life. Yet, if such a full participation of the divine in history is not possible under the present reign of sin, then a historical Church could not be an efficacious sign of Christ.

Attempting to solve this problem, Cullmann distinguishes between the historicity of the Christ-event which is accessible even to secular historians, and the historicity of the Church which is likened to the historicity of the risen Christ and

---

[264]Cullmann, *Salvation in History*, pp. 24, 25, 45. Faith and salvation rest upon our decision, not on any sequence of events. According to existentialist theology no sequence of events can ground faith. (p. 120)

therefore not accessible to historical research.[265] To comprehend the reality of the Church demands the light of faith. Otherwise, one's understanding is left frustrated in the face of that which transcends its capacity to comprehend, for the reality of the Church transcends any simply empirical explanation, because its historicity, like that of the risen Christ, transcends the empirical facticity of chronological existence.[266]

In this assertion, Cullmann implicitly rejects any monophysitic identification of secular historicity with the historicity of the faith. He understands salvation history to collapse into the eschaton, thereby sundering the salvation of the risen Christ from any historical mediation. Yet, the Christ-event, according to Cullmann, is the point at which salvation history and secular history are joined.[267] But after this one point world history and salvation history seem to part company. This separation remains until the eschaton.

Until the final consummation of the world, the mission of the Church is to preach the Gospel to all nations. "Since it is an essential mark of the Church that, in contrast to the other members of the *Regnum Christi*, those whom Christ rules and who rule with Christ have knowledge of him, so the first task of the Church is to preach the gospel."[268] During the present time the Church is called to bear witness to the Christ-event.[269] It is because of the Church's proclamation of the salvation of Christ that the present is included in the process of salvation history.

Although the time of the Church is an extension of the work of Christ through the preaching of the gospel, Cullmann claims that the proclamation of the Church differs greatly from the proclamation at the time of the Christ-event, the norm of all

[265]Cullmann, *Early Christian Worship*, p. 18.

[266]Cullmann, *Salvation in History*, p. 143.

[267]Ibid., p. 143.

[268]Oscar Cullmann, "The Kingship of Christ and the Church in the New Testament," *The Early Church*, ed. A.J.B. Higgins (London: SCM Press, LTD, 1956), p. 133.

[269]Cullmann, *Salvation in History*, p. 308.

88

proclamation.[270] (This period ends with the close of the apostolic age.) The apostolic witness distinguishes itself from the witness of the early Church by the fact that the apostles are the direct witnesses of the resurrection, whose witness is normative and safeguards the tradition.[271] The proclamation of the Church is not identical with the objective revelation of the divine Word, yet it has a special role in the economy of salvation. The time of the Church is understood, then, to be a prolongation of this central period. But the present Church unlike the apostles, cannot witness directly to the resurrection of Christ; it is a witness to a witness.[272]

Cullmann's theology is consistent with the *sola fide/sola scriptura* principles of the Reformation. The Bible alone is the norm which supplies the continuity for the preaching of the gospel, containing the apostolic witness to the fundamental facts of the work of the incarnate Word.[273] The Church's proclamation is important because it testifies to this apostolic norm, but it does not have the same clarity as the original apostolic witness. The Church's preaching is not only temporally distant from the Christ-event, but as sinful, it is fraught with all the ambiguities of life in fallen history and is doomed to err.[274] The Church, even her proclamation, is not infallible in what it

---

[270]Oscar Cullmann, "The Tradition," *The Early Church*, ed. A.J.B. Higgins (Philadelphia: Westminster Press, 1966), pp. 76ff. The center of all salvation history is the period from the birth of Christ to the death of the last eyewitness (1 A.D. - 80 A.D.). "If we consider the Christian faith from the point of view of time we shall say that the scandal of Christian faith is to believe that these few years, which for secular history have no more or no less significance than other periods, are the center and norm of the totality of time." (p. 76)

[271]Ibid., pp. 77ff.

[272]Ibid., pp. 78ff. According to Cullmann, the Roman Catholic Church fails to make this distinction. Catholics assume that apostolic authority is transferable, but this is actually not the case. Thus it is impossible for the Church to claim infallibility because the period of infallible witnesses ends with the close of the Apostolic Age; i.e., with the death of the last eyewitness to the Resurrection.

[273]Ibid., p. 87.

[274]Ibid., p. 85.

is or what it does, but for what it does not do. It is infallible in that it does not separate the believer from the true word given in the Bible.[275]

Even though the time of the Church is an ambiguous time characterized by the imperfect mediation of the Christ-event, it remains the time of the Spirit.

> Inasmuch as according to the Primitive Christian faith the Church now becomes the place where the Holy Spirit is active (Acts 2), the Church itself is included in the divine Lordship over time, and, so to say, takes part in it. For it now lives in this unique relation of tension between present and future, and it does so by reason of the Holy Spirit, who is powerful in it and who signifies the anticipation of the end.[276]

The Church lives by a "spiritual" continuity given initially at Pentecost.

> Pentecost is the beginning of the Church, the opening stage of the realization of the people of God in the end time. But the Spirit is the element of the future Kingdom of God. The miracle of Pentecost is that future element which is to provide the material of the new creation takes hold already of a part of old sin-corrupted creation in the present age, without being able to transform its outer framework. The miracle occurs from now on in the Church. That which took place at the ascension for the whole creation on the basis of the death and resurrection, the subjection to Christ in the end-time, here takes place for the people of God, on whom the highest mission in creation devolves: the realization in the end-time of a fellowship in Christ ordained by the Spirit of God - both on the way to the Kingdom of God.[277]

---

[275]Ibid., p. 91.

[276]Cullmann, *Christ and Time*, p. 73.

[277]Cullmann, "The Kingship of Christ and the Church in the New Testament," pp 116-117.

This eschatological community formed by the coming of the Holy Spirit after the glorification of Christ is the locus of God's redemption in the world. "That sin is still present, although the Holy Spirit is already at work, is definite proof that it is a 'redemptive necessity' for time itself to continue in order to carry the redemptive history to its goal."[278] The time of the Church remains an ambiguous time: a time after the decisive battle that awaits the final victory.

> The tension between the present and the future in the Church is not only due to the fact that it is the persecuted, suffering and crucified body of Christ, and at the same time the resurrection-body, the spiritual body. It goes much further and also arises from the fact that, though as a gift offered by God the spiritual body of Christ is a reality in the earthly world doomed to destruction, it cannot exert its full influence owing to the unworthiness of its own members, so that this body in which nothing corruptible should remain still contains sin, disease and death. The reason is that the Church is still made up of human beings who are still living in the carnal body, still living in sin.[279]

This eschatological Church lives in the present where sin and grace are both at work, awaiting a final future salvation. As the community of the Spirit, it awaits the future "recreation" of the fallen world.[280]

---

[278]Cullmann, *Christ and Time*, p. 93. This can be compared with the post-apostolic age. As it becomes further removed from the original witness of the apostles the Church no longer has the same authority. See, Cullmann, "The Tradition," pp. 68, 91.

[279]Cullmann, "The Kingship of Christ and the Church in the New Testament," p. 126.

[280]Like Fuchs and Ebeling, Cullmann has no present unambiguous mediation of God which causes the Church. The Church is ambiguous. It is locked in a world still bound to sin. The only solution is in the future, when the power of Christ will again make creation new. History, in the present, remains a history of sin and death.

F. Summary: The Church and worship

In Cullmann's theology, the historicity of the Church's faith is the historicity of the risen Christ, who is present *sola fide*, not *ex opere operato*, in the Church's worship.[281] "This very bold idea clearly assumes that the Supper is never eaten in a wholly worthy manner so long as the present age lasts. The risen body of Christ is never fully realized, as it should be by believers assembled for the meal."[282] Sin and death still exist and the fullness of the end time remains in the future.[283]

Cullmann's answer to the question of the historicity of the faith lies in the eschaton. Even though he emphasizes the fact that faith aligns us with a concrete salvation history there is no unambiguous locus of the presence of Christ in post-resurrection history. It is only in the light of this unambiguous point, a purely future point, that time and space have significance. That the end alone reveals the nature of the historicity of the faith is evidenced by his interpretation of the Eucharist. "In the risen body of Christ composed of the Church and realized in the Eucharist there should be no room for the power of death. So understood, the Eucharist is the supreme anticipation of the end."[284] Like the gathering of the early Church that looked only to the future, in faith, the Christian partakes of the future fulfillment; but it is never the full possession of redemption under the conditions of the fallen world.[285] In

---

[281]Cullmann, "The Proleptic Deliverance of the Body According to the New Testament," p. 171. It is true that Cullmann points to the flesh as being important, but for the Eucharist what is decisive is the Spirit. His difficulty is in making explicit the exact nature of the significance of the "flesh." cf. *The Early Church*, pp 100ff.

[282]Ibid., p. 171.

[283]Cullmann, *Salvation in History*, pp. 305ff. The difficulty with Catholicism is that it fails to heed the "not yet" dimension of reality. This is evidenced by the Catholic realism which comes close to repetition. See pp. 316ff.

[284]Cullmann, "Proleptic Deliverance of the Body according to the New Testament," p. 171.

[285]Cullmann, *Christ and Time*, pp. 75ff.

worship, the believer enters into the eschatological community of the "chosen people." This expectation of future fulfillment rests upon the already-present risen Christ, whose presence signals the end but awaits the transformation of the world. The reign is everywhere but it does not coincide spatially with fallen creation.[286]

As a representative of those who interpret the eucharistic symbols in terms of the primacy of the liturgy of the word, Cullmann is unable to locate in the present the fullness of the salvation given in Christ. There is a difference between the historicity of the Christ-event and the historicity of its sacramental re-presentation in the worship of the Church. For Cullmann, time is interpreted in the light of a future eschatological event. But the fullness of this future is not present anywhere in our present, except as promise. History, then, remains ambiguous.

---

[286]Cullmann, "The Kingship of Christ and the Church in the New Testament," p. 122.

Chapter IV: Moltmann - Liberation and History

Jürgen Moltmann begins his theology with a theology of history which is thoroughly Protestant. According to him, theology is the study of the effects of the revelation of God in history and the proclamation of that revelation. "The revelation of the special history that grounds faith in Christ takes place in the word that effects history. Thus history does not become revelation, but it becomes the sphere of revelation."[287] Although this theology emerges from the tradition of the theology of the word (like that of Fuchs and Ebeling), Moltmann's theological emphasis is much closer to Cullmann's in that he emphasizes the word as the word of promise, a word rooted in the Christ-event.[288] Like Cullmann, he understands history to be a most important theological concern.

The theology of Moltmann has as its main concern the development of an adequate hermeneutic. He finds the fundamental hermeneutical principle in the event of Christ. Not only is the Christ-event basic for the founding of the faith but it is also the foundational hermeneutical principle by means of which one judges the authenticity of the faith. He focuses, in particular, on the "crucified God." "In Christianity the cross is the test of everything which deserves to be called Christian. One may add that the cross alone, and nothing else, is its test, since the cross refutes everything, and excludes the syncretistic elements in Christianity."[289] The cross alone mediates the Kingdom of God in human history, freeing faith from all that which would seduce the

---

[287]Jürgen Moltmann, "Exegese und Eschatologie der Geschichte," *Evangelische Theologie*, 1962, vol. 22, p. 58.

[288]Robinson, *Theology as History*, pp 17, 89ff. Robinson points out that Moltmann, under the influence of the dialectical theology, holds that it is by means of the word that one is freed from the "objectifying idealistic interpretations of history." Nevertheless, Moltmann distinguishes his theology from other theologies of the word, like that of Fuchs and Ebeling, by his effort to ground his theology in the definitive historical hermeneutical point of the crucified God.

[289]Jürgen Moltmann, *The Crucified God*, trans. R.A. Wilson and John Bouden (New York: Harper & Row, Publishers, 1974), p. 7.

believer away from the unique redemption given in Christ.[290] Only in the light of the cross does the believer come to understand God, revelation and the meaning of history.[291]

In the world of the early Church, the idea of a crucified God was scandalous. "The idea of 'crucified God' to whom veneration and worship were due was regarded in the ancient world as totally inappropriate to God, just as for Israel the assertion that a condemned blasphemer had risen from the dead was bound to conflict with the righteousness of God revealed in the law."[292] Moltmann emphasizes that this belief in a crucified and Risen Lord is distinctive of Christianity and the beginning point for all reflection on that faith.

Moltmann understands all of theology to be hermeneutics. Accordingly, the dilemma of modern theology is the need for Christianity to speak meaningfully to the modern world while at the same time retaining its distinctive identity.[293] An authentic Christian faith, against all forms of dogmatism and fundamentalism, is a dynamic faith that is most fully alive when it meets the needs of others, no matter what the circumstances. Therefore, faith can never be reduced to an object, because the Christian faith must be open to the world, meeting the needs of the world.[294]

A. The hermeneutics of relevance

As a theologian who accepts the modern historicist premise, Moltmann understands Christianity's continual need to reinterpret the meaning of the faith for the

---

[290]Ibid., pp. 201, 205, 212.

[291]Jürgen Moltmann, "Hope and Development," *The Future of Creation*, trans. Margaret Kohl (Philadelphia: Fortress Press, 1979), p. 52.

[292]Moltmann, *The Crucified God*, pp 33, 34.

[293]Ibid., pp 7, 54.

[294]Ibid., p. 8.

present. The historicist premise is that each age has a unique view of the world, different from past ages. Consequently, if faith is to be a living faith it needs not simply to be preached, but reinterpreted to fit into the world and meet the challenges of the world in which it finds itself. The tendency of Christians to isolate their faith from the movements of world history must be resisted. Moltmann insists, on the one hand, that faith must be a living encounter in the day-to-day existence of the believer. On the other hand, Moltmann warns against the danger of over-accommodating the faith to the present times. The demands of faith transcend any simply human project and so it can never be reduced to human control. So in addition to interpreting the faith to meet the needs of a particular age, hermeneutics must protect the faith from becoming subservient to cultural trends diminishing that which gives the Christian faith its particular identity. The question which underlies the hermeneutical task, then, deals the relationship of faith to the believer's world.[295]

In answer to the "crisis of relevance," Moltmann asserts that it is not simply right beliefs, but also right actions and experience that constitute the essence of faith; it is "taking up" one's cross. Christian identity comes from the cross, an identity which, like that of Christ, calls for the believers to empty themselves and to identify themselves with the poor and outcast.[296] "Christian life is a form of practice which consists in following the crucified Christ, and it changes both man himself and the circumstances in which he lives."[297] Faith is a life of activity that by its very nature is relevant to life in the world.

The problem posed by the "crisis of relevance" is one which brings us directly to the question of worship. In worship the believer encounters that which is of ultimate significance for his life, the source of his faith. Moltmann understands this liturgical encounter to be mediated by the liturgy of the word. Today, the believer participates in

---

[295]Ibid., p. 17.

[296]Ibid., pp. 17-19.

[297]Ibid., p. 25.

the event of the cross through faith evoked by the preaching of the word of God. "The word of the cross enables one to participate in the divine event of the cross, and faith allows the godless to participate in this in fellowship with Christ. This is something more than merely conveying a piece of information or an arbitrary interpretation."[298] The word is a message about the cross and attests to the resurrection of the crucified Christ. In the cross the word is silenced, but in the resurrection this silence is smashed and the proclamation begins.[299] "Consequently, the event of revelation consists not only of the event of the cross and resurrection of Christ, but also the preaching of the gospel."[300] Preaching, then, not only stands in continuity with the revelation of God in Christ, but is a necessary part of the revelation of God. Nevertheless, preaching never fully realizes the Christ-event. "Although this preaching reveals him to the godless and brings them to faith, when Christ rose, he did not turn into words. The crucified Christ is more than the preaching of the cross."[301] It would be more accurate to say that the crucified Christ is the criterion of all preaching that appeals to him.[302]

This theology presents a problem. If one's access to the history of God is revealed in the crucified Christ and our access to the Christ-event is by means of an imperfect preaching, is there any unambiguous, perfect full revelation of God in the present? If not, then what is to be expected of Christian faith here and now? It might be helpful here to remember that the nature of Christian faith and the salvation it gives reflects the nature of the revelation given in Christ (Christology) and the way that

---

[298]Ibid., p. 73.

[299]Jürgen Moltmann, "The Theology of the Cross Today," *The Future of Creation*, trans. Margaret Kohl (Philadelphia: Fortress Press, 1979), p. 155.

[300]Moltmann, *The Crucified God*, p. 74.

[301]Ibid., p. 75. The Cross cannot be reduced to words or a mere interpretetation. Moltmann rejects the distinction between fact and interpretation. He understands this distinction to lead to control over the event by the word, by the interpretation. Moltmann insists on an intelligiblity of the Cross that cannot be reduced to any formulation.

[302]Ibid., p. 75.

revelation is mediated in fallen creation. The believer's faith is molded by the source of that faith and reflects the historicity of that mediation. So what the exact historical character of that mediation? In order to answer this question, it is helpful to look at what Moltmann says about the sacraments.[303]

B. The sacraments and the liturgy of the word

According to Moltmann, the liturgical life of the Church mediates the future of God. He notes that "the gospels and sacraments anticipate and celebrate the future glory of God by making the crucified Christ present."[304] By means of preaching and the sacraments, the believers now participate in the anticipated future of God.

It has already been noted that the word, as an imperfect means of "re-presenting" the crucified Christ, cannot mediate the fullness of this event. One must then ask if the sacramental re-presentation somehow brings the word to perfection. Does the attachment of the material sign to the word bring about a more perfect re-presentation of the Christ-event? In Moltmann's theology, how is the cross of Christ understood to be assimilated in worship?

According to Moltmann, in the history of theology this question has been answered in three ways. In the first answer, the cross is understood to be mediated by cultic worship: the best example is the Roman Catholic claim that the cross of Christ is present in the sacrifice of the Mass.[305] As Christianity spread into the pagan world, the cult was elevated to the center of Christian faith and worship. The original non-cultic

---

[303]The word, as only a partial expression of the Christ-event, gives the believer only an imperfect access to faith. One needs only to ask whether the fullness of the event of the crucified one is present anywhere in the present time. If not, then one must ask where the fullness lies. Do we find it in the past (faith and sacraments become transportation into the past) or is it future (faith then awaits the future fullness in the ambiguity of the present)?

[304]Moltmann, "Hope and Development," p. 54.

[305]Moltmann, *The Crucified God*, pp 41ff.

form of Christian worship absorbed the cultic character of pagan religions into its practice. In this process the Christian cult was altered, resulting in the suppression of what was unique and scandalous about the worship of the crucified God.

> But this means that basically the crucified Christ represents the end of the cult. He has died 'once for all,' as Paul emphasizes. His death is not a sacrifice which can be repeated or transferred. He has finally risen from the death which he died once for all, as Paul emphasizes again and 'will never die again' (Rom. 6:9), in either a bloody or an unbloody way. He cannot be turned into an eternally dying and rising cultic god. He is not drawn into the cycle of 'eternal return of the life' (M. Eliade), but breaks out of the compulsive repetition of the cult. It is true that the eucharist or the celebration of the Lord's Supper recalls and makes present the death of Christ 'until he comes' (I Cor. 11:26), but in the form of 'proclamation', not in 'repetition' of Christ's death on the cross.[306]

To understand Christian worship as cultic (as Mass) is to deny the difference between cult and Golgotha. It takes away the dangerous memory of the Cross of Christ and fails to see the sacrifice of Christ as the once-for-all definitive event in salvation history. The cult takes death out of the world and destroys its power, by making the death of Christ an arbitrary event.[307]

Against this cultic "repetition," which he considers to place the Christ-event in the hands of men, thereby abandoning the original meaning of the Christ-event, Moltmann proposes the memory of the cross as the proper way of understanding the worship of the Church. Anamnesis is our link to the Christ-event since the Eucharist is not repetition but proclamation. "Cultic religion must be replaced by the spreading of

---

[306]Ibid., pp 43, 44.

[307]Ibid., pp 44-45.

the word of the cross, the celebration of faith and the practical following of Jesus."[308] The proclamation of the word of the cross contains the *memoria passionis Domini*, a dangerous memory, which prompts the believer to partake of a practical following of Christ.

A second deformation of the relationship between worship and the crucified Christ Moltmann calls the "mysticism of the cross." This understanding of worship comes closer to the correct interpretation of the liturgical symbols, but still falls short. The key to this second interpretation of worship is that "Fellowship with God is not attained by the outward sacrifice and presence in the church's cult; the way of glory leads through personal suffering. Thus by meditation and adoration people have drawn closer to the sufferings of Christ, participated in them and felt them as their own sufferings."[309] Through a process of spiritual appropriation, by means of prayer and meditation, the sufferings of Christ become those of the believer. And, the sufferings of the believer are taken up into the obedient action of Christ's suffering.

The difficulty that Moltmann has with this second form of worship, the "mystical suffering with Christ," is that it tends to lapse into "bland inwardness." Faith, according to Moltmann, requires the activity of the believer, a participation in the suffering of Christ.

Also, Moltmann cautions that one must be careful not to use this argument to justify all suffering. The suffering of a Christian is not a passive suffering at the hands of fate; rather, it is an active suffering that leads beyond a mere conforming to the cross of Christ. "The poverty and suffering of Christ are experienced and understood only by participation in his mission and in imitating the task he carried out."[310] Only in this active suffering, understood in terms of the mission of the faithful, does faith become liberating; i.e., as implicit in praxis.

---

[308]Ibid., p. 44.

[309]Ibid., p. 45.

[310]Ibid., p. 52.

The third category which Moltmann uses critically to appraise the worship of the Church is characterized as "following the cross." To follow Jesus means that one is called to abandon everything.[311]

> Thus the motivation for the call to follow Jesus is eschatological, and must not be understood in a moral sense. It is a call into the future of God which is now beginning in Jesus, and for the sake of this future, it is not only necessary but possible to break one's links with the world which is now passing away and abandon a concern for one's own life.[312]

The cross of Christ is not simply an example. It is the result of the mission of Christ, a constitutive part of the faith and all who follow Christ will undergo this trial. The believer, now under the conditions of fallen history, must suffer and be rejected.

In his theology, Moltmann reacts against those theologies (such as theologies of the word) which minimalize the significance of the public expression of the Christian faith. For Moltmann, it is inconceivable for faith to exist which does not affect the world. Faith must take place actively in the midst of our fallen world just as Christ's suffering and death on the cross. To follow Christ is to have faith, "and faith is in fact an existential unity of theory and practice."[313]

The unity of theory and praxis in faith constitutes the inner dynamic of the mission of the faithful. Since this mission takes its meaning from the Christ-event, the believer must be in contact with and informed by this normative event. It is in this context that the Eucharist plays an important role.

> The gospel tells us about the suffering and death of Christ. The delivering up of God's Son for the

---

[311]Ibid., p. 54.

[312]Ibid., p. 55.

[313]Ibid., p. 60.

> reconciliation of the world is communicated to us in the
> eucharist in the form of bread and wine. When the
> passion of Christ becomes present to us through word
> and sacrament, faith is awakened in us - the Christian
> faith in God. The person who believes owes his
> freedom to Christ's representation. He believes in God
> for Christ's sake. God himself is involved in the history
> of Christ's passion. If this were not so, no redeeming
> activity could radiate from Christ's death.[314]

The emphasis here is not on a real presence of the event of Christ, for there can be no sacramental re-presentation of the full historical event in the present. Rather, in Christ's passion, God himself is active in history and the believer participates in this redemptive activity through the evocation of the dangerous memory of Christ by means of word and sacrament. For in preaching and in the Lord's Supper, the living remembrance and the history of the passion are made present.[315] Consequently, the source of faith cannot be ecclesiastical authority or any material "thing."[316] In essence, it can only be by the "individual insight into the truth of revelation" that these memories are kept alive.[317]

Once again, Moltmann's theology stresses the primacy of the liturgy of the word wherein the proclamation of the word dominates the sacraments. "The symbol in thought is matched by the conception of reality as a sacrament, that is, as a reality qualified by God's word and made the bearer of his presence."[318] The sacraments are

---

[314]Jürgen Moltmann, *The Trinity and the Kingdom*, trans. Margaret Kohl (New York: Harper & Row Publishers, 1981), p. 21.

[315]Moltmann, "The Theoloy of the Cross Today," *The Future of Creation*, trans. Margret Kohl (Philadelphia: Fortress Press, 1979), p. 62. It must be remembered that for Moltmann the sacramental sign is simply a supplement to the word, helping to materialize it. Also see, *The Trinity and the Kingdom*, pp. 21ff.

[316]Moltmann, *The Crucified God*, p. 202.

[317]Ibid., pp 78-79.

[318]Ibid., p. 337.

materializations of the presence of God which battle against all gnostic interpretations of the faith that abstract from the concrete historical activity of God. According to Moltmann, the word qualifies the sacramental sign. There is no intrinsic indispensable connection between the word and its materialization. This implies that a particular external sign is useful only so long as it mediates the word. Sacraments, then, are not unambiguous events, but like all temporal things they are subject to the movements of time and become outdated by that movement. As proclamation the sacraments must change to serve the word. The liturgy of the sacrament is secondary to the of the word.

The proclamation of the word of God leads the believer to faith, a faith that has its primary locus in the conscience of the believer, but is not simply an interior change. The word leads the believer out of apathy to fellowship with the oppressed, to a solidarity that makes faith concrete. Faith, then, can no longer simply be private, it must be political, because the believer must attest to the truth of the revelation as he lives out his life in solidarity with those who suffer.[319]

C. Faith, liberation and history

Any theology which does not begin with the crucified Lord neglects that dimension of the revelation which is most characteristic of the Christian faith. The cross, then, is not merely an example or pattern for behavior, nor does it simply lead to an inner union with the Christ of faith.[320] Rather, the cross is the unique, unrepeatable event of the abandonment of Jesus by his Father.

In the present age, the believer is locked in a struggle between the grace offered by Christ and the unfreedom of human idolatries. The cross breaks the power

---

[319]Moltmann, "The Theology of the Cross Today," pp 62ff.

[320]Moltmann, *The Crucified God*, p. 202.

of these idolatries, freeing man for faith.[321] In the act of faith, the believer is freed in faith from all those human conventions which distract him from his true end: life in Christ. A faith based on this action can alone become the source of true faith and freedom.[322] Faith, then, is inseparable from a process of Christian liberation.

The life of faith, according to Moltmann, is a life of action, praxis - liberating solidarity with the poor. Moltmann arrives at this interpretation of Christianity by following what he understands to be the two fundamental principles of Christian theology. They are the principles of the cross and the tension between relevancy and identity.

First, he interprets the *sola fide* principles of the Reformation as a theology of the cross. The cross breaks through any objectifications or ideologies which humans try to use to insure their salvation. It is such objectifications, such "dreamed of equality with God," that dehumanizes man by minimizing the suffering of Christ and imprisoning man in unreality. The cross alone sets man free from illusion and fear which is at the root of all human desires to dominate and control reality.[323] The suffering of God eliminates the need for human self-deification and self-justification.[324] It is especially against idolatry that the crucified God stands.[325] Moreover, this faith is not to be understood simply as a mental exercise. Rather, it is a liberating faith which calls man to action in the world.[326]

---

[321]Ibid., p. 127.

[322]Ibid., p. 57.

[323]Jürgen Moltmann, "Hope of Resurrection and Practice of Liberation," *The Future of Creation*, trans. Margret Kohl (Philadelphia: Fortress Press, 1979), p. 122. Also *The Crucified God*, pp. 301, 308ff.

[324]Moltmann, *The Crucified God*, pp. 69-70.

[325]The crucified God stands over against the God revealed in the law, all idolatry and all beliefs of the direct revelation of God. See *The Crucified God*, pp. 301ff.

[326]Moltmann, *The Crucufied God*, pp. 72ff.

104

Since Christian theology is always the theology of the cross, it cannot be simply a theology of the word or a pure theory of history.[327] Such Christian philosophies, like the theology of the cross, begin with the assumption that what is real is Christian.[328] But philosophies and theories of history have the tendency to reduce the Christ-event to a message and, in the process, they fail to deal with the fullness of this event. "A Christian theology which sees its problem and its task in knowing God in the crucified Christ, cannot be pure theory. It cannot lead to a pure theory of God as in the vision of God in the early Church."[329] The cross is more than precepts or an ethical message; it is a point from which Christianity takes its identity. "And yet it only remains *theologia crucis* in the context of critical and liberating practice in preaching and life. The theology of the cross is a practical doctrine for battle, and can therefore become neither a theory of Christianity as it is now, nor the Christian theory of world history."[330] The cross is the call to the suffering which constitutes Christian life in the present fallen world.

This faith cannot withdraw into a ghetto isolated from the world. Neither can it decay into an uncritical assimilation to cultural trends. For it can also happen that the more the Church goes about fulfilling the needs of society, the more the Church leaves the cross behind.[331] There is always the danger that Christianity will become more and more closely associated with the ideals and philosophies of the society at large. Any such identification destroys the true freedom of religion. Nevertheless, the cross guarantees the freedom of the Christian from any such perversion.

---

[327]Ibid., pp 67-68. Theology, simply focused on the word, separates the doctrine of God, what we can say about God, from God's economy. According to Moltmann, it is only in the economy of salvation that the true nature of God is revealed.

[328]Ibid., pp 67-68.

[329]Ibid., p. 68; also p. 247.

[330]Ibid., p. 72.

[331]Ibid., pp 15, 41, 56.

> To make the cross a present reality in our civilization
> means to put into practice the experience one has
> received of being liberated from fear for oneself; no
> longer to adapt oneself to this society, its idols and
> taboos, its imaginary enemies and fetishes; and in the
> name of him who was once the victim of religion, to
> enter into solidarity with the victims of religion, society
> and the state at the present day, in the same way as he
> who was crucified became their brother and their
> liberator.[332]

Moltmann considers all attempts to objectify or conceptualize the Christian faith to amount to a reduction of its content. Religions do this to faith whenever they attempt to reduce the faith to an institution or dogma; i.e., the different Christian confessions. True Christian faith breaks through all such attempts to objectify the faith by its memory of the cross, a memory never fully realized in human conceptions.[333] But such objectifications are not only found in the religion, but are reflected in all those ideologies which place the final redemption of humanity in human hands.

The rationalism and reductionism which has plagued Christianity from the early gnostics to the gnostics of the present age is symptomatic of a larger problem. Christians today are more than ever aware of the misery and suffering resulting from sinful social structures.[334] These structures are sinful because they claim, as do all ideologies, a legitimacy which contradicts the cross of Christ. Freedom from these idols, with their idolatrous promises of salvation, is alone possible through the power of Christ.

---

[332]Ibid., p. 40. It is important to note that following Schleiermacher, Moltmann distinguishes between faith and religion (pp 296ff). Religion can stifle the true revelation of God. See pp. 215ff.

[333]Moltmann, "The Theology of the Cross Today," pp. 60ff. Also see *The Crucified God*, pp 37, 96.

[334]Moltmann, *The Crucified God*, p. 23.

106

In faith, the tension between relevance and identity is solved. The very identity of the Christian faith, an identification with the cross of Christ, calls the Christian to solidarity with those who suffer persecution. This constitutes the emptying of oneself in loving union with those who suffer. In this act of solidarity, which is an essential aspect of faith, the believer becomes relevant. Faith in Christ is always a socially active faith which engages society and the structures of society in the present.[335] In faith, the believer is called upon to suffer for those who are oppressed in fallen history. History, here, consists of conflict and oppression, a history to be overcome by the future fullness of Christ.

D. The cross, resurrection and the opening of history

Moltmann's understanding of the Cross as the center of the Christian faith has always made the Christian message difficult to accept and this is especially true today. Moltmann identifies the tendency of contemporary theological scholarship to be moving away from the crucifixion and emphasizing the resurrected Christ.[336] This triumphalism has led to a dehistoricizing of the faith since it inevitably fails to recognize the full historical character of the cross and the implications of this for the faith.[337]

Moltmann believes his theology to better reflect the true nature of the faith by placing the crucified Christ at the center of his Christology, his ecclesiology[338] and his

---

[335] It is in this argument that the political theology of Moltmann becomes evident. It is on the point of solidarity that his theology can be understood most clearly as a form of liberation theology. See, The Crucified God, pp. 30ff.

[336] According to Moltmann, such an emphasis has often lead to the support of monarchical and despotic forms of government. See The Crucified God, pp. 301ff.

[337] Ibid., pp 96ff. According to Moltmann, the anthropological historical consciousness strips away the Christ of tradition and turns him into someone who is more human and acceptable to us all (p. 118). But the Cross cannot be reduced to such a portrait.

[338] Ibid., p. 123. The Church has been and must be altered by the death of Christ.

understanding of history.[339] "All Christian statements about God, about creation, about sin and death have their focal point in the crucified Christ. All Christian statements about history, about the Church, about faith and sanctification, about the future and about hope stem from the crucified Christ."[340] All theology of every interest begins and ends with the cross.

Time and again Moltmann stresses that the key to understanding faith is the cross,[341] for only in the light of the cross does the real meaning of the Christ-event become lucid. This "light" is only partial under the present conditions of fallen history. In the cross a glimpse of the "new creation," the order of the end time, is revealed. During the present age, faith lives by the promise of the "new creation" and the believer awaits the time when the actions of Christ will be made fully intelligible.[342] The cross of Christ reveals that which is essential to Christian faith, but the full understanding of this faith remains an eschatological event.

In this economy of salvation Moltmann describes the cross as imposing a silence on the words of men, and it is only in the resurrection that the silence is broken. There is silence because man cannot speak of those salvific events which transcend his power and it is only in the resurrection that we come to partake of that life and grace by which we are saved. If the life of faith in the present is founded on the proclamation of the word of God, it is a proclamation held within the tension of the Cross, where all human efforts are silenced, and the resurrection where the triumph of the grace of Christ is given as promise, since this proclamation reflects the presence of the

---

[339]Ibid., p. 124.

[340]Ibid., p. 204.

[341]Ibid., p. 120. Here he differs with the existentialist theologians. For Bultmann, the preaching, not the content, is decisive. Jesus is identified with his word. Of this theology Moltmann asks if in the death of Jesus the continuity of his message is broken. Does not his death destroy the meaning of this message? According to Moltmann, such theologies leave a gap between the death of Jesus and the present. (pp 120ff) Is the death a refutation of his message? Is the past proclamation a refutation of his death?

[342]Ibid., p. 106ff.

108

resurrected one, our faith in the present must reflect not only the historicity of dying Christ, but also the historicity of the Risen One as well.

At the center of the faith stands the Cross and resurrection, the crucified and risen Christ. In Moltmann's view of the Risen Christ it is important to recognize that he is trying to hold together the historical and the eschatological dimensions of faith. He does this in the simple proclamation that Christ is both crucified and risen.[343] On this basis, Moltmann critizes most contemporary Christians who, as he insists, see Christ and the faith primarily in terms of the resurrection. Moltmann is careful to show that despite the profound effects of the resurrection, the significance of the Cross is not negated. Rather, the resurrection points to the saving significance of the Cross.[344]

> The resurrection 'does not evacuate the cross' (I Cor. 1:17), but fills it with eschatological and saving significance. From this it follows systematically that all further interpretation of the saving significance of Christ's death on the cross 'for us' must start from his resurrection. Furthermore, when it is said at length that only his death has saving significance for us, that means that his death on the cross expresses the significance of his resurrection for us and not, vice versa, that his resurrection expresses the significance of his cross. The resurrection from the dead qualifies the person of the crucified Christ and with it the saving significance of his death on the cross for us, 'the dead.' Thus the saving significance of his cross manifests his resurrection.[345]

The resurrection is a prelude, an anticipation of the future that opens up the transitory present to the future of God.[346] It begins to bridge the gap between the history of God

---

[343]Ibid., pp. 160, 184.

[344]Ibid., pp. 161, 182.

[345]Ibid., pp. 182-183.

[346]Ibid., p. 163. Also, Moltmann, "Hope and Development," pp 52, 53.

and the history of fallen creation. In the crucified one, the future is initiated in the fallen world.

The emphasis on the historical reality of the cross gives Moltmann a locus, a historical event in fallen history, where the unambiguous future salvation of God has begun, making the reality of salvation a concrete actuality. "In the crucified Jesus the risen Christ is present on earth - present and seeable and tellable. But if God himself is near in the risen one, then the crucified Jesus is the face and the revelation of the coming God."[347] In the crucified one the future has dawned; Christ has come into the midst of struggle and death to bring reconciliation.[348]

In the light of the cross, as the hermeneutical principle by which all reality must be interpreted, Moltmann characterizes history as conflict. The conflict is centered on the struggle between order and chaos, God and gods, the divine and all idolatries. In any case, the time between creation and redemption is the history of fallen creation, a history of suffering.[349] The Fall has led to a total corruption of the once original good creation. There can be nothing new or creative, only the ever-increasing deterioration of the world.[350] It is into this history that Christ enters and brings salvation.

Like Cullmann, Moltmann emphasizes that the salvation of God is offered to man in concrete events and faith rests on these events. But unlike Cullmann, who sees this salvation working in the midst of fallen history (in that there are points at which salvation history and fallen history come together in certain kerygmatic moments), Moltmann understands salvation as an eschatological present. Salvation does not take place in fallen history, rather, fallen history is taken up into the salvific history of God. From this perspective one must distinguish between the salvation of human history, and

---

[347]Moltmann, "Hope and Development," p. 53.

[348]Moltmann, *The Crucified God,* pp. 171, 178.

[349]Moltmann, *The Trinity and the Kingdom,* pp. 36, 49.

the salvation of the faithful in the history of God. In the latter, salvation enters fallen history, but it does so only to save the believer from fallen history. There is no redemption of the original good creation itself, since it is lost to the power of sin.

According to Moltmann, because the history of the world, in which freedom and faith are considered foolishness, is an ambiguous history of struggle and sin,[351] present world history must undergo annihilation and be recreated in the history of God.[352] This redemptive process begins in the trinitarian history of God, a living history which finds its center in the cross, standing against the world as the world's horizon.

> This history of God or this history in God begins with the sending and the delivering up of the Son, continues with his resurrection and the transference of the rule of God to him, and only ends when the Son hands over this rule to the Father. The delivering up on the cross is the central point of this history in God, not its conclusion.[353]

We know God by means of his revelation in history, as he reveals himself in the suffering Christ.[354] He goes out of himself, becomes involved in a sinful world and takes the world up into his life. He is a suffering God whose very nature is self-sacrificing love.[355]

---

[350]Jürgen Moltmann, "Creation as an Open System," *The Future of Creation*, trans. by Margret Kohl (Philadelphia: Fortress Press, 1979).

[351]Moltmann, *The Crucified God*, pp. 171, 178.

[352]Ibid., p. 218.

[353]Ibid., p. 265.

[354]Jürgen Moltmann, "The Trinitarian History of God," *The Future of Creation*, trans. Margret Kohl (Philadelphia: Fortress Press, 1979), pp 83ff. Also *The Trinity and the Kingdom*, p. 153.

[355]Moltmann, *The Trinity and the Kingdom*, pp. 4, 27, 32, 34, 51ff.

This history of God, present in Christ and in the Spirit, opens our present world history, which has been closed by sin, to the trinitarian history of God.[356] As creation enters into this history of God, the bonds of sin are broken. Creation is transformed and created anew in the history of God.[357]

It is difficult to tell in the theology of Moltmann whether in the process of salvation the history of God annihilates the history of man or fulfills it. Moltmann appears to avoid the alternatives of a total annihilation and a total assimilation. Moltmann simply insists that salvation history, the history of God, is the only true history that enters into world history and takes fallen world history into itself.

> We can therefore term this 'history of God' in the cross of the Son the history of history. World history - creation's history of suffering and hope - is integrated in the trinitarian process of God and is experienced and formed theologically in the light of this presupposition. To recognize the crucified God therefore means seeing oneself together with suffering creation in this history of God.[358]

Given in the Christ-event is the anticipation of the future of God. "This anticipation of the future which can be recognized in his whole manifestation, in his person, his functions and his history of crucifixion and resurrection, has led to his being seen as the unconditional and universal realization of the promise."[359] In Christ, God does not become simply spiritually present, but he enters fallen creation and embraces the whole of human reality. "He lowers himself and accepts the whole of mankind without limits

---

[356]Ibid., p. 210. Also, Moltmann, "Creation as an Open System," p. 122.

[357]Ibid., pp. 100ff, 117ff.

[358]Moltmann, "The Theology of hte Cross Today," p. 75.

[359]Moltmann, *The Crucified God*, p. 256.

and conditions, so that each man may participate in him with the whole of his life."[360] In the light of the cross, the event where God enters fallen history, the Christian comes to understand himself and his relationship to creation.

This means that history is time interpreted in the light of the Christ-event, or better, that history is time interpreted in the light of the history of God. And the meaning of faith definitive of all time, is accessible to us here and now in the midst of time.

In this understanding of the faith, only in the future history of God will that which makes the believer whole be present to man in its fullness. "But what is meant is that the person and history of Jesus have been manifested and understood as open to the future of God in the way that was characteristic of the distinctive existence of Israel amongst all other nations."[361] This opening up of the present age is characteristic of Christ's redemptive activity and the proclamation of the word of God. The Kingdom of God, initiated in the Christ, fulfills the covenant with Irsael. Yet a complete clarity is not given in the present, because both faith and sacraments remain ambiguous mediations of the grace of Christ. They elicit a solidarity of the believer with Christ, which nonetheless remains partial in fallen history. This leaves one with a question as to the extent to which the believer is able to participate in the Christ-event in the present. Since there is no unambiguous re-presentation of this event in the present, the present must remain under the bondage of fallen history. In the sacrament, this present faith looks backward to the dangerous memory and forward to the promise of future salvation. The unambiguous points of contact with the source of our faith lie in the past and in the future, but not in the present.

Faith, then, is a response to the call to leave behind one's narcissism and to be taken up into the history of God.[362] In baptism, one enters into a union with Christ in

---

[360]Ibid., p. 276.

[361]Moltmann, "The Theology of hte Cross Today," p. 75.

[362]Moltmann, *The Trinity and the Kingdom*, p. 5.

the history of God and one's life is shaped by the Spirit.[363] "Whereas in the sending, in the surrender and in the resurrection, the Spirit acts on Christ, and Christ lives from the works of the creative Spirit, now the relationship is reversed: the Risen Christ sends the Spirit; he is himself present in the life-giving Spirit; and through the Spirit's energies - the charismata - he acts on men and women."[364] Given in the Spirit is the new creation, an eschatological future not yet realized in the present.[365] We are left, then, in Moltmann's theology, with a faith based upon an unarticulated unity with the history of God, given in the Spirit.

Moltmann is aware of the fact that a faith based on the Spirit can easily be dehistoricized. In his theology, he tries to prevent this by insisting that faith is an anticipation of future fullness. This does not mean that faith is a spiritualization, an enclave in a fallen world or a haven for redeemed souls in an unredeemed world; rather, faith is an eschatological anticipation.[366] It is a faith which concretizes itself in the present struggle for justice and love, a public testimony to the freedom of Christ.[367] And despite the fact that faith calls for such actions, Moltmann is careful to avoid the tendencies toward pelagianism which are so rampant today. He insists that this faith relationship with God is made possible by the power of God, not by any human effort. In the Christ-event, God opens up the history of man, a history of sin and death, to the history of God.[368] "Man is taken up, without limitations and conditions, into the life

[363]Ibid., pp 156-157.

[364]Ibid., p. 311.

[365]Ibid., p. 89.

[366]Moltmann, The Crucified God, p. 101.

[367]Ibid., p. 145.

[368]Ibid., p. 275.

and suffering, the death and resurrection of God, and in faith participates corporeally in the fullness of God."[369]

Within his perspective, Moltmann affirms the full historicity of the faith in the present by insisting that faith does affect the whole self and our struggle in fallen creation. "We shall thereby take as our premise that the Christian faith is due to the word of Christ, and we shall ask solely about the boundary at which faith has to be present today if it wants to participate in the transcendence of God's presence."[370] In the proclamation the believer is given a promise of future salvation, a salvation that transcends fallen history, a future that is qualitatively new. Only on the basis of such a future can the present be understood.[371] But the fullness is only given as promise.

F. Summary

History, the meaning of time, can only be interpreted in the light of ultimate meaning -- the unambiguous, full revelation of God. "For the Christian faith the two things - history and the future - come together in Christ in whom the qualitatively new future is present under the condition of history."[372] But the Christ-event is nowhere unambiguously mediated in our present. The present is time in between significant times (past Christ-event, future consummation), taking its meaning from the Christ-event yet awaiting a future fulfillment. The liturgy of the word is the sole bridge between the event of Christ and the present that alone unites the faithful with the promise of future salvation given in Christ.

---

[369]Ibid., p. 277.

[370]Jürgen Moltmann, "Future as a Paradigm of Transcendence," *The Future of Creation,* trans. Margret Kohl (Philadelphia: Fortress Press, 1979), p. 2.

[371]Ibid., p. 5.

[372]Ibid., p. 16.

A problem that arises in Moltmann's theology is the problem of the nature of faith in the present, a problem associated with the relationship of creation and redemption. Moltmann holds that fallen creation is annihilated in the process of redemption. He certainly does not want to gloss over the discontinuity between fallen and redeemed creation by some notion of grace that simply transforms the "old creation" into the "new creation." It is apparent that it is precisely the tension between the fallen history and the history of God that is the focal point of his theology. In this he believes himself to be faithful to the *sola fide, solus Christus* emphasis within Protestant theology, where it is in the cross that this tension finds its focus. And it is in faith in Christ that we overcome the consequences of fallen creation. This faith looks to the future, since the full redemptive activity of Christ is promised. But the relationship of faith to the future and the continuity of the faith in the present remains obscure.

A way to solve this might be to return to an examination of Moltmann's Christology. In his Christology, he rightly focuses on the Cross as the center of history where the link between human fallen history and the history of God is made. Here the sinful history is taken up into the history of God, a future history somehow inititated in Christ. Nevertheless, Moltmann fails to consider Christ's role in the order of the good creation (now fallen) and the history of God. Remember if Christ is present from the beginning, (it is he "through whom all things came to be" (Jn 1:10)), then there is a continuity between fallen creation and the history of God that needs to be explained. No doubt that without creation-in-Christ as a primary Christological category, one will most likely be left with a radical discontinuity between this world and the next, between "old" and "new," between a world bound to sin and one that is free. For the unity is free, given in Christ who is, was and is to come and there can be no other unity for the present, past and future. Moltmann appears to understand this unity, yet neglects to give an adequate account of it.

The result is that liturgy the nexus of unity between God and man, is understood to be an identification of the believer with Christ by means of the proclamation of the word of God and praxis - the mission of the Church. It is this unity of faith in praxis that constitutes the act of faith and is the norm by which history is interpreted. In praxis, the believer is taken up into the history of God and fallen history is redeemed. But like the proclamation, in the present age praxis remains ambiguous, failing to realize the fullness of the salvation of Christ. No earthly mediation can effect the history of God.[373]

It should be noted that there is in Moltmann's theology what appears to be an effort to make praxis the real locus of liturgical life, for in praxis the salvation of Christ given in the proclamation and sacrament finds its fullest articulation. According to Moltmann, it is by acting as Christ did, that one truly comes to understand and participate in the life of faith. The primary liturgical form becomes a solidarity with the poor; i.e., praxis.

---

[373]Moltmann, *The Trinity and the Kingdom*, p. 197. This is a rejection of the sacramental nature of the good creation, the Church and the Papcy. It is consistent with the *sola fide* rejection of all works and their claim to mediate the grace of Christ in any definitive manner. Such a mediation is not possible in fallen creation. Faith is free. It transcends any worldly mediation except for Christ. Also see Robinson, *Theology as History*, p. 17.

Summary of Part I: The Liturgy of the Word and the Historicity of the Faith

The Protestant theologies of Ebeling and Fuchs, which stress the liturgy of the word, are also characterized by an insistence upon the absence of any unambiguous encounter in history with the fullness of the Christ-event. Given in the word-event is the promise of future fulfillment, but our access to that future in the here and now is always partial and fragmented, for the proclamation of the word by the Church is always ambiguous: its sole function is to instill hope in our future salvation. Cullmann and Moltmann attempt to ground this proclamation in concrete historical events. Cullmann does this by pointing to the present workings of salvation history. Moltmann does it by making faith concrete, by anchoring it in the suffering of the world. But in all cases the present remains ambiguous. It is not possible to find anywhere in the present the full realization of the Christ-event. Consequently, one finds in these theologies an emphasis on the "not yet" pole of the eschatological tension.

These remarks are not made to condemn. Rather they are made in the light of the Roman Catholic emphasis on the re-presentation of the Christ-event in the sacrifice of the Mass. The Catholic position holds to the view that by the power of Christ the fullness of the Christ-event is present in the worship of the Church. In the light of this position, the implicit understanding of the historicity of faith in the Protestant liturgy becomes clearer. It is to the Catholic position that I now turn.

Part II: Roman Catholicism and the Liturgy of the Sacrament

The Roman Catholic interpretation of the eucharistic symbols upholds the primacy a sacramental understanding of the liturgy and lends a certain character to a faith informed by this worship. In order to understand the meaning of the relationship of eucharist and faith, this section begins by presenting a brief survey of some of the modern statements the magisterium of the Roman Catholic Church has made concerning the Eucharist. The focus is on the Church's Eucharistic teaching and the relationship of the Eucharist to the Church. This type of analysis is particularly appropriate to the Roman Catholic tradition where there is a special emphasis upon the Eucharist as the historical cause of the historical Church. Consequently the Eucharist plays a major role in Catholic ecclesiological discussion, the underlying assumption being that the nature and quality of the Church's history, the sacramentality of its present life of faith, is understood to be an implication and consequence of the sacramentality of her Eucharistic worship.[374]

It must be noted that the question of the historicity of the faith is not explicitly treated in the Church's teachings, but her teachings do hold an implicit and consistent understanding of that historicity. The Roman Catholic teachings on the historicity of the faith and of Church will differ significantly from what has been said about the the nature of the Church in Protestantism. The locus of that difference can best be found in each denomination's statements on the Eucharist.

The three final chapters in this section will examine the understanding of history implicit in the Roman Catholic interpretation of the Eucharistic symbols currently found in several Roman Catholic theologies. To do this, it will be necessary to look at some

---

[374]This same connection between worship and ecclesiology explored in the previous chapters will be tested again here. It should be pointed out that the Roman Catholic understanding of the Church posits a teaching authority which is normative for the understanding of the life of faith. So, contrary to Protestant ecclesiology where preaching and theology have the primary teaching function, any analysis of Roman Catholic thought must begin with the teachings of the Magisterium.

representatives of contemporary Roman Catholic theology and unearth the "theology of history" which results from their particular interpretations of the Eucharistic symbols. Three Roman Catholic theologies will be considered in this connection: the theologies of Hans Urs von Balthasar, Yves Congar and Henri de Lubac.

Chapter V: Modern Catholic Teachings on the Sacred Liturgy[375]

The teachings of Vatican II and many other modern Church documents affirm the centrality of Eucharistic worship to the life of the Church. According to Pope John Paul II, the eucharistic worship "constitute[s] the soul of Christian life."[376] In Roman Catholic teaching, the Eucharist is not interpreted in subordination to a confessional insistence upon the liturgical presence of the Christ in the Church *sola fide*, but in terms of the Catholic doctrine of the Eucharistic liturgy. The Eucharist is understood to be a sacramental representation of the one sacrifice of the Cross, and to be constituted by a presence of the Risen Christ, the prior cause of all faith and of the Church. Only on this basis can the Roman Catholic affirmation of the historicity of the Church, the Church's worship and the Church's faith be understood.

By focusing on this relationship, it becomes evident that a consistent understanding of the historicity of the faith can be found as one moves from an examination of the Church to an examination of the sacrament, and vice versa. There is a continuity between the Body of Christ as the Incarnate one, as represented in the Eucharist, and the Church. The life of the Church is informed by its encounter with Christ in the sacraments, and reflects the real presence of the resurrected Christ. It is the historicity of this relationship that is at issue here; i.e., the relationship between the Christ-event, sacrament and Church

---

[375]It would be beyond the limits of this work to show the development of the Church's interpretation of the Eucharistic symbols in terms of the liturgy of the sacrament. A brief summary of the Church's sacramental interpretation of the Eucharistic liturgy will be presented here, together with the view of the historicity of the faith corresponding to this understanding of the Eucharist. Although the historicity of the faith is not explicitly developed in this section on the Church's teachings, it is present there by implication. This will become evident in our examination of the Roman Catholic understanding of the sacraments and the life of the Church.

[376]Pope John Paul II, "Mystery and Worship of the Holy Eucharist," *Origins*, March 27, 1980; Vol. 9:No.41, p. 657.

122

A. The Church and salvation

As in the case of the Protestant theologies we have examined, the Roman Catholic ecclesiologies view the Church from the standpoint of her role in the economy of salvation. With the Fall, God did not abandon man to sin; rather, he gave man his Church to continue to mediate his salvation in fallen creation. The Church is his instrument in the work of salvation, a work never separated from his own presence in his Church.[377] Vatican II affirms this when it affirms the sacramental character of the Church.[378] *Lumen Gentium* describes the Church as not only containing sacraments, but as a sign, presence and fullness herself of the redemption of Christ. The Church is the all-embracing agent of salvation because Christ now lives in her. "For it is indeed Christ who lives in the Church and through her teaches, governs and sanctifies; and it is also Christ who manifests Himself in manifold guise in the various members of His society."[379] The Church, in her role in the process of salvation, offers Christ's redemption to man.[380]

Although the Church is the locus of the redemption of Christ at work in the world, she remains a Pilgrim Church.[381] "The Church, however, drawing sinners to her bosom, at once holy and always in need of purification, follows continually the path of

---

[377]*Lumen Gentium, Vatican Council II*, ed. Austin Flannery, O.P. (New York: Costello Publishing Company, 1975), p. 351.

[378]*Lumen Gentium*, pp. 350, 361ff. Also see Herbert Vorgrimler, ed., *Commentary on the Documents of Vatican II*, (New York: Herder & Herder, 1967), pp 149, 186.

[379]Pope Pius XII, *The Mystical Body of Christ*, trans. Canon G. D. Smith, in *Selected Letters and Addresses of Pius XII*, ed, Catholic Truth Society (London: Kiliken, Hudson & Kerns, LTD, 1949), p. 99. This threefold authority of Church is affirmed in *Lumen Gentium*, para 21. Also see Aidan Nichols, O.P. *Holy Order* (Dublin: Veritas Publications, 1990), pp 10ff.

[380]An expression of this is the papacy. Christ is *de facto* concretely present to his people. See Vorgrimler, *Commentary*, pp 149ff.

[381]*Sacrosanctum Concilium*, in *Vatican Council II*, ed. Austin Flannery, O.P. (New York: Costello Publishing Co., 1975), p. 1. *Lumen Gentium*, pp 356, 358, 422.

penance and renewal."[382] The sinfulness of the individual members of the Church does not destroy the Church as a sign of salvation. As the Bride of Christ, the Church is sanctified by the blood of Christ and remains holy, thereby free to mediate the grace of Christ amid fallen creation.[383] The bond between Christ and the Church is maintained, the Church remaining a sign of the salvific will of God in the world.

The Church itself becomes a sign and the sacrament of salvation in whom is the fullness of Christ, the Head, who brings perfection to His Body.[384] She, the Church, calls all men to salvation and stands before the world as the witness to the salvation wrought by Christ and the offer of that grace to the world.[385]

Since the Church is said to contain the fullness of the Christ-event, it would appear that the sacraments and the sacramentals of the Church are the extension of the divine redemption given in the Church. It may even appear that the Church claims control or power over the sacraments, but in reality the sacraments have a certain priority in the Church. It must be remembered that the Church receives its life and being from the Christ-event.[386] Therefore, neither the sacraments nor the Church receive their life from any human agency, but from the grace of Christ alone.

> The divine Redeemer began to build the mystical
> temple of His Church when he was preaching and

---

[382]*Lumen Gentium*, p. 358. Also see Pius XII, *Mystici Corporis*, p. 62.

[383]Vorgrimler, *Commentary*, p. 169. Despite sin by members of the Church, she remains here and now the sign of salvation. Also see Yves Congar, "The Church and the People of God," *Concilium*, January 1965; Vol. 1: No. 1, pp 15ff. There is a tension in the Church between the unbreakable relationship of Christ to his Body, his spouse, the Church, which is purified by the Blood of Christ, and the totality of Christians in the world who are sinners. This is an important aspect of the eschatological tension between the already and the not yet. Congar warns against degrading the "is now" in favor of the "not yet." From our limited human experience this would seem to be the primary temptation.

[384]Pius XII, *Mystici Corporis*, p. 62.

[385]*Lumen Gentium*, pp. 351, 364. Also see *Mystici Corporis*, pp 60f.

[386]Pius XII, *Mystici Corporis*, p. 63.

giving his commandments; He completed it when He hung in glory on the Cross; He manifested and promulgated it by the visible mission of the Paraclete, the Holy Spirit, upon His disciples.[387]

From this redemptive event, an event that the Church has access to primarily through her sacramental life, the Church alone receives its life.

Since the sacraments draw their life from "the Paschal mystery of the Passion, Death and Resurrection of Christ," in the sacraments the power of Christ which builds up the Church is given to the Church.[388]

In that body the life of Christ is communicated to all those who believe and who, through the sacraments, are united in a hidden and real way to Christ in his passion and glorification. Through baptism we are formed in the likeness of Christ: "For in one Spirit we were all baptized into one body" (1Cor. 12:13). In this sacred rite fellowship in Christ's death and resurrection is symbolized and brought about: "For we were buried with him by means of baptism into death"; and if "we have been united with him in the likeness of his death, we shall be so in the likeness of his resurrection also" (Rom. 6:4-5). Really sharing in the body of the Lord in the breaking of the eucharistic bread, we are taken up into communion with him and with one another.[389]

By means of the sacraments the Church has contact with the source of her life. And though it is true that there are other means of access to the grace of Christ, it must be emphasized that the most perfect means during the present age are found in the sacramental life of the Church..[390]

---

[387]Ibid., p. 63.

[388]*Sacrosanctum Concilium*, p. 20. Also see Pius XII, *Mystici Corporis*, pp 66, 67.

[389]*Lumen Gentium*, p. 355. Also see Pius XII, *Mystici Corporis*, pp. 60ff.

[390]Pius XII, *Mystici Corporis*, pp 86ff.

Since the Church draws its life from the Christ-event and it is by means of the sacraments that the Church in the present has access to the source of her faith, it must be concluded that although Christ is the formal and final cause of the Church, the sacraments now are the historical locus of that "causing" from which the Church in the present draws its life. The sacraments, then, are not under the power of the Church; rather, they are the cause of the Church and therefore prior to the life of the Church. They are prior, not in a chronological sense, but as the font from which the Church takes its life.

One way that one might describe this unity of the visible sign and the results of the sacramental actions is to say that they are efficacious, mediating the grace of Christ by the power of Christ. This means that they are under the power of Christ alone.[391] Yet often Roman Catholic sacramental theology has been accused of "perverting" the sacraments by reducing them to human "control." There may well have been grounds for this charge, but according to the explicit teachings of the Church, it is the sacraments which control and inform the life of the Church, not the opposite.[392]

At Vatican II the Church reaffirmed the worship of the Church to be at the center of Christian life.[393] It was once again stated that the Church was from its very origin a cultic community.

> From that time onwards the Church never failed to come together to celebrate the paschal mystery reading those things "which were in all the scripture concerning

---

[391] John Paul II, "Mystery and Worship of the Holy Eucharist," p. 664.

[392] Pope Paul VI, *Mysterium Fidei* (Washington, D.C.: National Catholic Welfare Conference, 1965), p. 4. Paul VI warns against subjecting the revelation to rationalisms. The primacy of the sacraments to the Church is evidenced in particular in the sacraments of marriage and Holy Orders. The Church witnesses a marriage and can judge if the conditions are right for a free entrance into this covenant, but it cannot "undo" this sacrament or any other. This is the basis for the *res et sacramentum* analysis, a doctrine developed by Augustine in response to the Donatist controversy. It is now being attacked on generally Reformation grounds.

[393] *Sacrosanctum Concilium*, pp 1, 7. Vorgrimler, *Commentary*, p. 161. They see the Church as the "cultic Community."

126

> him"(Luke 24:27), celebrating the Eucharist in which
> "the victory and triumph of his death are again made
> present," and at the same time "giving thanks to God
> for his inexpressible gift" (2Cor. 9:15) in Christ Jesus,
> "in praise of his glory" (Eph. 1:12) through the power
> of the Holy Spirit.[394]

Pope John Paul II notes that the liturgy is more than simply an expression of faith, it is the source of the Church's life.[395] In worship the believer encounters his Savior, the source of his faith.[396] And, just as the Roman Catholic Church has always affirmed the importance of the sacramental life, she has also asserted the primacy of the sacrament of the Eucharist. "For if the sacred liturgy holds the first place in the life of the Church, the mystery of the Eucharist stands at the heart and center of the sacred liturgy because it is in fact the font of life; purified and strengthened by it we live not for ourselves, but for God and are joined together by the strongest bond of love."[397]

> Moreover in a manner even more sublime, Christ is
> present in His Church when she offers the sacrifice of
> the Mass in his name. He is present when she
> administers the sacraments. In regard to the presence
> of Christ in the offering of the sacrifice of the Mass it is
> well to recall what St. John Chrysostom, overcome
> with admiration, said with no less truth than eloquence:
> "I wish to add something thoroughly amazing, but do
> not be astonished or disturbed. What is it? The
> sacrifice is the same, no matter who offers it, be it Paul
> or Peter, it is the same sacrifice which Christ gave to
> his disciples and which priests now offer; the offering
> made today is not inferior to Christ's because it is not
> men who make this offering holy, but He himself who

---

[394]Ibid., p. 4.

[395]Pope John Paul II, "Mystery and Worship of the Holy Eucharist," p. 664.

[396]Ibid., pp 655, 656.

[397]Paul IV, *Mysterium Fidei*, p. 2. Also see John Paul II, "Mystery and Worship of the Holy Eucharist," p. 658.

sanctified the first. For just as the words which God spoke are the source of those which the priest now uses so also is the sacrifice the very same." . . . . But there is another way, and indeed most remarkable, in which Christ is present in His Church in the sacrament of the Eucharist which is therefore among the rest of the sacraments "the more pleasing in respect to devotion, the more noble in respect to understanding and holier in regard to what it contains" for it contains Christ Himself and is "as it were the perfection of the spiritual life and the goal of all the sacraments."[398]

The priority of the Eucharist in the Church and among the sacraments reflects the very nature of the Eucharistic presence.

B. The liturgy of the sacrament and the sacrifice of the Mass

In the Eucharist, the unique presence of Christ is caused by the power of Christ. "From this it follows that every liturgical celebration, because it is an action of Christ the Priest and of his Body, which is the Church, is a sacred action surpassing all other. No other action of the Church can equal its efficacy by the same title and to the same degree."[399] This Eucharistic encounter with the source of our faith is different from the encounter in the other sacraments. One dimension of this unique sacrament is it's communal character. Since the Spirit given in the Eucharist unites the believers with the source of their faith, the Eucharist is often referred to as the "sacrament of Christian fraternity."[400]

---

[398]Ibid., p. 11. The reference to St. John Chrysostom is taken from "Matthaeum Homilia," 82, 4 *Migne P.G.* 58, p. 743.

[399]*Sacrosanctum Concilium*, pp 4, 5. Also see Paul IV, *Mysterium Fidei*, p. 5.

[400]Joseph Ratzinger, "Pastoral Implications of Episcopal Collegiality," *Concilium*, January 1965, Vol. 1:No. 1, p. 10.

This unity is indeed one of the results of the liturgical life of the Church, but the experience of unity and brotherhood are not the causes of the Church's existence.

> The Church is brought into being when, in that fraternal union and communion, we celebrate the sacrifice of the cross of Christ, when we proclaim "the Lord's death until he comes," and later, when being deeply compenetrated with the mystery of our salvation, we approach as a community the table of the Lord in order to be nourished in a sacramental manner, by the fruits of the holy sacrifice of propitiation.[401]

The Roman Catholic teaching on the Eucharist retains and emphasizes the sacrificial character of the Mass, for it is only in the sacrifice of the Mass that the fullness of the Christ-event is present in the Church.

A central point of the Roman Catholic discussion of the Eucharist is the belief that the Eucharist has the character of an "event." As an "event", the Eucharist cannot simply be reduced to the remembrance of a past event or a "spiritual" encounter that takes place solely in the interior life of the believer. Rather, it is the encounter with Christ, a participation in the Christ-event; i.e., the whole Christ, born of the Virgin Mary, who suffered, died, rose from the dead and is now seated at the right hand of the Father.[402] This is the "real" presence.

---

[401] John Paul II, "Mystery and Worship of the Holy Eucharist," p. 656. Also see Paul VI, *Mysterium Fidei*, p. 10.

[402] A distinction must be made at this point between the two notions of sacrifice operative in the tradition: the *sacrificium crucis* and the *sacrificium laudis*. See "Catholic-Lutheran Agreed Statement on the Eucharist," *Origins*, January 1979, Vol. 8:No. 30, pp 416-480. "According to Catholic teaching, in each eucharist 'a true and proper sacrifice is offered' through Christ. 'This sacrifice is truly propitiatory and has this effect that we "obtain mercy and find grace to help in time of need" (Heb. 4:16). For the victim is one and the same, the same offering by the ministry of the priests then offered himself on the cross, the manner of offering alone being different..... Wherefore according to the tradition of the apostles, it is rightly offered not only for sins, punishments, satisfactions and other necessities of the faithful who are living, but also for those departed in Christ but not yet fully purified.

As members of his body, the believers are included in the offering of Christ."

"On the other hand, the Lutheran reformation affirmed the understanding of the Lord's Supper as a sacrifice of thanksgiving in return for the sacrifice of the cross present in the

The presence is called "real" - by which it is not intended to exclude all other types of presence as if they were not "real," but it is the presence *par excellence*: because it is a substantial presence by which the whole and complete Christ, God and Man, is present. One would therefore falsely explain this manner of presence by conceiving a so-called "pneumatic" nature of the body of the glorified Christ everywhere present, or by restricting it to the limits of symbolism as if the most august sacrament consisted of nothing else than an efficacious sign "of the spiritual presence of Christ and of his intimate union with the faithful members of His Mystical Body.[403]

The Catholic understanding of this sacrament emphasizes this sacrificial aspect of the Eucharist, for it is on the Cross, in that historical action, that redemption was accomplished for the whole of creation. The participation of the believer in that event is not simply pneumatic; rather it is the participation in the mystery of the whole Christ. In the event of the Cross, the person of Christ, his actions, his place in the order of salvation, are expressed completely. A full faith cannot be founded simply on an internal experience of God, mystical and private (although this is part of the experience of faith), but it must encompass the fullness of created reality as does the event which is the source of our faith. Consequently, we are saved in and through the sacrifice of the

---

sacrament. This sacrifice is an expression of faith and happens in such a way 'that we offer with Christ,' that is, that we cast ourselves upon Christ with unwaning faith in his testament and we do not appear otherwise before God with our prayer, praise and sacrifice than through him and his means (of salvation) and that we do not doubt that he is our pastor and present before God's face in heaven. The "eucharist sacrifice" thus understood is performed by those reconciled in faith, and is expressed in thanks and praise, in invoking and confessing God, in suffering and in all the good works of believers. These are the offerings which are particularly emphasized in the Reformation teaching in connection with I Peter 2:5 and Romans 12:1." (p. 474)

[403]Paul VI, *Mysterium Fidei*, pp 11-12. "The Council of Trent, basing itself on this faith of the Church, 'Openly and sincerely professes that in the Holy Sacrament of the Eucharist, after the consecration of the bread and wine, our Lord Jesus Christ, true God and true man, is really, truly and substantially contained under the outward appearances.'"

Cross. And in the eucharistic worship, the sacrament takes on the character of the original event.[404] The sacrament is informed and enlived by that primary event.

In this one sacrifice of Christ, then, a sacrifice represented in the sacrifice of the Mass, the fullness of salvation is given to history.

> At the Last Supper, on the night he was betrayed, our Savior instituted the eucharistic sacrifice of his Body and Blood. This he did in order to perpetuate the sacrifice of the Cross throughout the ages until he should come again, and so to entrust his beloved spouse, the Church, a memorial of his death and resurrection; a sacrament, a sign of unity, a bond of charity, a paschal banquet in which Christ is consumed, the mind is filled with grace, and a pledge of future glory is given to us.[405]

Because of the Eucharist's unity with the one saxrifice of Christ, the presence of the sacrifice of Christ in the liturgy of the sacrament is the source of unity and continuity in the Church.[406] In the sacrifice of the Mass, the Church is united with the Christ who, as both Priest and Victim, is the source of life for the Church.[407]

Although the Roman Catholic Church interprets the Eucharistic symbols in terms of the liturgy of the sacrament, it also recognizes the importance of the liturgy of the word. "The two parts which in a sense go to make up the Mass . . . are so closely

---

[404]It is here that the difficulties with the nature of real presence can find deeper meaning. For if the Mass is a sacrifice, then the concern shifts from a discussion of presence and the efforts to describe such a presence, to an understanding of the sacraments that are as dynamic and free as the events of Christ's life. And Eucharistic realism has a covenantal structure, just as the Cross. It is an invitation given in Christ, the invitation of the Cross.

[405]*Sacrosanctum Concilium*, p. 16.

[406]Pius XII, *Mystici Corporis*, pp 67, 93; John Paul II, "Mystery and Worship of the Holy Eucharist," pp 656, 659. Paul VI, *Mysterium Fidei*, pp 10-11.

[407]*Lumen Gentium*, p. 363.

connected with each other that they form but one single act of worship."[408] From the beginning of the apostolic period the Church gathered together to hear the teachings of Christ and to celebrate the Eucharist.[409] Yet the Catholic Church affirms that this preaching always takes place in the community of the Church, which is the result (*res sacramenti*) of the sacramental worship of the Church. The preaching helps to build up the Church, but this preaching is not the final end of the faith act. Preaching serves as a means of bringing the believer into a more complete participation in the life of the Church by preparing the believer for entrance into the sacramental life of the Church.

> Therefore the Church announces the good tidings of salvation to those who do not believe so that all men may know the one true God and Jesus Christ whom he has sent and may be converted from their ways, doing penance. To believers also the Church must ever preach faith and penance; she must prepare them for the sacraments, teach them to observe all that Christ has commanded, and encourage them to engage in all the works of charity, piety and the apostolate, thus making it clear that Christ's faithful, though not of this world, are to be lights of the world and are to glorify the Father before men.[410]

The proclamation of the word of God prepares the faithful to partake of the sacrifice of the Mass which is the summit of Christian life.[411] Just as in the preaching of Jesus to the apostles the Church is inaugurated, it is in the person of Jesus that the Kingdom is principally revealed. So too, the promise of the fullness of Christ is given in the

---

[408]*Sacrosanctum Concilium*, p. 19. Also see pp. 29, 30.

[409]Ibid., p. 4.

[410]Ibid., p. 6.

[411]Ibid., p. 6. Also *Lumen Gentium*, p. 362.

preaching of the Church, but it is only in the sacrifice of the Mass that the fullness of Christ is present to the Church in space and time.[412]

C. The Eucharist and the historicity of the Church

Some of the implications of this interpretation of the Eucharistic symbols for the historicity of the Christian faith and the resulting ecclesiology should now be evident. Since the Eucharist is understood to be the representation of the sacrifice of Christ, the deed of Christ and not of the Church, this worship has its origin and cause outside of the Church. The Church is caused by the *ex opere operato* efficacy of the sacramental worship of the Church, which finds its origin in the action of Christ.

> The liturgy is the summit towards which the activity of the Church is directed; it is also the font from which all her power flows. For the goal of the apostolic endeavor is that all who are made sons of God by faith and baptism should come together to praise God in the midst of his Church, to take part in the Sacrifice and to eat the Lord's Supper.[413]

In the Eucharist, Christ, the High Priest of the New and Eternal Covenant, perpetuates the sacrifice of the Cross until he comes again in glory, an act in which the continuity of the Church, as the Bride of Christ, is maintained.[414]

---

[412]*Lumena Gentium*, pp. 352-353. The other sacraments also come to be understood in terms of the Eucharist. All the sacraments serve to strengthen the Eucharistic community, the Church. See *Sacrosanctum Concilium*, p. 6. "From the liturgy, therefore, and especially from the Eucharist, grace is poured forth upon us as from a mountain, and the sanctification of men in Christ and the glorification of God to which all other activities of the Church are directed, as toward their end, are achieved with maximum effectiveness." Also see Pius XII, *Mystici Corporis*, pp. 60-61; and Vorgrimler, *Commentary*, pp. 160ff.

[413]*Sacrosanctum Concilium*, p. 6.

[414]Ibid., pp. 16, 24. *Lumen Gentium*, p. 381.

The primary effect of the liturgy, then, is the formation of the Body of Christ, the Church under its Head Christ.[415] Only in the Church, as the Body of Christ, does the believer come to experience and recognize the fullness of the redemption of Christ.[416] One of the implications of this is that the true nature of the Church can only be understood after an examination of the Eucharist.

> For it is the liturgy which, especially in the divine sacrifice of the Eucharist, "the work of our redemption is accomplished," and it is through the liturgy, especially, that the faithful are enabled to express in their lives and manifest to others the mystery of Christ and the real nature of the true Church.[417]

The very existence of the Church is informed by those Eucharistic symbols and becomes intelligible in all its fullness only in the light of this life-giving source.

In the Roman Catholic tradition, the theology of history finds its locus in the worship of the Church. Since the present time has meaning only in terms of the definitive action of Christ's life, death and resurrection, history (in this instance Christian history) will reflect the manner in which Christ is present to his people in the

---

[415]Pius XII, *Mystici Corporis*, p. 58. *Lumen Gentium*, p. 355. John Paul II, "Mystery and Worship of the Holy Eucharist," pp. 657-658.

[416]One of the results of this emphasis on the Eucharist is a renewed understanding of the primary effect of the Eucharistic worship. The effect is not simply the faith of the individual believer, but of the Church. The whole Church is present in this worship. The emphasis is placed on the community over against (but not to the exclusion of) the individual. Incorporation into the Mystical Body is incorporation into the historicity of the Mystical Body. Rahner, referring to St. Thomas, points out that the "*Res sacramenti est unitas corporis mystici.*" (*Summa Theologica*, III, p. 73, a.3c). Also see Vorgrimler, *Commentary*, p. 161. "We may no doubt deduce from this that incorporation into the unity of the Mystical Body is the primary effect of the Eucharist and the instrumental cause of all other effects." Ratzinger ("Pastoral Implications of Episcopal Collegiality," p. 28) affirms this. He points out that the separation of the doctrine of the eucharist and ecclesiology has not been unfortunate.

[417]*Sacrosanctum Concilium*, p. 1.

midst of fallen creation. The historicity of the faith, then, is determined by the presence of Christ in the Church.[418]

Since the Church is visible in its worship, the historicity of the Church reflects the presence of Christ in that sacramental event, and the Roman Catholic tradition teaches that "the whole and complete Christ, God and Man," is present in the sacrifice of the Mass.[419] The Catholic doctrine of transubstantiation affirms this.

> Not that there now lies under those species what was already there before, but something entirely different; and that not only because of the faith of the Church, but in objective reality, since after the change of the substance or nature of the bread and wine into the Body and Blood of Christ, nothing remains of the bread and the wine but only the appearances, under which Christ, whole and entire, in his physical "reality" is also bodily present, although not in the same way that our own bodies are present in a given place.[420]

The Church, through this Eucharistic mediation, is made historical by this actuality and retains the full historicity of the Christ-event in its own life.

Since the mystery of the Church is "the historical embodiment and manifestation of the universal salvific will of God in the world," the Church, as realized by the power of Christ, is the sign of the salvific presence of Christ in the world.[421] "Christ as the one mediation remains the real way to salvation. The Church, as his

---

[418]Vorgrmler, *Commentary*, pp 161, 162.

[419]Paul VI, *Mysterium Fidei*, pp. 11-12.

[420]Ibid., p. 4.

[421]Vorgrimler, *Commentary*, p. 168; *Lumen Gentium*, p. 366.

body, is the place where his presence is accessible."[422] It is the visible sacrament of the union of Christ and the Church.[423]

As a sign of the offer of salvation given here and now, the Church, as concrete, must be both invisible and visible. "Not only must it be one and undivided, it must also be something concrete and visible, as our Predecessor of happy memory, Leo XIII, says in his Encyclical *Satis Cognitum*: 'By the very fact of being a body the Church is visible.'"[424] The Church cannot be conceived as simply a spiritual "corpus." Rather, it must be visible, concrete and publicly accessible.

> The mystical Body of Christ is like Christ Himself, the Head and Pattern of His Church, who is not complete if we consider in Him only His visible humanity. . . . . or only His invisible divinity, but is one, for and in both natures. For the Word of God assumed a passible human nature so that this invisible society being founded and consecrated by the divine blood, man might be brought back to things invisible by means of visible government.[425]

"It means this, that our Savior so shares with His Church the goods that are especially His own, that the Church in the whole of her manner of life, visible and invisible, portrays most perfectly the likeness of Christ Himself."[426]

One cannot conclude from this that the external structure of the Church is the full realization of the grace of God. For the Church exists within a fallen history. On the other hand, the visible is not simply arbitrary and expendable. This is affirmed by

---

[422]Ibid., p. 175.

[423]*Lumen Gentium*, 360.

[424]Pius XII, *Mystici Corporis*, p. 58.

[425]Ibid., p. 83.

[426]Ibid., p. 78.

Vatican II when it is stated in *Lumen Gentium* that full membership in the Church includes membership in the visible Church.

> Fully incorporated into the Church are those who, possessing the Spirit of Christ, accept all the means of salvation given to the Church together with her entire organization, and who - by the bonds constituted by the profession of faith, the sacraments, ecclesiastical government and communion - are joined in the visible structure of the Church of Christ, who rules her through the Supreme Pontiff and the bishops.[427]

The Church, as the continuation of the presence of the incarnate Christ, must include a visible dimension. She has a "sacramental" character. Both the visible and spiritual aspects are essential and neither can be reduced to the other.

The relationship of the visible structure of the Church to the invisible Church is a matter of debate again today.[428] This is most evident in the ecclesiological discussions between Roman Catholics and Protestants. The same tension is also present, no less obviously, among contemporary Catholic theologians. Nevertheless, the Catholic Church insists that the full realization of the Christ-event entails the fullness of human historicity, so as the effect of that event the Church must also realize in itself this same historicity. By affirming this, the Roman Catholic Church is fighting against all partial and fragmentary evaluations of the faith which fail to realize that the fullness of the Church lies in the union of both the visible and the invisible dimensions.[429] The Catholic Church goes so far as to hold that despite the effects of sin, sin does not destroy this wholeness, the integrity of the good creation. Further, it affirms that the fullness of that good creation, which is the result of the grace of Christ,

---

[427] *Lumen Gentium*, p. 366.

[428] Vorgrimler, *Commentary*, pp. 169ff.

[429] Ibid., p. 181.

and the salvation of Christ, both as visible and invisible, is present here and now in the life of the Church.[430]

Another fruitful way to consider this might be in terms of Vatican II's characterization of the Church as the People of God. There is much theological discussion today as to the adequacy of this term, but the term People of God is especially helpful in pointing to the historicity of the Church within the economy of salvation.[431] Here the process of salvation takes the form of the "constitution of a community of salvation."[432] It begins in the Old Testament community of worship which takes its life from God's actions.

> At all times and in every race, anyone who fears God and does what is right has been acceptable to him (cf. Acts 10:35). He has, however willed to make men holy and save them, not as individuals without a bond or link between them, but rather to make them into a people who might acknowledge him and serve him in holiness. He therefore chose the Israelite race to be his own people and established a covenant with it. He gradually instructed this people - in its history manifesting both himself and the decree of his will - and made it holy unto himself. All these things, however, happened as a preparation and figure of the new and perfect covenant which was to be ratified in Christ, and

---

[430]Paul VI, *Mysterium Fidei*, p. 2. Also see Pius XII, *Mystici Corporis*, pp. 78, 84, 85. One of the most controversial topics today, which touches directly upon the question of the nature of the historicity of the faith, is the infallibility of the pope. *Lumen Gentium*, pp. 370ff. The Church as a whole is understood to be infallible. In the *sensus fidei* the Church expresses "universal consent in matters of faith and morals." (p. 360) It is understood that by the fullness of his revelation God makes the people of the New Covenant infallible. See Vorgrimler, *Commentary*, p. 165. Something new is not given in the Church, but the fullness of the revelation in Christ. What is given as infallible are statements in conformity with that revelation. Its goal is to preserve the faith. *Lumen Gentium*, pp. 380ff.

[431]Yves Congar, "The Church the People of God," *Concilium*, Vol. 1: No. 1, Jan 1965, pp. 7-19.

[432]Vorgrimmler, *Commentary*, p. 154.

of the fallen revelation which was to be given through the Word of God made flesh.[433]

This New Covenant community stands in continuity with the people of the Old Covneant, but as a community in Christ it takes its life from the sacrifice of Christ. "Christ instituted this new covenant, namely the covenant in his blood, (cf. ICor 11:25); he called a race made up of Jews and Gentiles which would be one, not according to the flesh, but in the Spirit, and this race would be the new People of God."[434] The Old Covenant gives way to the New, and the Mass, as the celebration of the new covenant, is the source of its life. The New People of God, then, is a sign of the salvation of Christ in the fallen creation.

This covenantal relationship is expressed in terms of marital imagery. The power of Christ is the source of the life of the Church, causing the Church and purifying His Bride, the Church.[435]

> The Church, whose mystery is set forth by the sacred council, is held as a matter of faith to be unfailingly holy. This is because Christ, the Son of God, who with the Father and the Spirit is hailed as "alone holy" loved the Church as his Bride, giving himself up for her so as to sanctify her (cf. Eph. 5:25-26); he joined her to himself as his body and endowed her with the gift of the Holy Spirit for the glory of God.[436]

The unfailing holiness of the Church caused by Christ is not solely a future reality, simply to be consummated in the eschaton; rather, it is a historical, sacramental event. Given in the Christ-event and represented in the sacramental life of the Church is the

---

[433]*Lumen Gentium*, p. 359.

[434]Ibid., p. 359.

[435]Ibid., p. 360. Also see Pius XII, *Mystici Corporis*, pp. 80-81.

[436]Ibid., p. 396.

offer of salvation and the grace which enables the Church, his Bride, to accept the offer of grace. The salvation of the New Covenant, as a free offer of the grace of God, requires the free response of man - - a response made possible only through the redemptive activity of Christ. Through his death the Church and the believer are purified by Christ, freeing the Church from the bondage of sin and enabling the Church to accept the offer of salvation. Both the offer and the means of acceptance are given in the Eucharistic sacrifice, the New Covenant in the blood of Christ.

Vatican II utilizes the relationship of Christ and Mary to help explicate the covenantal relationship of Christ and his Church.[437] Mary is free from sin, "but this does not diminish the power of Christ, for her salutary effect flows from the power of God. It flows forth from the superabundance of the merits of Christ, resting on his mediation, depending entirely on it and drawing all to its power from it. It does not hinder in any way the immediate union of the faithful with Christ but on the contrary fosters it."[438] This same power, working in the Church, sanctifies it and enables it to mediate, like Mary, the salvation of Christ.

> By reason of the gift and role of her divine motherhood, by which she is united with her Son, the Redeemer, and with her unique graces and functions, the Blessed Virgin is also intimately united to the Church. As St. Ambrose taught, the Mother of God is

---

[437]Vorgrimler, *Commentary*, p. 156. The Church, then is not simply assumed into Christ, but remains distinct, freely responding to the sacrifice of Cross (*sacrificium crucis*) with it own sacrifice a praise (*sacrificium laudis*). Neither can be reduced to the other. By holding this, the Roman Catholic tradition avoids kind of spiritualizing which, by dehistorizing the Church, induces a quasi-monophysitical identification of the Church with Christ.

In addition see Pius XII, *Mystici Corporis*, pp. 94, 95. This covenantal structure is indicated by Vatican II's discussion of Mary. It is the grace of Christ which constitutes Mary in her freedom, while at the same time her free and responsible appropriation of the salvation offered is a constituting element of the New Covenant which is the immanence in history of the Emmanuel.

Also, it should be noted that Vatican II does not refer to the Church as mediatrix. But this term is used to describe Mary in the discussion of the relationship of Mary and the Church. It does refer to Mary as "Advocate, Auxiliarix, Adjutrix and Mediatrix." (*Lumen Gentium*, para 62)

[438]*Lumen Gentium*, pp. 418, 420.

a type of the Church in the order of faith, charity and perfect union with Christ. For in the mystery of the Church, which is itself rightly called mother and virgin, the Blessed Virgin stands out in eminent and singular fashion as exemplar both of virgin and mother. Through her faith and obedience she gave birth on earth to the very Son of the Father, not through knowledge of man but by the overshadowing of the Holy Spirit, in the manner of a new Eve who placed her faith, not in the serpent of old but in God's messenger without wavering doubt. The Son whom she brought forth is he whom God placed as the first born among many brethren (Rom. 8:29), that is, the faithful in whose generation and formation she cooperates with a mother's love.[439]

It is said of the Church as of her antitype, "She herself is a virgin who keeps in its entirety and purity the faith she pledged to her spouse."[440] Like Mary, the Church is an instrument of God in the plan of redemption, mediating, here and now, the New Covenant, which as the Covenant of Christ offers salvation and makes the free acceptance of that offer possible. The Eucharist, the source of the life of the Church, mediates this covenant to a sinful people.[441]

It should be mentioned, if only briefly, that the documents cited from Vatican II take note of the importance of the eschatological dimension of the Church. The Catholic Church believes that the Church will reach her perfection only in the future glory of heaven. So during the present eon, the Church remains the "pilgrim Church."[442] Yet the distinctive character of the Roman Catholic understanding of faith

---

[439]Ibid., pp. 419–420.

[440]Ibid. p. 420.

[441]Vatican II affirms this sacramentality of the Church time and time again. The Eucharist is the source of the life of the Church; as the New Covenant, it is the offer of the full salvation of Christ.

[442]*Lumen Gentium*, pp. 407–408.

and the economy of salvation is its emphasis upon the belief that the restoration of the fallen creation has already begun and is taking place now. "Already the final age: it is even now anticipated in a certain real way, for the Church on earth is endowed with a sanctity that is real though imperfect."[443]   But he question remains: what exactly does it mean to say that this sanctity is actual and real in the Church, but still not perfected?

The Protestant theologians whom we have discussed tended to see the sanctity of the Church as separable from her situation in fallen creation. Since the Church under the present sinful conditions is not holy, their thological writings emphasize the transcendent, eschatological character of the Church. The Roman Catholic tradition distinguishes the sanctity of the Church, which is hers by her Eucharistic union with her Lord, from the sinful condition of her members, sinners whom she continually invites to that union which is hers in its fullness. It is believed that the Church under the present conditions of fallen creation contains the fullness of Christ. There are at work here two different understandings of history, two different notions of the historicity of the faith which find their loci in the two different interpretations of the Eucharistic worship.

D. Summary

Because the Church's documents do not set forth explicitly her understanding of history, in this section a theology of history has not been developed; rather those teachings of the Roman Catholic Church have been singled out which imply an understanding of the historicity of the faith.   As has been shown, the Church understands itself to be formed by its Eucharistic worship, which it interprets in the light of the liturgy of the sacrament. Her focus is on the encounter with the salvation of Christ in the sacrifice of the Mass in which the "whole" Christ is present. The Church's understanding of the historicity of faith corresponds to this Eucharistic realism since it is the source of the life of faith, an act of worship given in response to the Cross - the

---

[443]Ibid., p. 408.

source of all salvation. It is a realism which goes beyond that of the sacramental presence of Christ in a linguistic community. For the event of the sacrifice of the Mass cannot be reduced to its proclamation; rather, the proclamation is always measured by the event. As a consequence, the proclamation of the Word is always to take place within and as a preparation for the representation of Christ in the sacrifice of the Mass. For it is here that the believer participates in the prius of the faith, the life, death and resurrection of Christ as the event by reference to which all reality is to be understood and judged. History as understood within the Roman Catholic tradition is, therefore, time concretely interpreted by the liturgy of the Mass as the offering of the One Sacrifice of the Cross, sacramentally re-presented by the authority of Him who offers it, Jesus the risen Lord. In this liturgy, the time of the Old Covenant is made historical by its fulfillment in the New Covenant, whose time is opened upon the Kingdom by the concrete presence within the Church of He who is risen, the Lord of history whose lordship is Eucharistic.

Chapter VI: Hans Urs von Balthasar - Catholic Historicity and the Eucharist

One finds in the theology of Hans Urs von Balthasar that his primary concern is with the question of the relationship of God to the world. In his early work, this theological problem found its focus in the question of history. Later, in his theological aesthetics and his "theo-drama," he again takes up the question of the relationship of the infinite to the finite, of the creator to the creature, of the universal to the particular. This foundational question finds its resonances in Catholic theology's discussion of the "real distinction" and the *theologia entis*.[444] This question of the relationship of man and God is the fundamental question for man, the question of the meaning of history. Here once again the question of the meaning of the particular is raised.

According to von Balthasar, the priority of this question was not new to Christianity - the same question can be found at the heart of most mythical, religious and philosophical traditions. Yet, he quickly notes that outside Christianity, no suitable answer can be found. The problem with these non-Christian traditions is the almost universal resistance to historical fact.[445] Von Balthasar understands this to be the product of the tendency in human thought to abstract from the particular, to move toward the eternal, the infinite. In the end, the pre-Christian and non-Christian answers to this question are inadequate, lapsing either into a dualism separating the finite and the infinite or a monism reducing the particular to the One. Despite the inadequacy of these non-Christian alternatives, von Balthasar is aware of the value of natural religion; but ultimately such religions point only to the predisposition of nature to revelation and fail to note the fullness of the revelation given in Christ[446].

---

[444]Hans Urs von Balthasar, *Explorations in Theology I: The Word Made Flesh*, trans. A.V. Littledale and Alexander Dru (San Francisco: Ignatius Press, 1989), pp. 169ff.

[445]Hans Urs von Balthasar, *A Theology of History* (New York: Sheed and Ward, 1963), pp. 7-17.

[446]von Balthasar, *Explorations in Theology*, vol I, pp. 59ff.

144

Finally, according to von Balthasar, it is only Christianity and the Christian revelation that can give an account of the meaning and purpose of the relationship of the infinite and the finite, the creator and the creature, and the universal and the particular. Such a solution is possible because only in Christianity does the infinite enter the finite, revealing the nature of the finite in its relationship to God. This, the incarnation, is the starting point for theology, a starting point to which theology must remain faithful unless it lapses into some gnostic abstraction.[447] The revelation governs theology, informing and shaping it.[448]

In his theology, von Balthasar is aware of the need to start with the revelation and remains faithful to this need. Some have criticized his work, noting that at times von Balthasar is guilty of the abstraction that he works to guard against.[449] At times he appears to abstract from the historical event, lapsing into some gnostic interpretation of the faith. But if one carefully reads the *Theo-drama* and his writings in the theology of history, it becomes clear that he is intent upon preserving the historicity of the faith. This is particularly evident in his later work, the *Theo-drama*. Von Balthasar himself claims that the theo-drama surpasses the earlier efforts of aesthetics more carefully supporting the proper understanding of the historicity of the faith.[450] In this work, the event character of the faith is given priority, shaping the concrete nature of a faith informed by those events. The "act" of revelation is primary to the faith. For this study of the relationship of worship and history, only an analysis of the nature and significance of the "act" of revelation and its mediation by the Church can shed light on his understanding of the historicity of the faith.

---

[447]Ibid., pp. 67ff.

[448]Ibid., p. 156.

[449]This is especially true of the criticisms of his work *The Glory of the Lord*. Von Balthasar is aware of the criticisms and his *Theo-drama* is a response in part to those criticisms. The *Theo-drama* is to go beyond the aesthetics. See *Theo-drama I: Prolegomena*, trans. Graham Harrison (San Francisco: Ignatius Press, 1988), pp. 15ff.

[450]See *Theo-drama I: Prolegomena*, pp. 16ff.

This chapter will outline the approach that von Balthasar uses to articulate his understanding of the faith. First, he begins with a discussion of the nature of revelation and its meaning for the faith. In this discussion he introduces the idea of theo-drama, using this analogy to describe the dynamic nature of creation and redemption. Next, the meaning of the theo-dramatic action will be shown in its relationship to Christ. In Christ the true meaning and significance of the drama between God and man becomes apparent. In this relationship, Christ's authority in the process of salvation includes his role in the created order as well as in salvation history. One finds that reality itself is rooted in Christ, and it takes on the structure of the response by Christ to the Father's free offer of salvation; i.e., it is covenantal. Finally, in the worship, the believer comes to participate in the offer of salvation given in Christ. Von Balthasar, distinguishing between the liturgy of the sacrament and the liturgy of the word, shows that in her worship the Church takes on the form of Christ, participating in those events which reveal and mediate the grace of Christ. As the Church comes to participate in the redemptive activity of Christ in her worship, the historicity of the faith is determined by those redemptive events and by her participation in those events. The historicity of the faith, then, will reflect the historicity of the Church. In the theology of von Balthasar, this discussion finds its most profound expression in theo-drama.

A. Revelation and theo-drama

The priority of the "act" of revelation is reflected in von Balthasar's theology in numerous places. It has already been noted that in the *Theo-drama*, aesthetics give way to drama.[451] Here he states that from the very beginning revelation is thought to be an event, an act, a drama.[452] In the theo-drama, that constitutes life, reality is act. "What takes place in the world is neither feeling nor narration (however "dangerous" it

---

[451]Ibid., p. 16.

[452]Ibid., pp. 15, 16.

may be) but simply action."[453] Acts supercede dialogue. One can never reduce an act to narration.

This understanding of reality is based on a specific understanding of the nature of God, who himself is mysterious and transcendent yet active in history. This is the drama at the heart of reality. God is the Author of the drama, the one through whom all things come to be, and at the same time an Actor in the play.[454] The revelation is about these actions of God and reflects the drama of the trinitarian life as it manifests itself at the center of reality. Consequently, this drama includes the whole of reality, both creation and history. History then can and must be seen from this Christian perspective.

Within this view of time, temporal existence has a meaning that cannot be reduced to mere flux. Nor does it permit the kind of abstraction that allows for one to formulate a theology which lapses into a theology of essences.[455] Such an abstract theology fails to capture the actions of God which make temporal existence intelligible. Rather it is in the light of God's acts alone that one can come to understand history.

Discussing the relationship of the Son to the Father, von Balthasar points out that history is more than secular history, since there is no such thing as "time in itself."[456]

> To have time means, for him, to have time for God, and is identical with receiving time from God. Hence, the Son, who has time, in the world, for God, is the point at which God has time for the world. Apart from the Son, God has no time for the world, but in him has

---

[453]Hans Urs von Balthasar, *Theodrama III: Dramatis Personae: Persons in Christ*, trans. Graham Harrison (San Francisco: Ignatius Press,1992), p. 531.

[454]Ibid., p. 532.

[455]von Balthasar, *Dramatis Personae*, p. 194.

[456]von Balthasar, *A Theology of History*, p. 34.

all time. In him he has time for all men and all
creatures: in relation to him it is always Today."[457]

One discovers that there is no simply secular history, since any attempt at a purely
secular account of history fails to understand the dynamic relationship between God
and man at the very heart of reality. Yet this dynamic relationship does not undermine
the external dimension of history by dissolving it into mere illusion (dualism), nor does
this relationship identify with temporality by merging with it (monism). Rather, the
Word is pre-historical or prior to history in a metaphysical sense. "We might say that it
pervades all history, meaning thereby that we are concerned with an event which took
place at a certain historical time, and also, since it comes from God, that it touches the
whole of history and every moment of it."[458] This comprehensive understanding of
time indicates that time is sacramental, opening and mediating some larger dynamic
process.

According to von Balthasar, the key to understanding Christianity is to see that
the revelation is not an escape from time, but that it is historical. As a matter of fact, it
is the real locus of history: i.e., meaningful time. The simple fact that revelation seems
to be timeless is not because it leads outside of time, but because it appears foreign to a
fallen world.[459] This revelation, this grace, enters the world converting the sinners,
revealing the meaning of time. It is no longer simply a time of sin and death, but a time
of salvation.[460]

Temporal existence in this instance must not be juxtaposed to eternal life as a
mode of deficient existence, defined in a neoplatonic manner as a fall from unity with
the primordial one; rather, man's fall is the product of a free decision, distancing man

---

[457]Ibid., p. 34.

[458]von Balthasar, *The Word Made Flesh*, p. 138.

[459]von Balthasar, *A Theology of History*, pp. 33, 34.

[460]Hans Urs von Balthasar, *Man in History* (London: Sheed and Ward, 1968), pp. 28-29.

148

from God. The results are the fragmentation and paralysis of man: i.e., original sin, the loss of the ability of man to respond to God's grace. "Original sin, as the loss of the original reciprocity of the love relationship between God and man, involves for man the loss of that 'power to become a child of God,' without his therefore losing, or wanting to lose, the will to be God's child."[461] This fragmentation, which cripples man under the present condition of fallen creation, culminates in death. Death reveals the gradient in life away from wholeness, towards a loss of our fundamental relationship with God. Still the effects of the fall are not total. Worldly existence is not simply evil.[462]

Within the dynamic relationship between man and God, man can flee from God, but this need not be the case. In and of itself the spatio-temporal existence is good. The materiality and temporality of creation are principles of differentiation from God that do not express a fall or opposition to God.[463] They are constitutive of the Creator-creature relationship of the original creation.[464] Time becomes a time of sin only when man uses time to flee from this relationship with God, disrupting the original "good" order of creation. As a matter of fact sin is the attempt to usurp God's power, to escape time. It is a failure to be historical.[465]

Likewise, time is not only experienced as sinful, but it can also be experienced as redemptive. In the revelation of God, man becomes aware of the redemptive quality of temporal existence. (In religions without historical revelation, time is often seen as destructive.) Von Balthasar insists that there is no simply "natural time," a neutral flow without redemptive significance. For it is precisely in time that one's redemption is at

---

[461] von Balthasar, *Man in History*, p.205.

[462] von Balthasar, *A Theology of History*, p.34.

[463] von Balthasar, *Man in History*, p. 23.

[464] Ibid., p. 23.

[465] von Balthasar, *A Theology of History*, pp. 29ff. Man experiences time as a time of sin, as punishment. Consequently man tries to flee time, yet it is only in time that man can become human.

149

stake, thereby revealing the true meaning and purpose of temporal existence.[466] Time is really where man discovers himself and is redeemed. This is possible because God acts in time.[467]

In the history of salvation, the actions on the part of God whereby man is called to redemption are characterized as the covenant. The covenant refers to the dynamic relationship between God and man that encompasses the whole of the created order and the order of salvation. The covenant reflects, first of all, the dynamic relationship between God and the world. God is a personal God who in his being is trinitarian. Out of this trinitarian life flows not just the "divine plan" but the very Word of God.[468] This interpersonal nature of God is manifest not only in God's relationship with man but in the order of creation and salvation itself. This is particularly evident in the life of Christ. "He did not live an 'abstract' human life, but in a living way took hold of and experienced the checkered, crude, historical reality of humanity, and in obedience to the Father recapitulated the whole concrete historical reality of his Father's creatures, in order to set free their true meaning and thereby honor and justify the Father and creator of the world."[469] The coming of Christ and returning to the Father is the central dynamic of history, a dynamic relationship opened up to man in the incarnation. Human history is therefore initiated by God and made possible by God, when in his love he sends the Son, who in turn sends the Spirit, thereby reestablishing the grace present from the beginning but lost to sin.[470]

---

[466]Hans Urs von Balthasar, *Word and Revelation*, trans. A.V. Littledale (New York: Herder and Herder, 1964), p. 92.

[467]von Balthasar, *Man in History*, p. 23.

[468]von Balthasar, *Dramatis Personae*, p. 220.

[469]von Balthasar, A Theology of History, p. 70.

[470]Ibid., p. 66. Also see *Persons in Christ*, p. 13 and *Man in God*, pp. 178, 189.

Such a dynamic relationship must not be seen as a narrowing, a movement from what is natural to something religious, thereby stifling the natural freedom of man. Rather, this dynamic relationship at the heart of Christian faith opens up history. History becomes the medium where man's existence is opened up to the true meaning and purpose of his existence.[471] "Since it is the manifestation in this world of the eternal life of God, it always has a dimension open to that which is above. Its meaning, the number of its possible applications, is, even at its own historical level, something limitless, even before we come to the forms in which it is universalized in the Church and in individuals."[472] It is precisely this relationship that lies at the heart of human history, best understood through the analogy of drama.

Von Balthasar introduces theo-drama as the theological category for describing this historical relationship. In this drama man and God are placed in tension with one another. This is the drama at the heart of human existence. Within this drama God provides the background. He is the infinite and absolute beginning from which man comes and the end toward which he journeys. He provides the horizon that makes drama possible.[473]

B. Christ and theo-drama

The tension between God and man which is at the center of the drama of human existence finds its full expression in the life, death and resurrection of Christ. In Christ the true meaning and nature of the Christian faith is revealed. What took place in the incarnation reveals the unsurpassed truth about the world, man and God. Moreover, Christ opens up history to its fuller meaning in a way only possible in him.

---

[471] von Balthasar, *Persons in Christ*, pp. 19-20.

[472] von Balthasar, *A Theology of History*, p. 67.

[473] von Balthasar, *Person in Christ*, p. 13.

151

Since Christ enters time as the fulfillment of time, he is the measure of time and in him is revealed the meaning of temporal existence. This "vertical presentness," as von Balthasar describes it, becomes the measure of all historical moments.[474] In the humanity of Christ, the definitive word enters the void of fragmented human existence and experiences the emptiness of fallen creation.[475] In and through his life, Christ embraces the created order and restores it to the fullness for which it is intended. But this redemptive activity of Christ should not simply be understood as isolated events in which the transcendent is now present in history; rather, it must be understood to be a definitive event, both exhausting history and summarizing it at the same time.[476] Here von Balthasar's writings emphasize a special dimension of the Christ-event that is important for understanding the nature and dimensions of the faith. Like Irenaeus, whose doctrine of recapitulation shows how the whole of created reality is completed in the Christ-event, von Balthasar's also insists that it is precisely in Christ that all creation is renewed.

Perhaps the breadth and depth of the significance of the Christ-event is best articulated by von Balthasar in his discussion of the universal character of the mission of Christ. Remembering that von Balthasar's theology starts with his concern for the relationship of the finite to the infinite, the particular to the universal, it is within this context that one should come to understand who Christ is and what Christ does. For Christ is the answer to this problem. Therefore, it is precisely in the tension between the universal claims of Christ and his particular life that the real nature of the revelation and the historicity of the faith become evident.

One way von Balthasar enters upon a discussion of the unique character of Christ is by noting that in our common experience there can be no universal individual.

[474]von Balthasar, *Man in History*, p. 226. Also see *A Theology of History*, p. 39.

[475]Ibid., p. 236.

[476]von Balthasar, *The Word Made Flesh*, pp. 30, 93, 170.

152

An individual cannot be universalized. It is precisely this problem that philosophy has been unable to resolve.[477] Yet Christians claim that the solution is found in Christ. In speaking of this problem between the individual and universal von Balthasar says

> But here also the two are identical in God, and, in the incarnation of Christ, God is brought into the world. Christ is neither one individual among others, since he is God and not susceptible of comparison, nor is he the norm in the sense of a universal, since he is an individual. Because he is God, he is *Universale concretum*, a *Concretum universale*. It is for this reason that he is outside our most elementary modes of thought. . . . Theology, on the contrary, starts out from Christ who, as this individual, is universal, because embodying the absolute norm, and who, as this contingent being within history, is the necessary being above all history and nature; he it is to whom, as Head, all things in heaven and earth must be brought back.[478]

In Christ that which is beyond the finitude of any individual is revealed. As the Son of the Father, sent to reveal the Father and to send the Holy Spirit, the Son came to save all humanity and bring about the "new heavens and the New Earth." All things are subordinate to the universal claims of Christ, nothing is outside his power.[479]

It should be noted that the coming of Christ does not annihilate time, bringing about some eternal now that transcends temporal reality, nor does it reveal a sacred history alongside secular history. Rather, the salvation brought by Christ is essentially linked to temporal existence and encompasses the whole of reality. This is affirmed by the unique character of the Christ-event and the nature of Christ's mission.

---

[477] von Balthasar, *A Theology of History*, pp. 69-70.

[478] von Balthasar, *The Word Made Flesh*, pp. 170-171.

[479] von Balthasar, *A Theology of History*, pp. 12ff.

Perhaps the most difficult teaching within Christianity, the stumbling block to the Jews and Gentiles alike, is the idea of the incarnation. First, it is this unique claim that God, the infinite, entered into history that is the definitive belief of the Christian faith, the foundation for its understanding of the world. In this context von Balthasar first affirms the importance of the life of Jesus for our faith by affirming that the scriptures accept the historicity of the life of Christ.[480] The scriptures defend this historicity, thereby thwarting all attempts to mythologize the faith. What this means is that the particular life of this individual man who lived in the past is somehow definitive for all human life.

Second, in the *Theo-drama*, von Balthasar describes the life of Christ within the context of his mission. In this theology the idea of mission finds its meaning in the drama that constitutes life. For it is only in responding to the call of Christ that the believer takes on an identity; that is, in this response the believer partakes of the mission in Christ. In this process, as each individual takes on their particular mission within the history of salvation, the individual becomes a person. Humans are of course free to accept the mission or reject it partially or completely. Yet it is in their mission that believers come to be who and what they are called to be. Describing this call to mission von Balthasar says: "All the same, this *a posteriori* synthesis cannot be termed 'accidental' because, in fact, in the plan of God, each conscious subject is created for the sake of his mission - a mission that makes him a person."[481] According to this plan, individuals are called to participate in the larger plan of God where the believer finds an identity and almost a "reality." Therefore, the mission is not a mere addition to human life; rather, in our response to our mission humans become persons, from a theological perspective. For it is only in relationship to God in the last analysis that man finds himself.

---

[480]von Balthasar, *Persons in Christ*, p. 141.

[481]Ibid., p. 208.

154

On the other hand, mission of Christ is different. Christ does not become a
"person" in accepting his mission, because from the very beginning his identity and his
mission are one.[482] In this mission Jesus completely abandons himself in obedience to
the will of the Father. "The whole person of the Son is involved in his work for the
world, and his whole human nature, in all its aspects, ministers to it. It is for this work
that the Son was sent."[483] As proceeding from the Father as the "act of God,"[484] the
Son's mission comes from the Father and is in complete unity with the will of Father.
Not only then is the mission of Christ unique, as directly in communion with the will of
the Father, but it is universal in its scope. The mission of Christ embraces all other
missions, judging both Jew and Gentile who now stand under the judgement of
Christ.[485] Believers, as being-in-Christ, participate in a limited manner in the drama
which is the person of Christ.

The mission of Christ is the drama of salvation history that unfolds in the
created order embracing the totality of that order from all eternity.

> By virtue of his mission, he must *already* be identical
> with him and having included him within his mission's
> embrace. It follows that this one Man among millions
> (as he seems to be) has not been given this world-
> embracing mission *subsequently*: he must know that he
> is identical with his mission from the very beginning. . .
> Thus the mission of salvation encompasses this totality
> - which reinforces the point we have just made: in
> God's foreknowledge of what is to become of it, the
> world cannot be created without account being taken
> of this sending of the "beloved Son"; this means, in
> turn, that he-who-is-sent cannot be given this mission

---

[482]Ibid., pp. 171ff.

[483]Ibid., p. 157.

[484]von Balthasar, *Prolegomena*, p. 26.

[485]von Balthasar, *Persons in Christ*, p. 179.

> *subsequently,* a posteriori, without having been
> consulted when the original decision was made. His
> readiness to accept the mission cannot have been
> elicited from him by persuasion, as it were; rather, it
> must be in him a priori, he must spontaneously have
> declared his readiness.[486]

The mission of Christ includes the whole order of salvation from creation to his death and resurrection, until his second-coming. Christ is at the center of it all. Notably he is not only at the center of a particular aspect of reality, but at the center of reality itself. However, one must be careful to preserve the belief that the center of reality becomes incarnate in the life of a particular man.

At this point, we see the particularly rich dimensions of the mission of Christ which mediate the universal truths of God through the life of Jesus. The historical mission of Jesus mediates the fullness of the truth of Christ.[487] For it is in history that this plan unfolds. "The mission of Jesus has no conceivable temporal beginning. But as it unfolds through historical time, it enters increasingly into history. It awaits God's signal for its fulfillment not only purely from within: it also awaits it from without, because the mission will be fulfilled essentially in the fulfillment of history."[488] Not only then is history the medium through which God communicates himself, but history itself is ordered and shaped and made intelligible only in the light of Christ, whose existence alone encompasses all dimensions of reality. Discussing how the believer comes to understand his or her individual mission. von Balthasar says:

> The access is through salvation history which means
> that the creaturely order and all it comprises is always
> undergirded by the order of salvation history, which
> gives a goal and a meaning to the former. Yet identity

---

[486]Ibid., p.516.

[487]Ibid., p. 157.

[488]Ibid., p. 178.

156

is only attained in the concrete Epitome of the order of salvation history called Jesus Christ, in whom we who have yet to be created have been "chosen" and "predestined" for our mission "before the foundations of the world" (Eph 1:4f.) Furthermore, if this identity constitutes the "peak" (Eph 1:10) of the whole creation, it is only possible on the basis of an (entirely different) distinction within the One who exhibits this identity, namely, the distinction between the Son who eternally comes forth from the Father (*processio*) and the Son who is sent and goes forth into the world of time (*missio*).[489]

In his "creation-embracing" mission, not only is the truth about the individual mission of each man revealed, but the very meaning and order of the whole of the good creation is revealed. This is, of course, made most evident in the Cross.

If there is an event in the life of Christ that sums up his life, his preaching and the salvation that he offers, it is the Cross. One need not scan the whole of the life of Christ to see the meaning of his life; rather, one need simply look to the Cross. If the goal of his life and his mission is to embrace all of creation bringing it back to Father, the key event is the Cross, which summarizes the mission of Christ. It is not some abstract speculation on the nature of reality that is the center of the faith, but Christ's person given in the Cross. It is in the Cross that the drama of salvation unfolds. "Here the nub of the theo-drama must lie; God must bring it to this point so delicately, on the one hand, nothing godless is imported into God and, on the other hand, man's freedom is not overridden by a drama within the Godhead that seems to have nothing to do with him."[490] In Christ the drama of human existence which began with the incarnation comes to completeness, revealing the depth of his love for man and the redemptive power of that love. Von Balthasar notes that "God's self-disclosure is based on the

---

[489]Ibid., pp. 156-157.

[490]von Balthasar, *Man in God*, p. 194.

Cross from the very outset."[491] Nothing in the life of Christ transcends what is contained in revealed in the crucifixion. In this event, the vertical and horizontal dimensions of reality definitively cross.

If it is in the particular life of Jesus of Nazareth that the revelation of the infinite, the Trinitarian life of the God, is revealed, then his life is the center of salvation history. It is only in Jesus, who becomes man, that this salvation can take place. In his life, the "epitome" of salvation history is reached. In Christ "history" becomes intelligible in a definitive sense, since it is not only in history that the full revelation of God takes place, but history takes its meaning from this event. So that according to von Balthasar history is only possible in Christ. Only with the presence of God in time does time become meaningful, opening itself to the drama between God and man.[492] At the same time, only in and through historical time is the revelation possible.

> The mission of Jesus has no conceivable temporal beginning. But as it unfolds through historical time, it enters increasingly into history. It awaits God's signal for its fulfillment not only purely from within: it also awaits it from without, because the mission will be fulfilled essentially in a fulfillment of history; the Father's will is encountered in history no less than in interior inspiration.[493]

History, then, becomes a central theological category, where in the mission of the Son the universal enters the particular, the infinite into the finite. This means on the one hand that in Jesus the fullness of God is offered to man. In the mission of Christ, the meaning of the theo-drama is revealed and the invitation of the life of Christ is offered to every individual. At the same time this revelation opens up history to the larger

---

[491]von Balthasar, *Persons in Christ*, p. 47.

[492]von Balthasar, *Theology of History*, pp. 59ff.

[493]von Balthasar, *Persons in Christ*, p. 178.

dimensions of reality, the created order itself whose existence is made possible in and through Christ.

With his insistence upon the normative and historical character of the Christ event, von Balthasar is writing a theology that attempts to preserve the historical nature of the faith by insisting upon the original historical character of the revelation given in Christ. He insists that the historical character does not delimit or diminish the essential nature of the revelation. Likewise, our faith, rooted in the events of this historical revelation, must also be a historical faith. Not only then does our faith have its origin in those past events, but the very nature of the faith is informed by those events. The question becomes for the believer, living almost two thousand years later: how do we come to participate in those events at the origin of the Christian faith and do the means used affect the historical nature of the faith in the present?

In his Christology, von Balthasar is careful to extend the authority of Christ beyond salvation history to include the whole of the created order.

> In concentric rings around the nondeducible and sovereignly free fact of the Son's Incarnation-Cross-Resurrection, we can discern, according to the laws of theology, all the events of salvation history and world history, and of nature too, since ultimately everything exists for the sake of this center: "For . . . all things were created through him and for him" (Col 1:16)[494]

All of creation is through Christ and finds its completion in Christ. Consequently, the universal claim of Christ is now extended beyond salvation history to include the created order.

On the one hand, the created order provides the backdrop within which the revelation of Christ takes place. The incarnation requires creation. On the other hand, the created order is not prior to Christ, but is created by Christ and finds its meaning in Christ. In describing how one comes to know Christ, von Balthasar says, "The access

---

[494]von Balthasar, *Man in God*, p. 281.

is through salvation history, which means that the creaturely order and all it comprises is always undergirded by the order of salvation history, which gives a goal and meaning to the former."[495] The Christ-event becomes the source not only of salvation history but of the whole of the created order. "So we arrive at the fundamental conclusion: it is not only the Logos but Christ who is the *mediator of creation*. It means nothing less than this: all things could only be created with a view to their being perfected in the Second Adam - something that only truly comes into the light in the being and the consciousness of the Son as he carries out his mission of bringing everything to perfection."[496] So from the very start the created order was understood in terms of the plan and order given in the relationship of the Son to the Father. As such it is totally contingent for the whole of its being upon Christ, the ground of its being.

> But, being totally dependent on divine freedom, the world can receive its possibility and reality nowhere else but in the eternal Son, who eternally owes his being to the Father's generosity. If the Son is the Father's eternal Word, the world in its totality is created by this Word (Jn 1:3), not only instrumentally but in the sense that the Word is the world's pattern and hence its goal.[497]

Within this theological metaphysics, creation is not some inert object beyond or prior to God's act of salvation; rather creation is based on the fundamentally free act of God, a personal act, that is intelligible only in the light of Christ's salvific activity. The "good creation" comes to be through Christ, "through whom all things came to be, apart from him nothing came to be" (Jn 1:3). The locating of the act of creation within salvation history adds depth to the believer's understanding of the authority and activity of Christ, thereby expanding our understanding of the meaning of the historicity of the faith. It is

---

[495] von Balthasar, *Persons in Christ*, pp. 156-157.

[496] Ibid., p. 257.

[497] von Balthasar, *Man in God*, p. 261.

160

also only within this understanding of the dependency of creation upon Christ that the meaning of the relationship of nature and grace is understood.

Von Balthasar describes the relationship of nature and grace as two poles in constant tension. The relativity of these two poles provides the framework in which the world becomes intelligible. God stands in relationship to his creation but can never be reduced to that creation. Such monistic attempts at reducing the divine and the created to the same reality are characteristic of all non-Western religions and philosophies.[498] Contrary to this position, the Christian contention is that despite the origin of creation in God, it is not God. Nevertheless this does not mean that the created order is not contingent, directly and constantly dependent upon God. In this relationship grace must not be seen as simply an epiphenomenon of nature, a secondary addition to a nature which has its own complete integrity. Nor must grace be thought to so completely dominate nature that it excludes the freedom of God to reveal himself to his creature.[499] God must retain a freedom in order to enter into a covenant with man.

Likewise, the grace of Christ creates an openness where the believer can respond to the offer of God's grace. The order of grace is the goal and object of all human life.

> Naturally, in a world in which God desires all men to be saved, there is no room for a "*purely* natural" event, either in God's objective offer of salvation or in man's subjective appropriation of it. Paul too, if we consider his whole presentation of the plan of salvation, always brings out the interpenetration of natural and "graced" revelation and knowledge of God. We must always take into account man's spiritual nature which even at the natural level has a transcendent openness to the absolute, undergoes a supernatural modification.[500]

[498] von Balthasar, *Explorations in Theology*, pp. 173ff.

[499] Ibid., p. 60.

[500] von Balthasar, *Persons in Christ*, pp. 410-411.

Since the created order is fundamentally graced, there is no possibility of a "purely" natural knowledge of God, for all things are created by God and for God. This, of course, leads to the fundamental paradox of human life: that the finite creature is ultimately created for a goal that lies beyond it.

> But God's seal is set on spiritual nature in this way only because, in the first place, nature was created so that, through grace, it might behold God: the *desiderium naturalle* with a view to the *visio*. (Left to itself, the *desiderium* could not attain to *visio*, but the latter could be freely granted to it.) Thus nature is totally encompassed by grace, and this certainly has the effect of elevating it and enabling it to pursue its ultimate goals.[501]

Perhaps the best way to understand this is to focus on the universal character of the mission of Christ, for it is precisely in this universality that he embraces all of creation, including it in the plan of salvation. The meaning of the natural and the supernatural is found in the new covenant, Jesus Christ.

Since it is in Christ that the created order comes to be, one needs to look at who Christ is in this regard. Von Balthasar notes that Christ has a pre-eminence in the order of creation that is reflected also in his pre-existence. He is the "first-born of all creation" (Col 1:15). This pre-existence places Christ not simply chronologically prior to creation, but ontologically, as the one through whom things came to be. Therefore, creation reflects the very nature of Christ, the New Covenant. Most importantly, then, the question of nature and grace needs to be seen within the mission of the Son and, in particular, in terms of his role in salvation history.[502] "There is no common measure between nature and grace, reason and faith; only the order grounded in the person of

---

[501]Ibid., p. 417.

[502]Ibid., pp. 250ff.

Christ: nature as the expression and servant of the supernatural. In this service it will not be found wanting."[503]

C. Christ and the faith of the Church

As noted, von Balthasar describes the relationship of Christ to the world as "theo-drama." In this drama, at the center of the created order, the covenant between man and God unfolds. At the core of this drama, of course, is the Christ-event. In the revelation of Christ, the full meaning of man and God is revealed, as well as the meaning of the created order. But the question now must be raised that if the unique life of Christ mediated the universal truth about God, the very truth by which we are saved, how can we come to participate in that truth? How are we who are temporal, finite beings able to participate in the infinite events by which we are saved? And if what is significant about the revelation of God is the act of God, then how do we come to participate in those acts in our act of faith? The answer, according to von Balthasar, lies in the nature of the Christ-event and in the subsequent life of the Church.

According to von Balthasar, the incarnation is where God enters into the world. And when he departs from the world he does not abandon it, but opens it up so that man might respond to his offer of grace. This befits what happens in the mission of Christ. Remember that the universal mission of Christ is inclusive of all other missions. Likewise in his mission the nature of his person is revealed. "When a human becomes a person, theologically, by being given a unique vocation and mission, he is simultaneously de-privatized, socialized and made into a locus and bearer of community."[504] One sees this in the life of Christ. He calls followers who become incorporated into his mission and continue that mission after his death. Likewise,

---

[503]von Balthasar, *Explorations in Theology*, p.168.

[504]von Balthasar, *Persons in Christ*, p. 271.

believers today are called to participate in the mission of Christ, not alone, but by entering into the community of the faithful, the Church.

All are called to enter into a relationship with Christ, to participate in the "sacramentality" of the person Christ.[505] As sacrament, Christ both is and mediates the salvation, the grace for which we were created. Yet one must observe how the participation in the life of Christ can and does take place here and how.

As noted at the beginning of this study there is a relationship between faith, history and worship. Worship should be informed by the original revelation and communicate the content of that revelation, at the same time preserving the historicity of the faith as it informs the life of the believers. By examining the nature of worship, one can better understand the nature of the faith. In addition, it is the worship of the Church that bridges the gap between the Christ-event and the present. So depending on how one interprets the liturgy of the Church, one will have a certain understanding of the Christian faith.

As a Roman Catholic, von Balthasar interprets the primary liturgical action of the Church to be the liturgy of the sacrament, especially the Eucharist, where the event of the Cross is represented in the sacrifice of the Mass. Accordingly, the Mass is the context where the Church finds the source and continuity of the faith in the present. But such an interpretation of the liturgical symbols, this issue of liturgical mediation, is a matter of dispute within Christianity. It is precisely the question of the historical mediation of the grace of Christ that now, all too evidently divides Christians.

According to von Balthasar, the key complaint against the Roman Catholic position is against the "innovations" of Roman Catholicism; i.e., innovations without biblical warrant.[506] For the most part, these critics claim that these "innovations"

---

[505]Ibid., p. 278. Also see Hans Urs von Balthasar, *The Office of Peter and the Structure of the Church* (San Francisco: Ignatius, 1974), p. 278. This text examines the individual ministries of the Church in the light of the universal mission of Christ. Here, discussion of the role of Mary in the process of redemption is important. This will be done later in this chapter.

[506]von Balthasar, *Man in History*, p. 125.

elevate something in fallen creation to mediate between God and man. They therefore reify the faith, failing to maintain the proper distance between the personal act of faith and any ambiguous external mediation. According to their opponents, the Catholics fail to realize that everything in fallen creation is finally "external and alien to the Christ-form, and in the end acts only to obscure it."[507] The good creation, now under the effects of sin, cannot mediate the grace of Christ.

In Protestant theology, the world is understood to be intrinsically sinful and under the judgement of God in all its dimensions. There is no special, sacramental mediation in the world, for all would-be mediations share the same fatal ambiguity: in fallen history there is no complete sacramental access to the Risen Christ[508] and the revelation remains hidden *sub contraria specie*.[509] The *sola fide* emphasis within Protestantism means, then, that one must be suspicious of all external mediations of the faith.[510] This is particularly evident in the Protestant treatment of aesthetics.

According to von Balthasar, Luther's theology begins with the Cross, cutting through any abstraction of the faith that might view the faith as ontology, thereby robbing the Cross of its significance.[511] From this hermeneutical basis, Luther battles to preserve the purity of the faith from any rationalistic systemization. But according to von Balthasar, Luther fails. Instead of protecting the faith, von Balthasar claims that

---

[507]von Balthasar, *The Glory of the Lord: Seeing the Form*, ed. Joseph Fessio, S.J. and John Riches, trans. Erasmo Leria-Merkakis (San Francisco: Ignatius Press, 1982), p. 528. Von Balthasar also discusses this in terms of the offices of the Church in *Church and the World*, pp. 80-114.

[508]von Balthasar, *Word and Revelation*, pp. 37-38.

[509]von Balthasar, *The Glory of the Lord*, vol. I, pp. 57ff.

[510]von Balthasar, *Word and Revelation*, pp. 37-38.

[511]von Balthasar, *The Glory of the Lord*, vol. I, pp. 57ff.

Luther robs the faith of the significance of its expression.[512] He does this by separating the object of faith from any adequate present historical mediation. As a consequence of the Protestantism emphasis on the fallenness of creation, all that is within the created order is subject to the ambiguity of fallen existence and cannot mediate the divine.

> It is evident that, from the standpoint of Protestantism, beauty has to be transferred wholly to the sphere of event. For from the Protestant perspective, any kind of regularity, of immanence which is seen as perduring, inherent *qualitas*, as Being-in-repose, as *habitus*, as something that can be manipulated, is already by that very fact identified with demonic corruption.[513]

According to the Protestant view, the dichotomy between God's revelation and human history is the result of the fall. The sense of total corruption that often pervades the Protestant description of the world denies an intrinsic goodness to the fallen creation. All that is good is found in God alone, who imparts goodness where he will. So, just as beauty cannot remain incarnate in fallen creation, all fallen creaturely modes of mediation are likewise restricted to the realm of the tragic[514]- a consequence of the failure of any temporal mediation of the divine. This rejection of the possibility of the mediation of the divine glory, beauty, by fallen creation likewise can be extended to theo-drama.

As noted, the theo-drama has at its center the relationship between God and man given in Christ. Unlike the Lutheran position, it emphasizes the continued historical presence of Christ in history. As a matter of fact, it is that continued presence

---

[512]Ibid., p. 49. An example of this logic is provided by Kierkegaard, who separates aesthetics from Christian religion. This results in the dehistoricization of the faith. Like Bultmann, Kierkegaard retreats from history to the inwardness of faith. (pp.49-52)

[513]Ibid., p. 67. *Sola fide* implies an absolute sovereignty on the part of God. This leads to a kind separation of God and man. Von Balthasar does not deny a separation, but asks whether the separation must be so construed.

[514]Ibid., pp. 68-69.

that constitutes history. Yet it is precisely the "theo-drama" that Luther rejects, rendering vacuous the historical character of the revelation.[515] Faith simply becomes an "internal" experience of Christ, absent any continuous public expression.[516]

It is exactly this point that Roman Catholicism fights against, interpreting the faith in such a way so as to defend the ability of the created order to mediate the divine. Therefore, Roman Catholic thought will always repudiate the idea that God and the world are totally at odds, recognizing not only that God is now present, but that since he is present, those who live in him have an authority in history.[517] "What is distinctively catholic is that this informed existence is posited within the objective, prescribed and, for the individual subject, the normative form of the Church. The hierarchical office is a form, the sacramental system is a form; and obedience to the Church according to her mind is how the individual appropriates the form."[518] Despite sin, von Balthasar understands that the created order can mediate the divine. This "ability" is something that is part of the created order, affected by sin, although never totally destroyed by sin. Also this "ability" is not a later addition, but part of the very good creation from the very beginning.[519] Instead, the ability of the spatio-temporal existence to mediate the divine is an intrinsic part of the order and meaning of creation and history.

---

[515] Ibid., p. 544. Von Balthasar does see Karl Barth as an opponent to this tendency within Protestantism (p. 53). Barth insists upon the inseparability of form and content in the revelation.

[516] This tendency has become continually more evident in much of contemporary theology, Catholic as well as Protestant. See the *Glory of the Lord*, vol. I, pp. 534ff.

[517] von Balthasar, *The God Question and Modern Man*, trans. Hilda Graef (New York: Sheed and Ward, 1955), p. 7.

[518] von Balthasar, *Word and Revelation*, pp. 158-159.

[519] von Balthasar, *The Glory of the Lord*, vol. I; pp. 440-453.

The sacramental nature of the reality is best affirmed in von Balthasar's *Theo-drama*.[520] The theo-drama mediates the whole of salvation history making that drama visible and bringing it to life. In a sense, the dramatic becomes the "ultimate, not to be surpassed; it does not point to some prior "wisdom" or "teaching" or "gnosis" or "theology" that could then be recounted in the epic mode; it remains at the center, as drama, as the action takes place between God and man, undiminished in its contemporary relevance."[521] It is within this drama, this action, that the faith lives and unfolds. By our participation in these actions we come to faith, to a life in God, which is offered to us here and now in the midst of fallen creation. To fail to see this is to fail to accept the full sacramental nature of creation and the true historical character of the faith.

Consequently, it is this sacramental focus at the center of the Catholic interpretation of the faith whereby the Church most concretely affirms the continuity of the faith with the events of Christ. To abolish this "sacramentality" would lead to the dehistoricization of the faith, a Christian faith that cannot be abstracted from history and remain true to its very nature. Such abstractions can only lead to the kind of gnosticisms that have plagued Christianity in every age. To guard against these mythologizing tendencies, the faith needs to be rooted in the Christian drama, the concrete life of the Church, which has its primary expression in the Church's sacramental life.[522]

Von Balthasar, as a Roman Catholic, understands the sacraments to be the center of the life of the Church and the focal point of faith. The sacraments render available to us in the present the drama of salvation, which finds its central locus in the

---

[520]The criticisms of von Balthasar's *The Glory of the Lord* are focused on this point. In that work he fails to affirm the historical nature of the faith. One might assume that he accepts it, but unlike the *Theo-drama* where the incarnational nature of the historicity of the faith is affirmed, *The Glory of the Lord* fails to do so.

[521]von Balthasar, *Man in God*, p. 49.

[522]von Balthasar, *Word and Revelation*, pp. 167ff.

Christ-event. "Herein too lies the meaning of the Catholic sacraments, which continually make the one event present; herein a more all-embracing sense, the meaning of the Church insofar as she is the re-presentation of the "drama of salvation" once for all on each particular occasion."[523] The sacraments act, therefore, as an extension of the grace of Christ, given definitely in the incarnation to believers in the present.

> For each of the sacraments it would be necessary to point out in this same way the personal, temporal-historical reality which is thrown open to the recipient, offered to him, made available for his participation, assigned to him personally. By becoming contemporaneous with the believer in the sacrament, the Lord bestows upon him, given him in faith, of becoming like him who became man. The grace he communicates is inseparable from his incarnation, his relationship to the Church , his historicity.[524]

This sacramental re-presentation makes permanently simultaneous in the present the fullness of salvation given in Christ. This mediation of the past is unique since no other past event has such a mediation (most past events are never fully recaptured at any later time) and because it refuses any abstraction from the present. The sacramental mediation takes place in a particular event, at a particular time, mediating the grace of Christ given in the particular life of Jesus of Nazareth.

As that which links the salvific events of the past with believers in the present, how one understands this mediatory role of the sacraments will greatly effect the manner in which the faith is structured and understood. According to von Balthasar, then, the sacraments take their meaning from and reflect the nature of the Christ-event. Therefore, as in the incarnation, the essence of the sacrament cannot be separated from the external form of its historical mediation. This grace is not a "formless grace" to

---

[523]von Balthasar, *Man in God*, p. 49.

[524]von Balthasar, *A Theology of History*, p. 93.

which is later added a physical sign, rather, both form and content are inextricably related.

> Christ's sensuous existence must necessarily accompany the appearance of his Word. And the Sacrament here is more than Old Testament rite, even if here too we are dealing with an essentially symbolic reality: namely, the thing itself in a veiled form that reveals it. The unprecedented hardness and exciting nature of the corporeal form of the sacraments, which simply demand to be enacted, call forth, not only the naked faith, but also the equally hard historical truth to which they owe their origin. Those who realize this stand in no danger of a sacramental holiness through works, for the sensory character of the event confronts them directly with the event which is made present *hic et nunc* in the sacraments. The image compels them to enter into the act by revealing to them the act which both instituted the image and is continued in the image.[525]

The sacraments are not simply human efforts, the product of the human experience of God, rather, it is by the power of God that these "symbols" mediate salvation: their source being the Christ-event. And just as the Christ-event is historical, the sacraments must have this historical dimension.

Therefore the sacraments are essential to our understanding of the faith. They are the keys to understanding where and how the divine and the human come together. Von Balthasar insists upon the importance of the historical nature of the sacrament, yet he realizes the difficulties in trying to conceptualize the relationship of the human and the divine that is realized in the sacraments. "These entities, possessing form and mediating the shaping deed, are particularly difficult to describe because, on the one hand, they are the Christ-form itself, but, on the other hand, in their communication to the world, they are already necessarily affected in their form by the world that receives

---

[525]von Balthasar, *The Glory of the Lord*, vol. I; p. 422.

them."[526] At this point the meaning of Christian faith and the historicity of that faith is once again raised, since the faith lives by its participation in the Christ-event, a participation mediated by the sacraments, which is affected by their reception in the world..

In his description of Von Balthasar describes the sacramental mediation noting that the sacraments must have a visible dimension. Nevertheless, despite the necessity of a "physical" dimension, the divine can never be restricted by that physical mediation, always transcending the visible. The Spirit always overflows its vessels; i.e., it can never be fully restricted to any physical mediation.[527] But this does not mean that the physical realm is inconsequential to Christian faith. On the contrary, the divine must be historically mediated if God and man are to be related. It is precisely in the role as mediator that the sacramental nature of the history comes to play an important role in von Balthasar's theology.

While developing his theology of history, von Balthasar discusses the relationship between *signum* and *signatum* in terms of materiality and form.[528] "The appearance of the form, as revelation of the depths, is an indissoluble union of two things. It is the real presence of the depths, of the whole of reality and it is a real pointing beyond itself to these depths."[529] In this theological aesthetics, the form, flowing from the love of God, is actualized in the material realm. To destroy either the sign or the signified would be to prevent the full sacramental mediation of the divine in material order. Nevertheless, in history there is a tension between the material sign,

---

[526]Ibid. p. 528.

[527]von Balthasar, *A Theology of History*, p. 103.

[528]von Balthasar, *Word and Revelation*, pp. 158-159.

[529]von Balathasar, *The Glory of the Lord*, vol. I, p. 118.

which is a necessary and essential witness to the presence of the infinite in time and space,[530] and the divine, which cannot be limited by material mediation.

Perhaps a better way of understanding the nature of this historical mediation is to look at it not in terms of a physical object mediating an abstract truth, but seeing it in terms of the act of revelation. To understand the nature of this material mediation one needs to look to the Incarnation. As noted, the Incarnation is the event where the universal mission of Christ, the relationship of all the created order to the trinitarian Godhead is revealed. It is in the historical revelation that we participate in the theo-drama at the heart of human existence. This drama is mediated by the revelation which, like Christ, is historical. Von Balthasar thus concludes that although faith can never be deduced from the particular historical events, its life is inseparable from them.

Faith, then, is based on a perception of sorts.[531] This perception, on the one hand, begins with faith, yet is at the same time the cause of faith. Faith is not simply the acceptance of certain facts, for one needs faith to see the revelatory character of historical events; rather, it is in the process of faith that the believer takes on the "form" of the revelation, enabling the believer to identify and grow in that truth.[532]

Although von Balthasar describes the faith act as taking on the "form" of Christ in his theological aesthetics, in his theo-drama he describes this act more concretely in term of a participation in the mission of Christ. The sacraments, like the Christ-event, bestow grace on the Church as they communicate the salvation accomplished by Christ. "All sacraments (and in this they are like the Eucharist) are a saving act that God performs in Christ Jesus for the ecclesial believer."[533] The events of our life find their meaning and significance in the concrete events of Christ's life. The sacraments,

[530] von Balthasar, *Word and Revelation*, pp. 172, 187ff.

[531] von Balathasar, *The Glory of the Lord*, vol. I, pp. 121ff.

[532] Ibid., pp. 125ff and 576-577. Also see *Man in History*, pp. 202ff.

[533] Ibid., p. 576.

since they have their origin in the Christ-event, share the character of that origin, and so must our faith. "His being born, his living and dying are a finite temporal process; but within this process God actually comes forth out of himself in order to be part of an interplay involving worldly beings."[534] Through the sacramental life the believer enters into this process.

D. Word and Sacrament

Von Balthasar interprets the Christian liturgy as giving primacy to the liturgy of the sacrament. In particular, it is upon the Eucharist, interpreted as the locus of this sacramental worship of the sacrifice of Christ, that the Church is built.[535] "There is not Christian liturgy without the sacrifice of the cross; in fact we might say that the two are one and the same."[536] It is precisely this sacrificial dimension that is central to understanding the role of the sacraments and the event-character of the sacramental mediation.

Von Balthasar affirms the primacy of the sacramental mediation in the Theo-drama where he describes the Eucharist as being at the center of cultic drama.[537] In the Eucharist, the believer is drawn into the center of the unfolding drama of salvation history. The Eucharist summarizes all of salvation history. Moreover, it is in the Eucharistic celebration that Christ remains simultaneously and countinuously present in his Church. "The seal of this simultaneity (which is also substantially conditioned by the Church's structure and ministerial authority) is the real presence of Christ in the eucharistic action, which - as Dom Casel emphasized - is drama: it is a re-presentation,

---

[534]von Balthasar, *Persons in Christ*, p. 53.

[535]von Balthasar, *Man in History*, p. 77.

[536]von Balthasar, *Word and Revelation*, p. 107.

[537]von Balthasar, *Prolegomena*, pp. 115ff.

each time, of the once-for-all divine action."[538] It is precisely this "action" that separates the liturgy of the word from the liturgy of the sacrament.

Perhaps more than most Catholic theologians since the Reformation, von Balthasar not only points to the differences between the liturgy of the sacrament and the liturgy of the word, but also to the ways they are alike and how they complement each other in the life of the Church. He understands both to be gifts of Christ to the Church.[539] Both the liturgy of the sacrament and the liturgy of the word are able to mediate the grace of Christ, incorporating the believer into the life of Christ. "So it is that he delivers himself over to the Church as eucharist and as scripture, places himself in her hands in these two corporal forms in such a wise that, in both forms, he creates a means of being present in the church as the one, ever active, unchanging life, life that is infinitely manifold, ever manifesting itself in new, astounding ways."[540] In the word, in scripture and through sacraments, the Spirit acts upon that which pertains to the Son, forming the mystical body of Christ through the universalizing of the historical Christ.[541] It is both the public expression of the preaching and the sacramental life that "universalize the body of Christ without making it any less concrete."[542] Despite the universal nature of the preaching and sacraments, they are personal calls to the believer in the midst of space and time.[543]

In comparing the word of scripture and the sacraments, von Balthasar asserts that they both have their origin in Christ and are concrete manifestations of the life of Christ. "Scripture makes the incarnate Lord present in a way analogous to that in

[538]von Balthasar, *Man in God*, p. 74.

[539]von Balthasar, *Explorations in Theology*, p. 16.

[540]von Balthasar, *Word and Revelation*, p. 20.

[541]von Balthasar, *Explorations in Theology*, p. 16.

[542]Ibid., p. 16.

[543]Ibid., p. 24.

which the eucharistic body makes present his historical body."[544] They do not replace each other but complement each other, "they make the event present as event."[545]

> Here it already becomes evident that Eucharist and Scripture belong most intimately together, that they can only be different aspects of the same thing, and this, furthermore, justifies the practice of the Church, as she remembers her Lord in celebrating her liturgical memorial as Christ's becoming present both in the Word and the eucharistic Sacrament.[546]

What is of significance here is that von Balthasar sees both the scripture and the sacraments to be essential to Christian life, and that he understands them to be complementary rather than the same. Both take their meaning from their reference point, the life of Christ, yet they seem to involve different dynamics. Despite the fact that they both mediate the grace of Christ, the nature of the mediation differs.

First von Balthasar describes the different modes of mediation by stating that the sacrament mediates *vita*, whereas the scripture mediate *veritas*. "They mediate the one, incarnate logos to the faithful, and make him who of himself is both origin and end the way (*via*); the eucharist does so inasmuch as he is the divine life (*vita*), and scripture inasmuch as he is the divine Word and the divine truth (veritas)."[547] The unity of truth and life in Christ, of course, unifies these two dimensions. But beyond this unity, von Balthaser asserts that the sacramental mediation is not only different, but more perfect. In order to explain this, he distinguishes between the Word of God and scripture.

---

[544]Ibid., p. 16.

[545]von Balthasar, *The Glory of the Lord*, vol. I, p. 596.

[546]Ibid., pp. 529-530.

[547]von Balthasar, *The Word Made Flesh*, p. 15.

The Word of God is more than the letter, it is the full revelation of God that surpasses all words about God.[548] As the language of God, it transcends all philosophy and takes up the fragmented words of fallen creation, transforming them in the death and resurrection of Christ, establishing a new covenant.[549] On the one hand, the content of the Church's proclamation takes up ordinary words and transforms them, giving them a richness beyond their ordinary meaning. Here language acts as a "sacrament" opening up the world, mediating a transcendent reality.[550] On the other hand, von Balthasar notes the limited ability of a word about God to mediate the Word of God. Just as the divinity of Christ cannot be comprehended completely through his humanity, "no more can the divine sense of scripture ever be fully plumbed through the letter."[551] The Word of God, the full revelation of God, did become incarnate and present in history, but the historical presence always points beyond itself. The scriptures bear witness to the Word, but the Word transcends that witness.[552]

Accordingly, Jesus is the original full expression of God, not the scriptures.[553] "We must, then, repeat that the Scripture is not the Word itself, but rather the Spirit's testimony concerning the Word, which springs from an indissoluble bond and marriage between Spirit and those eyewitnesses who were originally invited and admitted to the vision."[554] The unique character of the scriptures is that they attest to the concrete revelation of Christ in God, yet it is really only in the Christ-event itself that the words about the divine become concrete. He is their living commentary, the source of new

---

[548] von Balthasar, *Word and Revelation*, pp. 529-530.

[549] von Balthasar, *Man in History*, pp. 236ff.

[550] Ibid., pp. 63, 225. Also, *Man in History*, pp. 223ff.

[551] von Balthasar, *The Word Made Flesh*, p. 21.

[552] Ibid., pp. 11ff.

[553] von Balthasar, *The Glory of the Lord*, vol. I, p. 596.

[554] Ibid., p. 31.

life to which the scriptures testify.[555]   In the word of Christ, the divine truth is expressed to man.

Likewise, the gospel is a living doctrine, a testimony, that not only points to the revelation, but is the revelation. The exact unity of the scriptures with its source, the Word, enables the scriptures to mediate grace. "As we have already said on several different occasions Scripture does not stand over against this form of revelation by way of imitation as a second, antonymous form, complete in itself: for Scripture belongs to the sphere of revelation and, being the normative testimony, itself is part of revelation."[556] The scripture filled and shaped by the revelation of God in Christ must be consistent with that revelation and cannot but be understood to be an extension of that revelation. Yet the scripture is not the revelation. The revelation continues to be distinguished from scripture not simply as human to divine, as finite to infinite, but as testimony to act. As in his Christology, von Balthasar describes the unique character of the revelation as act, and the scriptures bear witness to those acts.[557] It appears that it is precisely at this point that the liturgy of the sacrament can be differentiated from the liturgy of the word.

According to von Balthasar, the liturgy of the sacrament has a normative mediatory character that surpasses that of scripture. Just as the words of Christ find their full meaning in light of his death and resurrection, the proclamation of the word of God takes its meaning from the Christ-event. Nevertheless, unlike the sacramental mediation, the proclamation of the Church is partial, in need of a supplement. "The word of revelation infinitely surpasses all that the word that testifies can possibly contain; and this superfluidity becomes available to the Church in the living eucharistic presence of Christ; the necessary reflection of this vitality in verbal form is the principle

---

[555]von Balthasar, *Word and Revelation*, pp. 12-13.

[556]von Balthasar, *The Glory of the Lord*, vol. I, p. 596.

[557]von Balthasar, *The Word Made Flesh*, p. 21.

of tradition."[558]   The Eucharist mediates the fullness of the revelation of Christ, where,
as in the Christ-event, the last words of man are taken up into Christ.

> The eucharist is the marvelous means of freeing Christ's
> historical humanity from the confines of space and
> time, of multiplying mysteriously its presence without
> forgetting its unity and, since it is given to each
> Christian as his indispensable nourishment (Jn 6:53-56),
> of incorporating all into the body of Christ, making
> them in Christ one body through which comes divine
> life.   Through the eucharist the church comes into
> being as the body of Christ; while the one flesh of the
> Lord is multiplied mankind divided is unified in it.
> "And the bread that we break, is it not the partaking of
> the body of the Lord?   Because the bread is one, we
> though many, are one body, all of us who partake of
> the one bread (I Cor. 10:16-17)."[559]

The Eucharist mediates the full redemption given in Christ, establishing a unity among
all those who believe, forming the Church.   This sacramental presence in the church
becomes the center of the Church's life, uniting all being in the cross of Christ.

In one place von Balthasar describes the presence of Christ in the sacraments,
in particular the Eucharist, as the presence of Christ during his forty days on earth after
his resurrection.   During those forty days, Christ remained present among his people
teaching, exhorting, bridging the gap between heaven and earth.   Also, during these
days, the bond between the earthly life of Christ and the Church is established.   "We
shall take as our first principle that Christ's existence, hence his mode of duration, in the
Eucharist and sacraments is, as far as concerns himself, no different from that which
belongs to the forty days."[560]   In those forty days the truth of the grace of Christ and

---

[558]Ibid., p. 19.

[559]Ibid., pp. 15-16.

[560]Von Balthasar, *A Theology of History*, p. 91.

the offer of salvation become visible in the Church. The Eucharist, then, as the forty days, links the Church with the historical Jesus, revealing and "externalizing" the meaning of the faith, so that which was given in the past is made contemporary. The historical body of Christ, born of Mary, whose full meaning is given in the death and resurrection of Christ, now causes the Church's existence, an existence informed by the sacramental mediation of the original definitive event.[561]

Further, the Eucharistic presence is likened by von Balthasar to the presence of the entire Kingdom of God.[562]

> In this light the Mass, as the eucharistic action, can be viewed within the bonds of the sacramental, though the "making present" is here given a new intensity. It is not, as in the other sacraments, some *one* special aspect of Christ's earthly existence which is here turned upon the Church and the individual, but his whole bodily reality in its supreme fulfillment as the bodily sacrifice of the Cross. In so far as the new and eternal marriage between Godhead and manhood was sealed in the blood on the Cross by the loving sacrifice of that one individual whose dual nature was itself the center and source of the Covenant, to that extent his *one* sacrifice to the Father, contains from the very start, a duality within itself: it is the sacrifice of the Head and the Body, of the Bridegroom and of the Bride. This one marriage in blood contains within itself in advance not only every bodily approach of the Lord to his Church until the end of the world but also every response on the Church's part: the Church whom the Lord had already drawn into his liturgy of the Cross by the liturgical con-celebration of the Last Supper. When, in the Mass, the Church is granted a true bodily contemporeity with her Head in his sacrifice, something takes place not only from the Church's point of view but from Christ's: something for which the closest comparison we can find lies in those meetings of the

---

[561]Ibid., pp. 84ff.

[562]Ibid., pp. 87, 91, 94.

> risen Christ - which were real meetings for *him*, too -
> with Mary at the seplechure, with the apostles, with
> Thomas and the others, or again in that breakfast by the
> lake-side.[563]

It is being made contemporary with the events of salvation that makes the Eucharistic presence so unique. This is the "real presence" of the Eucharistic sacrifice, a presence that images the events that are the source of the faith.

One sees that von Balthasar claims a unique form of mediation for the sacraments, at least more complete than the scriptures, yet that particular nature of that uniqueness is difficult to identify. In the tradition it was held that the unique character of the sacramental mediation of the grace of Christ worked *ex opere operato*. Like the focus on real presence and later transubstantiation in the doctrines on the eucharist, *ex opere operato* suggests that the sacraments have an objective character. This "objective character" refers, of course, to the activity of the Christ, the presence of the salvific activity of Christ wherever the sacrament is performed. "There is no Christian liturgy without the sacrifice of the cross; in fact we might say that the two are one and the same."[564] Von Balthasar recognizes the reality of an "objective dimension," rooted of course in the grace of Christ - Christ is present by the power of Christ, because he promised to be. Yet he is also reluctant to describe this presence and "objective dimension" using any kind of static language. Rather, he wants to see this "presence" as a dynamic process whereby the God calls man and man responds. So just as he understands revelation to be "act," the meaning of the sacraments can only be understood in terms of the actions of God. The real difference between the liturgy of the sacrament and the liturgy of the word, then, is that in the sacramental actions we come to participate in those very acts of Christ by which we are saved. Since history is

---

.[563]Ibid., pp. 94-95. The presence described here comes very close to the mode of Eucharistic presence as described by Calvin; i.e., as Christ was present to his disciples after the resurrection. But unlike Calvin, von Balthasar understands this relationship to be marital and covenantal.

[564]Ibid., p. 84.

ultimately theo-drama, it is the actions of Christ which constitute the center of reality and only by our participation in those actions do we come to share in the fullness of that reality

A noticeable absence in von Balthasar's theology is that he does not discuss the presence of Christ in terms of the traditional sacramental language; i.e., *ex opere operato*. Such attempts to conceptualize and systematize the faith fall short of their desired end and always lead to a reduction of the faith to rational categories, thereby distorting the full meaning of the revelation of God in history. Rather, the revelation must not be sacrificed to rational clarity.

In his sacramentology, von Balthasar insists upon a free sacramental presence not reducible to any deterministic structure which would reduce the divine/human relationship to the categories of the human mind. The divine/human relationship rests on the will of God, his providence, and therefore transcends human reason. As a result, he articulates his understanding of the real presence of Christ in the sacraments in terms of a marital/covenantal relationship.[565] "The accent that renders the Eucharist comprehensible falls on the real presence, in which the living Christ makes himself present to the Church by means of his deed of power; but this deed of power by no means neglects the realization of the community which, as it realizes him by remembering him, also realizes itself."[566] In the Eucharist, it is not a static entity of which we partake, but ultimately a personal relationship mediated in and by the sacramental life and the Church.[567]

Within this approach, transubstantiation must now be defined in terms of "eating" and "drinking" and not in terms of an "objective" external presence. "What is

---

[565]von Balthasar, *Church and World*, pp. 125ff. Here von Balthasar finds fault with the theology of *Mystici Corporis*. He believes that the church document overemphasizes the *ex opere operato* character of the sacraments.

[566]von Balthasar, *The Glory of the Lord*, vol.I, p. 573.

[567]von Balthasar, *A Theology of History*, pp. 80-81.

important for the Church is not that something is to be found on the table of the altar, but that by consuming this nourishment the Church becomes what she can and ought to be . . . The accent falls on the constitutive event occurring between Christ and the Church (which always has its concrete expression in a gathering community)."[568] Yet the difficulty that this leaves one is that if the faith cannot be located in a place - "on the altar"- how does one avoid a gnostic kind of abstracting where the faith is reduced to the "simply spiritual?"

The hesitancy of von Balthasar to use traditional language reflects his understanding of the faith in terms of aesthetics and drama. Both show the dynamic dimensions of the faith. But it is theo-drama that is particularly helpful in answering the problem of the relationship of faith and history. It does this by sustaining the privileged significance of the Eucharist. In the drama of salvation history, the Eucharist mediates the grace of Christ so that the believer can become a "child of God."[569] Yet his Eucharistic theology is less concerned with a presence defined by location than one that

---

[568]Ibid., p. 574. There is a shift away from ex opere operato and transubstantiation toward the Eucharist as the cause of the Church. One must wonder if the historicity of the faith is the same in both instances.

First, in the *The Glory of the Lord*, Von Balthasar seems to argue that in the sacraments the image-form of Christ is impressed on the believer. The sacrament mediates the Christ-event to the faithful. "But the event is nevertheless always aimed at the individual subject, who must discern the mediating, symbolic character of the form mediating the event if his conformation to Christ is to occur meaningfully and fittingly. A sacrament is an ecclesial gesture that Jesus Christ directs to man." (*The Glory of the Lord*, vol. I, p. 5478.) The effects of the sacrament do not simply rest upon those who receive them, infant baptism represents an inadequate paradigm for sacramental worship. (p. 579) This is a "quasi-natural" in that it is not ratified initially by the subject.

This "qualified meaning" of *ex opere operato* shifts the emphasis away from the working of the sacrament itself to the relationship between Christ and the believer. The historicity of the faith reflects this mediation and tends to downplay the *de facto*- historical presence. There is a tendency in this theology to collapse the *res et sacramentum* into the *res tantum* thereby questioning the *ex opere operato* efficacy of the sacraments. This endangers the efficacy of the visible signs in the mediation of salvation. Because when the presence of Christ is understood as a relation to the believer, it is much more difficult to locate in time and space. One must ask whether von Balthasar's theology of history is conformable to that implicit in Vatican II which reemphasizes the *ex opere operato* doctrine.

[569]von Balthasar, *Person in Christ*, pp. 38, 39.

has its reality and "objective" character understood in terms of the larger process of creation and particularly the Church.

In his discussion of "real presence," the emphasis is on the relationship of Christ to the Church. This reflects his understanding of the faith as taking place in relationship to the whole created order given in Christ. The act of faith stands beyond the subjective definitions sometimes given in modern theology. The objective character of the faith is neither a local presence nor a simply internal experience of faith. Rather, it has the character of action, event or drama where the participant partakes of the Eucharist that mediates the fullness of the historical revelation of Christ and reflects the very covenantal structure of reality itself and the economy of salvation. In the present, this realization and unfolding take place in the life of the Church.

What is really at the heart of this "New Covenant" during the present time is the relationship of Christ to his Church. In and through Christ, the Church has her existence. She is the "body of Christ," the final form and extension of the one body that became incarnate.[570] Yet, the Church is not Christ but stands in relationship to Christ. "For, as Christ's concrete partner, she has a visibly defined form; yet she becomes his partner only through a special influence on the part of the Savior - it is only because she is his 'Body' that she can be his 'Bride.'"[571] The Church, then, is the *primal sacrament*, "infallibly receiving her life from receiving her own being from the being of Christ (*ex opere operato*)."[572] The Church does not exist in isolation but always in people, who are called in and through the Church to respond to the call of Christ. The Church, then, is able to mediate the grace of Christ, to speak with authority since the source of her life continually sustains her, still recognizing her continued dependence upon the grace of Christ.

---

[570]von Balthasar, *The Word Made Flesh*, p. 15.

[571]von Balthasar, *Persons in Christ*, p. 429.

[572]Ibid., pp. 429-430.

In this dependence a unity is created, in which the will of Christ and that of the Church become one. Like Christ, the Church has a universal mission and now has a privileged role in the plan of salvation. The Church's role in this plan is to mediate Christ; she is the *sacramentum mundi*. In a sense she has no reality of her own but is an extension of the mission of Christ into the world.[573]

Within von Balthasar's theology, the Eucharist and the Church both reflect the covenantal structure of reality and salvation given in the life of Christ. They reflect in their structure the covenantal nature of the whole process of redemption in which and by which the Eucharist and Church have meaning and life. In the present time, the Eucharist mediates in a special way between Christ and the Church. The Eucharist is the "cause" of the Church, vivifying and unifying the Church. This sacrament has a way of mediating the grace of Christ to many without destroying the unity of the body of Christ nor undermining the historical character of the Christ-event. "Through the eucharist the Church comes into being as the Body of Christ; and while the one flesh of the Lord is multiplied, mankind divided is unified in it."[574] The Eucharist, as the New Covenant, is our access to the unfolding of the covenant in the economy of salvation.

> In this communion between the Lord and his Church there comes into existence a kind of time which is sacramental, and most especially eucharistic. Its peculiar character is that the eternal Lord is constantly coming afresh into contemporaneity with his Bride, but without becoming subject to or measurable by passing time. It is a time stripped of corruption, of everything negative, but containing everything positive which characterizes earthly time.[575]

---

[573] Ibid., pp. 441f.f

[574] von Balthasar, *The Word Made Flesh*, pp. 15-16.

[575] von Balthasar, *A Theology of History*, p. 95.

184

The nature of this eucharistic encounter between Christ and the Church reflects not only the unique character of this time, but von Balthasar insists that this encounter has the "ever-new" presence of the physical humanity that has now become pneumatic.[576] Nevertheless, this mediation remains uniquely concrete, sacramental. The spirit remains rooted in the flesh.

> This is what comes about in the bodily life of the Church, effected by the personal Incarnation of the Word. In virtue of his physical nature, the Son can fashion mankind as his "body" (ICor 12:27) by means of his Eucharist (ICor 10:16f.): he pours his "fullness" into a vessel which is formed by this very act of pouring (Eph 1:23). Thus the movement towards enfleshment is completed by becoming ecclesial and even cosmic (*ibid.*), whereas it was initially in the human figure of Jesus Christ that "the whole fullness of the deity dwelt bodily."(Col 2:9).[577]

The significance of this "bodily" presence, then, continues in the Church and von Balthasar is careful to preserve this dimension in his theology. Nevertheless, he emphasizes here not only a passive presence, but, as in the New Covenant, a dynamic process, where the incarnate word is mediated in the eucharistic "real presence" to the Church and accepted by the Church. Moreover, this presence is mirrored in the life and mission of the Church, including her institutional life.[578]

Seemingly at odds with his insistence that the Eucharist has a real presence and "bodily nature" that cannot be dehistoricized, von Balthasar at times refers to the eucharistic participation as anamnesis. But here, unlike Cullmann, Moltmann and others who emphasize this, he understands faith to be an ecclesial event, not simply an

---

[576]von Balthasar, *Persons in Christ*, p. 429.

[577]von Balthasar, *Man in God*, p. 412.

[578]von Balthasar, *Persons in Christ*, p. 431. Also *The Office of Peter*, pp. 162ff.

individual event. It is by the *memoria passionis* that the Church becomes existentially constituted. As such, the faith of the Church is internally constituted by this memory.[579] Yet, in the end, this memory is not enough and a fuller understanding is necessary.

In summary, one might say that for von Balthasar the concreteness of the Eucharist is not accidental, but constitutive of the sacramental actions themselves. Like the revelation it does not have an "abstract" content but as sacrament mediates the "act" by which we are saved. The concreteness then lies in the dynamic of our participation in the events of the New Covenant. Put differently one might say that von Balthasar accepts the original historical character of the faith, which remains part of that faith,[580] and that the Church has as the source of his historicity the continued presence of this concrete revelation in the Eucharist

E. The Church, Mary and historicity of the faith

In the theology of von Balthasar the historicity of the Church's life reflects the historicity of the Eucharist, the cause of its life. This understanding of the Eucharist is built upon a Christology that focuses upon the historical character of the redemptive activity of Christ. This is especially true in the *Theo-drama*, where the created order is made and given reality in the light of the relationship between God and man which stands at the center of reality, constituting the drama itself. The Eucharist is the effective sign, the extension of this historical redemption accomplished by Christ, in his creation, and is caused by the presence of Christ, a presence that mirrors the presence of the incarnate Christ. In the worship of the Church, the Church takes on the form of Christ by means of her free acceptance of the offer of grace in the Eucharist. Through the Eucharist the Church becomes the "Bride" anew, entering into the covenant from

---

[579]von Balthasar, *The Glory of the Lord*, vol I, p. 523.

[580]von Balthasar, *Word and Revelation*, p. 33.

which she has life and identity. In this dynamic, the Church receives her holiness from outside herself. In and through the Cross she enters into the Trinitarian life.[581] Perhaps the best way to articulate this sacramental relationship is in terms of the covenantal relationship exemplified by the relationship of Christ and Mary.

Von Balthasar is particularly aware of the importance of Mary in the economy of salvation .

> It is undoubtedly true for the Christian, however, that the relation of God to mankind possesses a concrete, sacramental covenant nature in the personal relationship between Christ and the Church, the "bride without spot or wrinkle" (Eph 5:27), which finds its personal concrete embodiment in the immaculately conceived mother-bride, Mary.[582]

In this economy the Church is not a secondary addition, an afterthought, but the "objectification of Christ," the intersecting point between time and eternity. In this relationship, the Church is not Christ, but the concrete presence of Christ in history. She is the "Body of Christ" and the "Bride of Christ." Yet this objectification takes place most completely in the personal relationship of Mary and Christ, thereby making Mary the epitome of the Church.[583] In her innermost being she is identical with the *ecclesia immaculata*.[584]

Like the Church, Mary's mission alone is universal, mediating the fullness of the grace of Christ. But just as important, in the relationship of the Christ and Mary, the original order of creation is restored. Upon Mary the perfect form of Christ has been bestowed by the power of the Holy Spirit and the oppositions within man due to sin are

---

[581]von Balthasar, *Persons in Christ*, p. 431.

[582]von Balthasar, *Man in History*, p. 188.

[583]von Balthasar, *Persons in Christ*, p. 431.

[584]Ibid., p. 327.

destroyed. "But in one specific instance such opposition appears perfectly abolished - in the instance of Mary, virgin and mother and in her two things become visible: first, that here is to be found the archetype of the Church that conforms to Christ, and second, that Christian sanctity is *Christ-bearing*, *Christophorous* in essence and actualization."[585] In Mary one finds the only adequate response to the call of Christ.

> As the mother chosen for the birth of the Son and freed in advance from the corruption of original sin, Mary is necessarily the object of love that adequately corresponds to the Son and is presented by him to himself (Eph 6:27) as that "bride" and (seen eschatologically) "wife", who concludes in advance for all and in all the love contract between God and the world, between the eternal and the created heart.[586]

The relationship between Christ and Mary reveals the "form" of the relationship between Christ and the Church. At the same time in the economy of salvation the mystery of the Church is revealed in Mary. "Mary is the *typos* of the Church and of the new birth that takes place in the Church. Indeed, she is more: she is the *Realsymbol* and epitome of the Church herself."[587] Mary stands as the paradigm for the relationship of Christ and his Church. She *is* the means by which the free salvation of creation is concretely actualized in history. Through her free acceptance, her "fiat," the Christ-event was made possible and all creation came to participate in the order of salvation. "It is a real two-sided mystery of love through the bridal consent of Mary acting for all the rest of the created flesh. In Mary's flesh is meant "all" created "flesh" (Jn 17:2) to which God wills to expose himself: and since Mary is *caro ex qua*, she is

---

[585] von Balthasar, *The Glory of the Lord*, vol. I, p. 562.

[586] von Balthasar, *Man in History*, p. 75.

[587] von Balthasar, *Persons in Christ*, p. 333.

188

also *fides ex qua.*"[588]   The love contract between God and man is concluded in
advance.

The relationship between Christ and Mary, Christ and the Church is described
in terms of mystical and marital imagery whereby the Church is understood to be the
bride of Christ (Eph 5). This relationship is precisely the center of the covenantal order
of creation and redemption which avoids the monadic reduction of the Church to
Christ; rather the Church stands as the bride to whom Christ commits himself and for
which he pours out the fullness of his being.[589] It is the union of "one flesh", a fully
human union, which finds its fullest realization in Mary and the eucharistic presence.
The Church, then, is not simply an extension of Christ, but an entity which is
empowered by Christ to give itself over to the form of Christ. As Mary, she too awaits
the form of Christ, which is freely offered to her and to which she must respond.[590]

Furthermore, von Balthasar articulates the relationship between Christ and the
Church using the nuptual imagery which likens the Christ/Church relationship to the
relationship between the sexes. In this relationship the man claims a natural superiority,
but he remains dependent on the woman.[591]

> Mary is the subjectivity which, in its womanly and
> receptive manner, is enabled fully to correspond to the
> masculine subjectivity of Christ, through God's grace
> and the overshadowing of his Spirit. The Church
> flowing forth from Christ finds her personal center in
> Mary as well as the full realization of her idea as

---

[588]von Balthasar, *Church and World*, p. 24.

[589]von Balthasar, *Man in History*, p. 72.

[590]Ibid., p. 231. Also see *Church and World*, p. 72.

[591]Ibid., pp. 309ff. Also, *A Theology of History*, p. 119. There is evidence in von Balthasar's
theology of a neo-platonism that affects his discussion of the man/woman relationship. He does
not describe the relationship as a covenant, but understands the relationship to be maternal: man
needs the womb to grow, the word needs the Church. Only by maintaining the full historicity of
the Christ-event can the proper understanding of the sexual imagery be maintained. See Keefe,
"A Methological Critique of von Balthasar's Theological Aesthetics."

Church. Her faith, with its love and hope, in its
womanly openness to the divine, the divine-human
Bridegroom, is co-extensive with the masculine
principle, embedded in the Church of office and
sacrament, even though it is not part of the its womanly
character to comprehend totally, in the manner of the
bridegroom, the objective spirit therein contained. She
is not the Word, but the adequate response awaited by
God from the created sphere, and produced in it by his
grace through the Word.[592]

Mary's response to the offer of grace is the proper response on the part of the humanity
to the definitive offer given in Christ. Note, that as nuptial and covenantal, such a
relationship is free and redemptive. In this dynamic, man can never be seen as simply
passive. Rather the Church, like Mary, responds freely on the part of humanity.[593] It is
in this continually free acceptance of the continually free offer of the grace of Christ
that the union between Christ and the Church, the historical body of Christ, becomes
united with the Church, his body, through the eucharistic body. The Church contains
the fullness of the redemption offered by Christ. Again, this is not a monadic unity but
a free covenantal unity made possible by Christ.

In this nuptual framework the relationship between Mary and the Church
reveals the nature of Christ's salvific activity.

On the same plane on which Mary (the Church) is
spiritual and bodily, at the same time, Christ (the
Word) is eucharistic. The mystery of the Eucharist
equally depends on the primacy of the virginal
renunciation in order to descend by this renunciation to
the plane of fleshly fruitfulness and there produce
immeasurable fruit through the sacrifice of flesh and
blood. One need not hesitate to see the natural
generative function of the male universalized in the

---

[592]von Balthasar, *Church and World*, p. 132.

[593]von Balthasar, *A Theology of History*, p. 121.

190

> eucharistic Lord and extend to his whole corporeal nature. The flesh sacrificed on the cross is the seed of new life throughout all the ages of the feminine Church and through her of the whole historical cosmos.[594]

In the sacrifice of the Mass, the representation of the cross of Christ, the Church is purified and made holy, enabled to respond to the call of Christ. At the same time Christ plants within her the seed of life, his own grace apart from which she can neither respond nor have life. But the effects of this relationship extend to the whole of the created order.

The Eucharist is the cause of the Church, it is the source of life and continuity within her. For at this point the drama of human existence, the relationship between man and God is fulfilled. All that is needed, the very end and goal of human life, is offered to the Church and the Church is freed, like Mary, to respond to the offer of grace. The "yes" of God to man and the "yes" of man to God are made concrete in Christ, the New Covenant. The Church in the world must be this continuous "yes" to the offer of the grace of Christ; the offer of the sacrifice of Christ: an offer given in the Mass.[595]

Acknowledging the fundamental role of Christ in this process, the Church then takes on the form of Christ, but is not identical with Christ.[596] Rather, like Mary, the Church responds to the mystery of salvation operative in the relationship between Christ and Mary. It is precisely this relationship and its corresponding insights that von Balthasar sees as central to the work of Vatican II, where Mary is once again shown to be an object of serious theological reflection. From Mary we come to understand the Church. "So we can hold fast to the assertion that the Church, as subject, is inchoately present in Mary and that she can be called the personal center of the Church insofar as

---

[594]von Balthasar, *Man in History*, p. 310.

[595]von Balthasar, *Who is a Christian?*, p. 65.

[596]von Balthasar, *Person in Christ*, p. 343.

she fulfills her personal mission by surrendering to her Son."[597] The historicity of the Church in the present reflects this Marian character.

Furthermore, it is interesting to note that despite von Balthasar's tendency at times to refuse to accept any external mediation of the faith that might be understood to be "mechanical," he staunchly defends the "institutional" dimension of the Church. "Far from being the antithesis of the nuptial 'event,' the institution makes it possible for this event to be a here-and-now reality at every point through history. The institution guarantees the perpetual presence of Christ the Bridegroom for the Church."[598] Not only did Jesus prepare the institutional aspects of the Church during his ministry, but continues to sustain them by "surrender of Christ's eucharistic body to the Church," a surrender that has the character of an "event" and a "sacramental-institutional side."[599] The institutional dimension, then, is like the sacramental dimension mediating and sustaining the Church in the midst of history. This concrete presence reflects the real historicity of the Church, from the incarnation to the present.

F. Summary: Von Balthasar and the historicity of the faith

Von Balthasar's theology of history reflects the ecclesiology of his eucharistic theology; in this he fulfills Ebeling's hypothesis. The Christ who is present in the Eucharist is the fulfillment of time, both vertical and horizontal.[600] He is the fulfillment

---

[597]Ibid., p. 352.

[598]Ibid., p. 354.

[599]Ibid.

[600]von Balthasar, *Man in History*, p. 162.

of salvation history and consequently the fulfillment of the history of man.[601] The history of salvation begins and ends with Christ.

The key to the Catholic view of faith as interpreted by von Balthasar is to understand that the faith of the individual is always informed by the Church. The present time, the time of the Church, lives in and by the fullness of the Christ-event.[602] In her worship, the Church takes on the form of Christ. The effects of the sacraments are not only individual, but primarily ecclesial, binding the individual to the fullness of grace offered through the Church and bringing the Church into existence.[603] So the effects of the sacraments are not simply a nonhistorical relationship between Christ and the believer; rather, it is the relationship between Christ who is historically present in the Church, the historical Church and the believer as he lives out his life in history. In the theology of von Balthasar, one must go a step further. Faith does not only take place in history but it is the revelation of God in Christ and the offer of salvation to man that constitutes history.

It should be remembered that the primary concern of von Balthasar is to articulate the relationship between God and man. It is precisely this drama, the relationship between the finite and the infinite, the creature and creator, that makes history. Therefore this relationship is the center of all reality and reality must be understood in the light of this order. This is consistent with his Christology which holds that in and through Christ, creation and redemption are united in his person, the New Covenant. The structure of the drama of existence unfolds in these acts that define and constitute history. These acts constitute the revelation of God to man reaching its climax in Christ. And these acts not only become the source of faith, but also reveal the true structure of the act of faith. Like the revelation, then, faith is a

---

[601]von Balthasar, *Word and Revelation*, pp. 33, 111; *Man in History*, pp. 111ff; *A Theology of History*, pp. 58, 60, 129; and *The Glory of the Lord*, vol. I, pp. 451, 459.

[602]von Balthasar, *Man in History*, p. 114.

[603]von Balthasar, *Church and World*, pp. 37ff, 46, 104.

historical act. So the revelation and the nature of the faith take on a certain meaning in the light of the acts of God.

Another dimension to this historicity is the universal nature of the faith. Unlike the gnostic dualisms that point beyond history to some paradise, the New Testament grace includes the whole creation. In time the true meaning of the faith has revealed the true meaning of the whole of creation, showing it to be part of a larger plan. In this plan one finds that real history includes all the dimensions of the created order. It is precisely in the foundational and comprehensive nature of the faith that its concreteness is to be found.

This is not to deny the presence of sin and its effects upon creation. In the present, the time of the Kingdom is not brought to completion. Throughout time, the struggle for the articulation of the fullness of Christ continues, resulting in the division of heaven and earth: the full realization of the love of Christ remains an eschatological event.[604] But this does not mean that Christ is not unambiguously present, for in the Christ-event the end of history, the fullness of the revelation of God, the end of all ambiguity, is given. It is this full revelation that needs to be grasped by the believer and appropriated by the Church. This time is not empty, but remains the locus of salvation, a eucharistic time.

The danger of dehistoricizing the faith lingers in von Balthasar's theology, stemming from his suspicion of the traditional eucharistic language such as transubstantiation and *ex onere operato*. Nevertheless, the Roman Catholic understanding of the historicity of the faith rests upon the presence of Christ under the eucharistic signs in history. This is the appointed space and time where Christ is present in his full historicity and the Church finds the source of its life in this unambiguous mediation of the revelation of Christ. And, as we have seen, this is the mysterious source of the life of the Church. If one limits the eucharisitic presence to a personal, individual acceptance of Christ, the problem of a "real"

---

[604] von Balthasar, *Man in History*, p. 328.

physical presence arises. Where is Christ really present? On the altar? In heaven? In the soul of the believer? If the answer is solely the latter, this results in a loss of concreteness that no longer corresponds to the interpretation of the eucharistic symbols as the sacrifice of the Mass. To fail to understand the connection and unity between the Cross and the sacrifice of the Mass is to view the sacramental life differently than Roman Catholics.

There is a sense in which von Balthasar has a tendency to reduce all historical mediation to passivity. In doing so, he is insisting upon the lone efficacy of God's action; in Christ alone are we saved. The result is a use of language that reflects a kind of platonism which destroys the historicity of the faith. This is especially true in *The Glory of the Lord*, where von Balthasar claims that in faith the "form" of Christ is imposed on man. Reference to this "form" parallels platonic philosophy not only in language, but in content. In his treatment of the sacraments he affirms this by describing the presence of Christ in the Eucharist as an encounter with the risen Christ (the Christ present forty days after the resurrection). Such an emphasis separates the sacramental presence from full event of the sacrifice of the cross, thus departing from the sacramental presence *ex onere operato* of the full Christ-event. The result is an apparent diminution of the historical character of this normative event, which undermines the historicity of the faith. In this instance the "de-emphasis" of the event character of the sacramental representation makes it difficult to distinguish between the sacrifice of praise (sacrificium laudis) and the sacrifice of the cross (sacrificium crucis). The tendency is for the structure of the faith to be reduced to mere passivity, because the full historicity of the covenantal relationship is not longer possible. Faith becomes a form imposed on the believer. The problem for von Balthasar is to identify the historical character of this form.[605]

On the other hand, in his *Theo-drama* von Balthasar points to the essentially historical character of the Christian faith. Not only is the revelation in history, but

---

[605]Keefe, "A Methodological Critique of von Balthasar's Theological Aesthetics," pp. 23ff.

history is itself part of the larger drama of God's relationship to his people and creation. In the theo-dramatic action, the meaning of the created order is revealed. Here the very covenantal structure of reality is disclosed in the light of Christ, the New Covenant. Within this theological account the historicity of the faith seems to be affirmed in two ways.

First, the faith is founded upon the Christ-event and continues to have the character of that event. Like the revelation of Christ, his life, death and resurrection, faith is an action. In the act of faith, the believer participates in the historical life of Christ by which and through which we are saved. In a sense, this participation cannot be avoided because it is found at the very center of the created order. Nevertheless it is an order and a structure that finds full articulation in the Eucharist.

Second, in the universal character of Christ's role in creation one discovers that the whole of the created order comes from Christ and will return to him. So Christ does not simply afterwards redeem a fallen creation, but from the beginning he both creates and redeems. In a sense, the whole of existence finds purpose and meaning in the unfolding of the trinitarian life of God. In the end this "concreteness" rests upon the comprehensive nature of the salvific activity that touches upon all aspects of human life.

The historicity of the faith in its concreteness can perhaps best be seen in the mission of Christ as presented in the *Theo-drama*. It is precisely in the concrete, unique mission of Christ that all other missions are included. It is the lone mission which embraces the whole history of salvation. One finds in the Church, as in Mary, this concrete presence of Christ in its proclamation and mediation of the event by which we are saved, the mediation of the universal mission of the Christ. In the present, it is in the Eucharist that this mediation takes place.

Chapter VII: Yves Congar - The Church and the Eucharist

Like the other Roman Catholic theologians discussed, Yves Congar is concerned with the problem of the historicity of the faith, a concern reflected in his work in the areas of tradition and ecclesiology. According to Congar, the question of the nature of the Church has dominated the theology of this century and will continue to be the center of ecumenical discussion for some time to come. He views this contemporary preoccupation with ecclesiology to be the result of the discovery of historical consciousness by modern philosophy. Consequently, the traditional understandings of the historicity of the faith are now being called into question, causing a fragmentation within Roman Catholic thought resulting from different interpretations of the historicity of the life of the Church.

From Congar's perspective, if one wishes to understand the historicity of the Church and solve the difficulties concerning her historicity, it is important to look at the sacraments and their significance for the Church and its life.[606] As a Roman CatholicCongar interprets the eucharistic symbols in terms of the primacy of the liturgy of the sacrament. This becomes clear in his discussion of the interrelationship of the word and sacrament.

---

[606] It must be noted that there are shifts in emphases Congar's ecclesiology. In his later work Congar is consciously "de-emphasizing" the stress of some of his earlier ecclesiological writings where he points out that there are two ways of viewing the Church: first, as sacrament, and second, as the People of God. See *The Wide World My Parish*, p. 19. The tendency of his later work is to emphasize the Church as the "People of God." In these works, Congar is primarily concerned with ecumenical questions and the role of the laity in the Church. In these latter cases, the emphasis on the Church as sacrament is almost totally neglected (whereas it dominated his early work). The sacramental model for the Church is secondary. See Yves Congar, *Diversity and Communion*, trans. by John Bowden (London: SCM Press LTD, 1984) and "The Church: The People of God," *Concilium*, vol. 1: no. 1, January 1965, pp. 7-19.

A. Word and sacrament

According to Congar, is by means of the word of God and the sacraments that Christ becomes present to the believer in fallen creation. "This mystical identity with Christ is essentially achieved through faith and the sacrament of faith to which there corresponds two main powers or activities of the ministry, the ministry of faith or the word, and the ministry of the sacraments of the faith, and pre-eminently of the Eucharist."[607] The two means are alike, both mediating the grace of Christ in fallen creation. As a means of comparing them, he states that the bread of life has two forms: the Eucharist and the word of God.[608] "The word of God was seen throughout as a *sign* of divine saving action, an *efficacious sign*, a sign of *grace*: and these are also the marks of a sacrament. Not surprisingly, then, the Word's sacramental nature has been traditionally recognized . . . ."[609] But for Congar the "efficacy" of the word is not that of the *ex opere operato* character of the sacraments, for Scripture, although an event likened to the sacrament, cannot stand on its own.

In order to clarify this point, Congar first of all insists that the word must be read in the context of the Church, especially its worship. Although these texts are inspired, what is given in the faith of the Church is more than the documents of scripture; they are the product of the living faith of the Church.[610] Therefore prior to scripture is the worship of the Church. Consistent, then, with the whole Roman

---

[607] Yves Congar, O.P., *The Revelation of God,* trans. A Manson and L.C. Sheppard (New York: Herder and Herder, 1968), p. 173.

[608] Ibid., p. 35.

[609] Yves Congar, *Tradition and Traditions*, trans. M. Norsby and T. Reinborough (London: Burns & Oates, LTD, 1966), p. 404. It should be noted that for Congar the Scriptures are part of a larger Tradition that mediates the grace of Christ.

[610] Congar, *The Revelation of God,* pp 32ff, 42.

Catholic tradition, he asserts a primacy of the liturgy of the sacrament that places the liturgy of the sacrament in a privileged position in the life of the Church.[611]

> The pulpit - the written and spoken word - communicates knowledge by means of conceptual signs and formulas; the altar communicates the very substance of the reality, in signs which contain it and produce its fruits. This is what differentiates sacramental communion from a single spiritual communion, whose efficacy depends entirely on the dispositions of the believer. . . In a sacrament more is received and transmitted, than could be experienced or grasped. . . The liturgy's own way of teaching in its confession of faith, or in the profession of faith it makes in its act of praise (the doxologies are of great theological value) is not the style a teacher, or even a theologian, would use: the liturgy simply goes ahead, calmly confident, with the affirmation of what it does and affirming the content of what it hands on in its celebration.[612]

Congar is aware that words are essential to the sacramental life, but to believe means essentially to "participate" in the sacramental life.[613] In the sacramental encounter, the fullness of the salvation of Christ is given *ex opere operato*. This "realism" surpasses that of the liturgy of the word which relies on the faith of the believer.

Congar undersands the sacraments to be essentially visible signs of redemption, they mediate the salvation effected by Christ. "In a general sense, we can speak of sacraments as those forms under which God visibly approaches us as Grace, and

---

[611] Congar, *Tradition and Traditions*, pp 353-354.

[612] Ibid., p. 35.

[613] Yves Congar, O.P., *The Meaning of Tradition*, trans. A.N. Woodrow (New York: Hawthorn Books, 1964), pp. 24, 36, 131. Also see *Tradition and Traditions*, pp 437ff. "For content it has, in a more concentrated way than Scripture, the truth of the Divine-human covenant relationship, finally confirmed in the death and Resurrection of Jesus Christ, the unique meeting-point between God and man."

200

through which, therefore, we can visibly and at the same time spiritually receive His action."[614]

> It is a whole complex of things and gestures of their very nature visible and social whereby our faith in Christ as Savior is given expression and which, through a special efficaciousness attached by Christ to their symbolism, links us to the unique event of the redemption and salvation wrought by Christ in his death and resurrection . . . (they are not new actions) but they are, in the spiritual mode of being, which is that of a celebration at once symbolical and real, the actual presence in his substance (in the Eucharist), or of his sanctifying power (in Baptism and the others), of Christ in his mystery of Redemption.[615]

It is this real, concrete, historical mediation of the sacramental life which is essential to the formation of the life of faith. "It is, indeed, the active celebration of the Christian mystery, and as it celebrates and contains the mystery in its fullness, it transmits all the essential elements of this mystery."[616] This complete worship informs the life of faith, the life of the Church.

As part of his development of a sacramental theology, Congar analyzes the sacraments in terms of their role in the final stage of the economy of salvation. The historicity of the sacramental life, thus the historicity of the faith, is linked to this larger historical process. "For since the incarnation, since Calvary and the resurrection, God's glory dwells in Christ's now glorious body, and Christians participate in it when the

---

[614] Yves Congar, *The Church that I Love*, trans. Lucien Delafuente (Denville, NJ: Dimension Books, 1969), p. 46. Also see Yves Congar, O.P., *The Mystery of the Temple*, trans. by Regnold Trevelt (Westminster: MD: The Newman Press, 1962), p. 142.

[615] Yves Congar, *The Mystery of the Church*, trans. A.V. Littledale (Baltimore: Helicon Press, 1960), p. 46.

[616]Congar, *Tradition and Traditions*, p. 354, also 350ff.

Eucharist is celebrated and received."[617] Within this perspective the liturgy is an active presence in which the realization of the whole of salvation history in the total reality of the "New Covenant" is offered to us and the universal Lordship of Christ is realized.[618]

The essence of the sacraments, like that of the Church, then, is the full realization of the New Covenant, the event of Christ.

> Thus, the real meaning and function of the sacraments is this, that by them Christians are placed in contact with Christ himself, their Redeemer, the one and the same Lord who, at a particular time, suffered and rose; that they receive the same life-giving sap that proceeds from the tree of the cross, in short, that the life by which they are to live is the very life of Christ.[619]

The sacramental life of the Church is the concrete realization of this life under the present fallen conditions of earthly existence, a realization fully expressed in the Eucharist.[620]

B. The Eucharist and the Church

In the Roman Catholic Church, by the power of the Holy Spirit, the sacraments, as the sensible means of re-presenting the sacrifice of Christ, join us to the mystery of our salvation given in Christ.

---

[617]Congar, *The Revelation of God*, p. 87.

[618]Congar, *The Meaning of Tradition*, pp 125-126.

[619]Congar, *Tradition and Traditions*, pp. 147, 344.

[620]Congar, *The Mystery of the Churc*, p. 77. Congar emphasizes the two great sacraments, Baptism and Eucharist. He gives priority to the Eucharist, because in it is realized the fullness of the life of Christ.

> The sacraments, in various ways, bring to us beneath a
> sensible form called for by our nature and the
> Incarnation which itself follows the logic of our nature,
> the redeeming and the life-giving power of the Cross;
> but among the sacraments, there is one which contains
> in itself and gives purpose and significance to all the
> others; this is the sacrament of the Holy Eucharist in
> which the redeeming Body and Blood of Christ are
> really present.[621]

By holding this sacrificial character of the Eucharist, Congar stands within his Roman

Catholic heritage.[622]

The Eucharist links the believer and the Church with the event of the New

Covenant, which finds its completion in the blood of Christ.[623]   In this sacrifice of

Christ we are reconciled to God.   And although all sacramental action takes its

meaning from the passion, the Eucharist is its re-presentation *par excellence*.[624]   The

Church, then, lives by the fact that it is united in the sacraments to the Christ-event as

the source of its life, its salvation.

> As a result of their strong grasp of these aspects of the
> Eucharist, some writers of today see, in its institution,
> the point at which the Church took its rise and, in the
> Eucharistic body, that which gives its name to the
> mystical body itself. For the same reason, theologians,
> both ancient and modern, are at one accord in seeing
> the unity of the mystical Body as the effect proper to
> the Sacrament of the Eucharist.[625]

---

[621]Congar, *The Mystery of the Church*, p. 113.

[622]Congar, *The Meaning of Tradition*, p. 36.

[623]Congar, *The Mystery of the Church*, p. 64. Also see *The Revelation of God*, p. 5. Because the sacrifice of the Mass is the sacrifice of the Cross, it cannot be reduced to the *sacrificum laudis*. See *The Revelation of God*, pp. 186ff and the *Mystery of the Temple*, pp. 170, 179, 191.

[624]Ibid., p. 75.

[625]Ibid., p. 76.

The Eucharist, the re-presentation of the sacrifice of Christ given in the sacrifice of the Mass, is the central link in the life of faith and the source of unity in the Church. As the representation of the Cross of Christ, it is the veritable center of historical unity, stretching from the Cross of Christ to each Mass now said.

> Every day, at Mass, we celebrate, we renew the alliance in his blood; we celebrate the memorial of the new and eternal alliance concluded in his blood. In the faith and worship of the Church this "memorial" is something much more than a commemoration or a mere memory; it is the actual reality of what is celebrated that is made sacramentally present and active.[626]

The presence and activity of Christ mediated by the Eucharist strengthen and quicken the Church.

Since the Church lives by its participation in the salvific offer of Christ in the Eucharist, the Church also functions as a sacrament. The Church, as sacrament, not only receives but contains and mediates the realization of the Kingdom of God in the economy of salvation.[627] "They are the sign and the promise that all will be made one, the visible and the invisible, the corporeal and the spiritual, in the one temple of God and of the Lamb."[628] In this process the Eucharist is the cause of the Church and the Church in its life reflects this Eucharistic presence as the "Body of Christ."[629]

---

[626]Congar, *The Revelation of God*, p. 181.

[627]Ibid., p. 107. Also see *The Mystery of the Church*, pp 80-82, 107.

[628]Congar, *The Mystery of the Temple*, p. 247.

. [629]Congar, as de Lubac, often discusses the relationship between the incarnate Christ, the eucharistic body and the Church as the Body of Christ. *The Mystery of the Church*, pp 242-243. The Church, as the Body of Christ, contains what it conveys, as does the Eucharist. It therefore mirrors in its life the historical realism of the Eucharistic sacrifice. See *Tradition and Traditions*, p. 345 and *The Mystery of the Church*, p. 80.

> But the Body of Christ is not invisible, it is not in the purely representational and interior order. It is sacramental and Eucharistic, it is the Church as community. In the first case, as far as the sacred species are concerned, it is palpable, extended, localized. This is why the places which are used for the sacramental celebration of the sacrifice of the body and at the same time for the assembly of the Church as a body, are themselves temples or churches.[630]

Because of its sacramental nature, the Church - like the Eucharist - has an event character which clarifies the meaning of human life and history. Both claim a historicity in which the fullness of time enters into history.

In the Roman Catholic tradition, according to Congar, the Church is an extension of the offer of the salvation of Christ in time and space. "The Church, the Body of Christ, is in a mysterious way formed by the Eucharist which she celebrates and in which she preserves, sacramentally re-presented, the reality of Jesus Christ and his Pasch, the true Temple of the messianic era."[631] The Eucharist as the unique continuing presence of the redemption of Christ is the heart of the Church, and the mystery which causes the Church. In this mystery, the Old Covenant is fulfilled by the new sacrifice of Christ, the new worship replacing the sacrifice of the Old Covenant. "In the Eucharist the final consummation in Christ is already present and active."[632] The power of the Church, then, is the power of this eschatological redemption, yet to be consummated, already at work in the Church. As St. Thomas asserts, "all such power over souls comes to the Church solely from the power and the ministry which

---

[630]Congar, *The Mystery of the Temple*, p. 191.

[631]Ibid., p. 290.

[632]Congar, *The Revelation of God*, p. 175.

she has in the celebration of the Eucharist the sacrament of Christ crucified, sacrament of our salvation."[633]

It should be noted that, unlike von Balthasar, who tends to play down the traditional eucharistic idiom, as expressed by *ex opere operato* and transubstantiation, Congar finds in the term transubstantiation a term of significant importance for understanding the Roman Catholic interpretation of the Eucharistic symbols. According to Congar, "Eucharistic transubstantiation should be envisaged as the supreme expression of the most definite aspect of God's purpose as revealed to us in the Bible."[634] The doctrine of transubstantiation leads the believer ever more deeply into the process of the successive unfolding of salvation history. "Thus, in the Eucharist and precisely in transubstantiation, it is the essential point of God's purpose that is fulfilled; our approach to him suddenly concludes because it has been met with a gift from above."[635]

In the Eucharist we attain the intimacy with God that the whole of creation desires. "Then, through transubstantiation, these humble signs of our return become the operative signs of the work accomplished, once for all time, for our benefit by the beloved Son."[636] There is a sense in which Congar might say that it is the believer who undergoes transubstantiation by the power of God, a "passing over," a gaining of one's inheritance.[637] The Eucharist is, in this sense, the sacrament of the passover to eternal life, the final things. But Congar nowhere substitutes this "transubstantiation of the believer" for the sacrifice of the altar.

---

[633]Congar, *The Mystery of the Church*, p. 115. Also see *The Mystery of the Temple*, p. 185. "The Eucharist, the sacramental body of Christ, is thus the means whereby the Church becomes supremely the body of Christ and the temple of God in the New Dispensation."

[634]Congar, *The Revelation of God*, p. 175.

[635]Ibid., p. 177.

[636]Ibid., p. 178.

[637]Ibid., p. 178. Also see pp. 190ff.

One way Congar avoids any subjectivist interpretation of the effects of the Eucharist is by insisting that in the economy of salvation, the Eucharist has a universal dimension, a dimension affecting all of creation. This follows Irenaeus, who taught that in the Eucharist "the first fruits of creation" are offered.[638] Congar says, "This doctrine is that Christ is the origin and conclusion of everything God has made, because, in his own being, in a manner beyond anything we could have imagined, he constitutes the union between God and creation."[639] The Christian faith needs to accept this order, and be informed by it. This is exactly the goal of faith, a faith received and mediated in the Eucharistic life of the Church.

Within this framework, the Church, as the community of the faithful, is the Mystical Body in which the re-creation of man to the image of God takes place.[640] This is possible because the whole world is involved in the spiritual destiny of man and the state of creation (and man) is changed by the Incarnation.[641]

C. The Christian faith and history

Like Oscar Cullmann, Congar situates the parameters of his discussion of the Church, the sacraments and the question of the historicity of the faith in the theological context of salvation history. The Bible as the record of salvation history, takes its meaning from the plan of God, witnessing to the revelation of God to man in time. "Revelation is a disclosure of his mystery which God makes to men; not the total disclosure of himself by himself which would freeze us forever in our chosen state and

---

[638]Ibid., p. 191.

[639]Ibid., pp. 193-194.

[640]Congar, *The Mystery of the Church*, p. 123.

[641]Congar, *The Mystery of the Temple*, p. 244.

put a stop to history, but a disclosure through created signs, guaranteed by God not to mislead us, though they may be very imperfect."[642]

At the heart of the revelation and salvation history is not some closed cosmology, but the relation between God and man, a living relationship.[643]

> If there is one obvious direction in the great story of God's presence to his creatures as it has been made known to us by Revelation, if this story has one overall movement, it is surely this - it begins by momentary contacts and visits, then passes through the stages of external mediations that draw God ever nearer to mankind, and finally reaches the state of perfect stable and intimate communion. Whether it be through the temple, the sacrifice or the priesthood, God's plan moves toward a communion of such intimacy that the duality between man and God, and therefore their external separation from one another, are both overcome in so far as this is possible without a meaningless confusion of beings or pantheism.[644]

This movement of salvation history does not take place in a cosmological, primordial time or an eternal now, an abstraction from human history, but this revelation is linked to a history, a time, in which God acts. "The God who manifests himself is also the condescending God who stoops down to us in order to raise us up to himself - in a word, the God of the Covenant and of Salvation, the God of the Incarnation. From beginning to end, for the Fathers, it is all a manifestation of this Reality."[645] "Revelation shows us God committing himself more and more deeply to his creation, giving himself more and more, to the point of admitting man to a participation in his

---

[642]Congar, *Tradition and Traditions*, p. 238.

[643]Congar, *The Mystery of the Temple*, p. X.

[644]Ibid, pp 231-232.

[645]Congar, *Tradition and Traditions*, p. 82.

life."[646] It is the activity of God, the revelation of God himself - his self-communication - which makes up this history. As historical, this plan or process of development is not internal or esoteric, but public. God acts in human history in a sequence of actions, thereby changing that history. "The major facts of the history of salvation are, as Fr. Danielou has rightly emphasized, events which, although they have occurred once only, change forever the course of spiritual history by introducing a new factor in the relations of man with God."[647] The individual events of this salvation history are part of the larger scheme, the stages of the plan of salvation.

According to Congar, the Bible plays such a central role in the faith because it witnesses to this salvation history.

> Consequently, the first events of Revelation and the texts which bear witness to them were understood as signifying, beyond their purely historical or literary reality, authentic as it was, other events and realities which they announced as yet only obscurely, and which would reveal the same law or basic structure. The internal ordinance of the total Plan involved renewal and correspondence, in other words *typology* . . . It consists in drawing out the relation between the various realities involved in the history of salvation at different moments of the unveiling and accomplishment of the plan of God.[648]

The history recorded in the Bible is not simple facticity, (although Congar does not question that they happened), but an interpretation of time in the light of the experience of God's presence to his people.

> The literary meaning of a text, its meaning as an event (événémentiel), does not exhaust its content because it

---

[646] Congar, *The Mystery of the Church*, p. 12. Also see *The Mystery of the Temple*, pp. 238ff.

[647] Congar, *The Mystery of the Temple*, p. 278.

[648] Congar, *Tradition and Traditions*, p. 69.

209

> is witnessing to events of revelation which have their place in a plan at the heart of which they have something more to say, something that goes beyond their immediate meaning, in a history which, while fully historical, is especially divine, the history of salvation: a history which is made by men and *the Holy Spirit,* together.[649]

This history is full of meaning and decisive for the Christian faith as the standard or referent by which the faith is understood and judged.[650] By means of this salvation history, the whole meaning of creation comes to light; a meaning measured by the covenantal relationship between Christ and creation.[651]

The Bible is the record of the stages of development of the plan of salvation in which each stage corresponds to a distinctive type of revelation of God. The first mode of presence is the presence of God in creation so that it might quite simply exist; i.e., creation *ex nihilo.*[652] In this stage, God as Creator brings all things into existence and sustains them.

The second stage in the process of salvation history is one characterized by a mode of presence in which God is present *with* his creature by means of grace.[653] "He gives us the power to be with him by possessing him as the content of knowledge and the love in which the life of a spiritual being is really lived."[654] This does not mean that there was no grace prior to this period; rather, it simply means that with the election of a "chosen people," salvation history entered a new stage. This is the stage of promise,

---

[649]Ibid., p. 75.

[650]Congar, *The Revelation of God,* pp. 30-31.

[651]Congar, *Tradition and Traditions,* pp. 495ff.

[652]Congar, *The Mystery of the Temple,* pp. 238-239.

[653]Ibid., pp. 238-239.

[654]Ibid., p. 239.

the time of the Old Testament.[655] It is the stage of foretelling and prefiguring,[656] characterized by both the transcendence and communication of God.[657] God is present among his people, but this presence is limited by its lack of permanence.[658] "God does not dwell fully and perfectly among his people because he is not yet fully given or communicated to them."[659] The virtues of the Old Dispensation are perfectly real, yet they are not complete.[660] Still, Yahweh formed a relationship with a people who became "his people." Where these people are to be found, there, too, is Yahweh.[661]

This covenant, an historical encounter of God and man, is at the heart of Israel's understanding of history. Man encounters God through the mediation of the created order. "It indicates in fact that God's presence and dwelling within man will not be purely "spiritual"; they will not only use sensible signs, but will literally become incarnate."[662] It is this process of God becoming incarnate that transforms the cosmological view of the world.[663] The historical now becomes normative, because time becomes the arena in which God acts.[664]

Israel understood God to be continually active in its life, nevertheless, it was in worship that the relationship with this God was most clearly and concretely discerned.

---

[655] Ibid., p. 5.

[656] Congar, *The Revelation of God*, pp. 168-169.

[657] Congar, *The Mystery of the Temple*, p. 13.

[658] Congar, *The Mystery of the Temple*, p. 13.

[659] Ibid., p. 18. Also see pp. 143-144.

[660] Congar, *The Mystery of the Church*, p. 33.

[661] Congar, *The Mystery of the Temple*, pp. 15-16.

[662] Ibid., p. 53.

[663] Ibid., p. 100.

[664] Ibid., p. 93. God is an active presence. He is present where he is active.

211

"It was in her feasts that Israel became conscious of her real existence as a people."[665] But like the revelation itself, the worship of the Old Dispensation was not yet complete. The prophets called for an ever greater prefection, proclaiming that the true sacrifice is the prayer of thanksgiving, not simply the temple ritual.[666] "In a word, over and above the presence of Yahweh in the act of public worship itself, they declared that he must also be present as the sovereign ruler of men's hearts, for Yahweh is a living God."[667] As such, the life and the worship of the Old Testament point to a fuller realization of the relationship between man and God. They point toward the Incarnation.[668]

The third and final stage of salvation is founded in the Christ-event. "In Jesus Christ, on the other hand, God unites himself in the field of existence itself to human nature, which becomes the human nature of the Word. The immanence, the indwelling, is total, ontological."[669] In the Christ-event, the full presence of God in the world is achieved and the revelation of God becomes finalized. "The incarnation and transition of the Lord Jesus do not destroy earlier revelation, but fulfill it. In succession, each of the events disclosing and establishing the true religious relationship was, in its own proper way, one of those events which, happening once only, change the spiritual conditions of the world for the rest of its history."[670] This event is not only

---

[665]Ibid., p. 88.

[666]Ibid., pp. 60, 90.

[667]Ibid., p. 59.

[668]Ibid., p. 53. "The Incarnation is the event towards which all things point, for in it, 'the whole plenitude of the deity is embodied, and dwells in him' (Col. 2:9) and the Church is none other than the Body of Christ (Col. 1:18, 2:19; Eph. 1:23, 4:12). The economy of the divine presence on earth will culminate in a bodily presence."

[669]Ibid., p. 239.

[670]Congar, *Tradition and Traditions*, p. 257.

212

the end of salvation history, but a fact of history. It is not simply a teaching, but an action on the part of God.[671]

The incarnation is the decisive act of God in favor of man in which the very economy of salvation, which began in the act of creation, is brought to completion in Christ, in whom the whole history of redemption is recapitulated.[672] He is the summation of what has gone before and the one who initiates the new and final stage of salvation. "Finally, if Christ is, both as second Adam and as Head, the source of the new order of things which is the Church, that is because he possesses in himself the fullness of the divine being and power."[673] This fullness reveals itself in the new and eternal covenant.

Within the economy of salvation Christ not only brings the Old to perfection, but initiates the New Dispensation. "It was a covenant consummated in the blood of Jesus, the new and final covenant that will have no successor."[674] It was founded in the event of the Cross, in the blood of the Pasch, and it revealed the new life in Christ.[675] "What the Alliance, the Blood of the New Testament, opens out to us is access to the heavenly inheritance (Heb. 9:15; Col. 3:24), an incorruptible inheritance (I Peter 1:4), the inheritance of the kingdom (Eph. 5:5; James 2:5), of eternal life."[676] The new alliance, the offer of fullness of life, is now present in time and space.

One of the consequences of this definitive act on the part of God is that the worship of the Old Covenant is now fulfilled.[677] So when Christ acted in the New

---

[671]Congar, *The Revelation of God*, pp. 72ff.

[672]Congar, *The Mystery of the Church*, pp. 142-143.

[673]Ibid., p. 67.

[674]Conger, *The Revelation of God*, p. 5.

[675]Congar, *The Mystery of the Temple*, p. 145.

[676]Congar, *The Mystery of the Church*, pp. 61-62.

[677]Congar, *The Mystery of the Temple*, p. 112.

Testament against the abuses of the worship of the Old Law, he did not simply call for a return to purity, "but proclaimed the real nature of the sacrifices which God desired, so Jesus indicates that the worship in Spirit and in truth is to replace the worship of the Mosaic regime. The sacrament of his body and blood, which he himself will institute, is to be the supreme communication of this worship in Spirit and truth."[678] "This worship takes into itself (in the one sacrifice of Jesus Christ that included them by anticipation and which is made actual through time and space by the celebration of the Eucharist), the spiritual sacrifices of the holy lives of the faithful, who thus become acceptable to God through Jesus Christ.'"[679] This new sacrifice, the spiritual sacrifice of Christ in which the believers now participate fully in the event of the one sacrifice of the cross, is decisive in the economy of salvation.

It has been noted that the Incarnation is the beginning of the end of salvation history, but it has not brought about that end. Rather, it has initiated the final period of this history which is now being lived out, a new age.

> Christ the Savior is, in the history of the world, the figure situated publicly in history, although in the humble and simple way becoming to the rule of faith, in which the realization of the absolute communication that God wants to make of Self is manifold to the world in a definitive and universally sufficient manner.[680]

---

[678]Ibid., p. 124.

[679]Ibid., p. 176. It should be noted that for Congar the term "spiritual" does not mean "non-corporeal." It also does not mean simple inwardness. "The spiritual character of the Christian system of worship is not derived from the 'spiritualization' of the literal, external and material worship which would then lose these characteristics; it is derived from the fact that Christian worship originates in the gift proper to the messianic era, which is the last epoch of time and will not be followed by anything substantially new." (p. 148) It is the time of the Spirit. Worship enters a new time - the final time and consequently, "spiritual" denotes this new relationship. "That is spiritual which corresponds to the nature of God." (p. 179) It is a relationship in which it is now possible for man and God to be united by the power of God.

[680]Congar, *The Church That I Love*, p. 42.

214

> This new manner of communication of God
> characterizes this final period of history. The Incarnate
> Word reveals the Father and establishes the new and
> eternal covenant in its full reality: he institutes the
> sacraments, the apostolate, and founds the Church.
> The Holy Spirit gives to this structure its vitality, the
> inner movement of its life, and interiorizes in men the
> gifts which Christ has acquired for them.[681]

This is the new and final period of the economy of salvation characterized by the sending of the Holy Spirit and the consequent working out of the salvation accomplished by Christ and given in the Church.

D. The Church and historicity of the faith

As noted, Congar begins his treatment of the problem of the historicity of the faith by noting that it is in the modern period that the problem of the historicity of the Church is once again at issue. The question of the historicity of the faith is one of those perennial questions that one finds again and again being raised throughout Christian history. Today, again, the nature of the faith is being called into question, and the question is essentially ecclesiological. "Note the strange phenomenon: it was at the very time when Catholic theology could at last command the resources of historical scholarship that it took to defending positions of uncertain historicity."[682] In the tradition, the Church's life is understood to reflect the character of the faith. Consequently, the question of the historical nature of the faith has ramifications for the whole of the life of the Church.[683] The answer to the question of the nature of the faith

---

[681]Congar, *Tradition and Traditions*, p. 265.

[682]Ibid., p. 290.

[683]Congar, *The Mystery of the Church*, p. 112.

215

and the historicity of the Church is an important issue that separates Roman Catholic and Protestant ecclesiologies.

According to Congar, Protestant ecclesiology rests on a certain single-mindedness, a one-sidedness which emphasizes the theme of sin - forgiveness, condemnation to death, and grace. It emphasizes the transcendence of God, but overlooks man's relationship with God,[684] isolating heaven and earth.[685]

> The difference between the Reformation Churches and us could well be one of ecclesiology rather than of hermeneutics here. Once again it seems to me that Protestant thought separates Christ in too radical a manner from his Body, the Church. Failing to recognize sufficiently that by the sending of Christ and his Spirit, God has truly entered into history, it isolates in an excesssive manner the *epaphax* of Christ from its effects in humanity, which effects it plays down in order to exalt the sovereignty of the Lord. It misconstrues the significance of the Mass, thinking this the better to preserve the uniqueness of the Cross, and ignores the value of Tradition, because it thinks it would be powerless otherwise to preserve that of God's written word.[686]

The result has been a certain understanding of the Church that limits its real significance in the present order of salvation, calling for more Christ, less Church.[687] This is the result of a new (or different) understanding of the historicity of the faith, an

---

[684]Congar, *The Revelation of God*, pp. 110ff.

[685]Congar, *Le Christ, Marie et L'Eglise*, p. 21.

[686]Congar, *Tradition and Traditions*, p. 409. Also see, pp. 61, 116, 148; and *The Meaning of Tradition*, p. 104.

[687]Ibid, pp. 61, 138.

216

understanding of man's relationship with God other than the one found in Roman Catholicism.[688]

As a result of their attempt to reinstate the absolute sovereignty of God, Protestant theologians end up believing that there remains one single mediation between God and man, the Scriptures.[689] Involved in this is an implicit denial of the value of tradition, for to accept tradition would be to submit the revelation to an alien history.[690] "For the Reformation, the only bond - not perhaps *de facto*, but the only certain, normative one, divinely guaranteed at least to a certain extent - which links the Church of today, and every believer in any age, to the unique fact of the apostles, is Holy Scripture."[691]

Congar sees two primary problems with Protestant ecclesiology which are derived from this understanding of the faith. First, Congar understands Luther to incorrectly identify the Gospel, Scripture and the Word of God.[692] As a consequence, Luther fails to accept tradition and thereby fails to properly understand Scripture (an understanding that is possible only in the light of tradition). Secondly, Luther is plagued by an inadequate Christology, based on his failure to appreciate the true nature of the Incarnation, an inadequacy reflected in Protestant theology.

> It seems to us that Protestant thought fails to see what the incarnation of the Son of God has introduced that is new and definitive. . . . . As a result the idea of the Body of Christ is not given its full value. There is a tendency to reduce the Church of the word Incarnate

---

[688]Ibid., p. 410.

[689]Ibid., p. 116. Also see *Le Christ, Marie et L'Eglise*, p. 28.

[690]Ibid., p. 269.

[691]Ibid., p. 146. Also see pp. 140, 150, 154.

[692]Ibid., pp. 273-285.

to the conditions of the People of God under the Old Dispensation.[693]

The results of this inadequate Christology is a return to the Old Testament understanding of the faith thereby failing to consider what is essential to the life of the Church.

> According to a theory frequently put forward by present-day Protestant writers (and we are not always sufficiently aware of its implications), the Gospel is the fulfillment of the promises in the sense that it tells us who is to fulfill them and where God is here and now at work. But God still works under the same conditions as formerly in Israel.[694]

The failure of this Christology rests on the failure of Protestantism to recognize the newness of redemption in Christ as operative in worship and so to miss what is novel in the Incarnation. Thus the Church and the sacraments are understood to be of the same nature as those of the Old Dispensation.[695]

One ramification of this theology is that Protestantism is unable to accept the holiness of the Church; i.e., its ability to mediate the grace of Christ amid fallen creation in a full and definitive sense. Congar writes, "It (the Reformation) replaced a religious

---

[693]Congar, "The Church: The People of God," p. 14. Also see *Sainte Eglise*, pp. 77; *The Mystery of the Temple*, p. 299; and *Le Christ, Marie et L'Eglise*. It should be pointed out that Congar would probably temper this criticism of Protestantism today. In a later work, *Communion and Diversity*, he argues that Protestantism did not destroy an original unity, because Christianity never possessed such unity. Rather, the effort for us today is to find a common agreement amid so much diversity. That is the goal of ecumenism: to create a harmony and unity previously unknown to Christians (pp. 132-152). This seems to imply that neither Protestant nor Catholic positions are definitive; they cannot stand on their own. Yet Vatican II affirms that the Catholic Church is the Church in which Christ subsists. *Lumen Gentium*, p. 360.

[694]Congar, *The Mystery of the Temple*, p. 284ff.

[695]Ibid., pp. 294ff. Also see *Le Christ, Marie et L'Eglise*, pp 18, 19; and Yves Congar, *Sainte Eglise: Etudes et Approaches Ecclesiologique* (Paris: Les Editions de Cerf, 1963), pp. 43, 55.

relationship that was intrinsically ecclesiastical by one in which the basic elements constituting it were of a purely personal nature; a certain communal note was added subsequently, but it was more of an external addition than an intregal part."[696] The Protestant emphasis on "God alone" is understood by Congar to deny any dependence upon any mediation said to bring about the spiritual relationship with God.[697] "It was the refusal to make it subject to a collective Church structure representing,, as the earthly Church had affirmed, a public order of faith, worship and salvation."[698] As a result of this refusal, faith becomes "non-ecclesial," reduced to an individual encounter with the word of God.

Perhaps the articulation of this problem most pertinent to our needs is Congar's assertion that this Protestant error is the result of a failure to understand the sacramental character of the faith. This failure amounts to the "single-mindedness" of which Congar accuses Protestantism.

> This supposed a refutation or a real ignorance of the ancient sacramental conception of the Church. This conception allowed for the Church's being, in a certain way, constitutive of the spiritual relationship; whereas for the Reformers the Church is consequent on the relationship which itself is a thing exclusively spiritual and personal.[699]

This Protestant ecclesiology has its foundation in an interpretation of the sacraments which reduces their significance in the life of faith. The tendency among the Reformers (especially evident in Zwingli and Calvin) is "to reduce the sacraments to the role of a mere sign or confirmation of the Word, and to deny their proper role, their special,

---

[696]Congar, *The Meaning of Tradition*, p. 61.

[697]Congar, *Tradition and Traditions*, p. 142.

[698]Ibid., p. 142. Also see *The Meaning of Tradition*, pp. 104, 148.

[699]Ibid., p. 142.

unique quality and modality in the communication of salvation, and so, therefore, to lose something of their realism."[700]   The result is an ecclesiology in which the sacraments are reduced to the proclamation of the word.[701] The locus of the faith is not the Church, but simply the individual personal spiritual experience.

> The Protestant Reformation tended to restrict the presence of the supernatural on earth to Scripture, just as it tended to restrict the action of God (God active for me) to his Word. We say "tended", to allow a place for the Reformer's statements or sacraments. In actual fact, one way or another, and especially with the theology called "reformed" (Zwingli, Calvin, Barth) the sacraments no longer constitute a genuine and original title to the corporal presence of the supernatural; the entire terrestrial moment of the supernatural is equated with Scripture. The unique events of the history of salvation have no other presence in our history than their appropriation by faith in the consciousness of each believer. They were once historical, at the time of the incarnation; the possibility of their exercising a direct action from heaven is always real; but they have not that existence recognized by the early Church, in a real historical continuity from the incarnation and the apostles.   There is an appropriation, by faith (and, certainly, by an act of God), of the salvation gained in Jesus Christ on the cross, and now hidden with Christ in God, but promised.[702]

In this Reform ecclesiology, the essence of life in the Church is therefore severed from the full historicity of the Christ-event, creating a discontinuity between the apostolic period and that of the Church in the present.[703] The result of this break is that the time

---

[700]Ibid., p. 147.

[701]Congar, *Tradition and Traditions*, pp. 146-148, 355.

[702]Ibid., p. 48.

[703]Congar, *The Revelation of God*, p. 32. Also see *Tradition and Traditions*, p. 290.

220

of the Church no longer permits a public expression of the faith and the faith is in consequence dehistoricized.[704] As a result of this failure to understand the sacramental nature of the Church (which was the result of an inadequate Christology and a therefore inadequate sacramentology), the Church can no longer be understood in its fullness. This concludes to a failure to accept the historicity of the life of faith, the life of the Church: this conception of the Church does not permit the fullness of the life of Christ to be continuously - historically - present within space and time.[705]

It is just this failure to account for the historicity of the sacraments and the Church that separates Protestantism from Catholicism. Unlike the Reformers, who, according to Congar's analysis, separate the Church from the Christ-event, thereby defining the Church to be simply prophetic, Roman Catholic doctrine understands the Church to be the sacrament of the grace of Christ, his Body.[706] As "apostolic," the Church is a continuation of the fullness of the presence of Christ of all that became present in history in the Incarnation.[707] "Together with the Fathers we see the Church as the continuous communication, through space and time, of the mystical community born from the Lord's institution and Pentecost."[708] Such a continuity of the life of faith remains only in the Church, where Christ, the source of faith, continues to be present. "In a word, the Catholic Church has its norm within itself: it is thus its own norm. In this way, any difference of kind between the Church's historical life and its divine source of revelation is abolished; no longer is there any dialectics between the Church

---

[704]Congar, *Le Christ, Marie et L'Eglise*, p. 15.

[705]Congar, *Tradition and Traditions*, pp. 148ff.

[706]Congar, *Sainte Eglise*, p. 85.

[707]Congar, *Tradition and Traditions*, pp 147ff.

[708]Congar, *The Meaning of Tradition*, pp 104, 105.

and its ideal."[709]   There is no separation of the present from the normative event of Christ and the apostolic period.

Roman Catholic historicity holds a historical continuity between the unique event of Christ and the present life of the Church in the history of salvation.[710]

> In these different cases, the time of the Church is not that of a purely human history during which the faithful would have to refer back to the ephapax of the incarnation and the apostles, as to a moment that was normative for them but separated from their history. The gift of revelation and of salvation made by God in Jesus Christ and by means of the apostles is the source of life in the Church, in the history of this Church on earth, a life of which the Holy Spirit is the divinely efficacious principle.   That is why an instituted magisterium founded on the unique and normative fact of revelation, ruled objectively by it, can in its turn, be a rule for the faith of the Church in history. *Regula regulata,*   yes, but also *regula (regulata et) regulans.*[711]

For the Roman Catholic, then, faith is based not simply on a private encounter with the Christ by the power of the Holy Spirit, but it is a faith mediated by the Church, a Church which stands in continuity with the central event of faith itself. "We twentieth-century Christians are accustomed to these ideas, at least in the Catholic Church, where the Presence of God, of Christ in his Eucharist, of God's mother and the saints, together with the reality of the mystical life, form the daily environment of the life of truly faithful souls."[712] The nature of the presence of the revelation of God in the

---

[709]Congar, *Tradition and Traditions*, p. 467.

[710]Ibid., p. 148.

[711]Ibid., p. 148.

[712]Congar, *The Mystery of the Temple*, p. 295.

present is ecclesial. It is both public and concrete; that is, it is present in its full historicity.[713]

E. The Church as sacrament and the New Covenant

Perhaps the best way to identify the historicity of the Roman Catholic understanding of the Church is to return to the notion of Church as sacrament. The Church acts like a sacrament in the economy of salvation, mediating in the present the grace initiated in the sacrifice of Christ.[714] Since the life of the Church is formed by the life and activity of its founder Christ, its very nature reflects this origin.[715] "If Christ is the foundation, if it is from him that everything begins and in union with him that everything is to be built, he is also the plan and the model that has to be materialized."[716] It is the light of Christ, the source of the life of the Church, who informs the very nature of the Church. And like Christ, the Church becomes the concrete offer of the salvation given here and now under the confines of time and space.

The historical concreteness of the present time of the Church is measured by its relationship to the Christ-event, the inauguration of the final dispensation. It is not a new stage in the process of salvation with its own identity; rather, it is the continuation of the definitive age initiated in the Christ-event. "In the context of salvation history, the time of the Church is the time between the synagogue and the Kingdom."[717] The mystery of the Church has already begun in the Old Testament covenantal relationship.

---

[713]Congar, *Tradition and Traditions*, p. 337. Also see *Sainte Eglise*, p. 44.

[714]Congar, *The Mystery of the Church*, pp. 89-90.

[715]Ibid., p. 154.

[716]Congar, *The Mystery of the Temple*, p. 163.

[717]Congar, *Sainte Eglise*, pp. 49ff. Also see *The Revelation of God*, p. 179.

Here the prophets understood the Church in the light of the Old Testament marital imagery.[718] Still, the Church of the present is not simply the people of God in the Old Testament. For it takes its life and identity not from the promises of the Old Alliance, but from the fullness of the New, the event of Christ. "As to the Church, Christ constituted it in being in the time of his life on earth, instituting the office of apostle, the sacraments, the primacy of Peter; then, by sending the Holy Spirit at Pentecost, he gave it the breath of life."[719] From this decisive point in salvation history the people of God now are formed in a new way. This new covenant, then, is synonymous with and informs the time of the Church.

> The Church of the apostles was still Israel, was still the People of God. But the regime had changed, the people of God are assembled and now live under a new dispensation, a new and eternal alliance, that will have no successor, a new and final dispensation that can be followed by nothing newer or more perfect.[720]

This is, in the end, not simply a period of greater presence of God (measured quantitatively), but it is a matter of a qualitatively new period, the last phase of salvation history.

The link between the Old and New Dispensation is not the presence of the Spirit but the historical/sacramental effect of the historical/sacramental cause, the Eucharistic sacrifice re-presented in the Mass. The historicity of this event, like that of Christ, surpasses the historicity of the proclamation of the word to which Protestantism links the event of faith. The Spirit is the gift of Christ given to the Church in the Eucharist, the New Covenant.

---

[718] Congar, *The Mystery of the Church*, pp. 58ff.

[719] Ibid, p. 15.

[720] Congar, *The Revelation of God*, p. 71.

224

Although the Church belongs essentially to the New Dispensation of the full revelation of God in Christ, it remains continuous with the Old. Like the Old, it takes its meaning from the revelation of God, but something qualitatively new is added. "The Church is the New Israel; and, like the Israel of old, it is a people of God with its own corporate life, its laws and its hierarchy."[721] But it is also true that this novelty is derived from the new and final Revelation, a revelation which informs the People of God in a new way, making them to be a New Covenant People, sustained in another desert by another Manna, however continuous their history is with that of the Old Covenant. "It follows that the work of manifestation or revelation of himself and his plan, which God initiated through the prophets, and then accomplished in Jesus Christ, to whom we have access through the witness of the apostles - this manifestation continues in the Church, through the action of the Holy Spirit."[722]

Perhaps the nature of this Church is best demonstrated by the manner in which it appears during this period of its mission. The present period of the New Dispensation is characterized by the tension between the given reality and the anticipation of the final consummation.[723] In one sense the Church possesses the fullness of the grace of Christ. "The Church is the realization of the New Covenant, the community of those who reconciled with God in Christ's death and resurrection, are called to live with God as his sons, citizens of the heavenly city and to enter a share in the inheritance of God."[724] The Church as the agent of the work of God looks back to its origin, taking all that is essential to its life from its source.[725] But the Church remains in a fallen world. So in all aspects of its life, since it has not yet brought all

[721]Ibid., p. 84.

[722]Congar, *Tradition and Traditions*, p. 131.

[723]Congar, *The Mystery of the Temple*, p. 246.

[724]Congar, *The Mystery of the Church*, p. 58.

[725]Ibid., p. 154.

things to completion, there is an openness to the future where the final fullness will be given.

> But God's plan is of such a character that although the cause of salvation has already come amongst us, it does not produce all its effects while the historical era endures in which the news of this salvation is to be spread abroad by the apostolic preaching and to receive the free welcome that men are invited to give it.[726]

This final stage of salvation history, then, is one in which the mission of the Church plays a significant role in bringing to completion the victory won by Christ.

So far it has been shown that the present period of the Church can and must be understood in terms of this economy of salvation. (Congar's description is much like that of Oscar Cullmann.)[727] This way of discusssing the Church is important to Congar because it locates faith within the plan of salvation, understood as an intelligible process taking place in space and time. But for Congar, such an analysis is not sufficient. If one wishes to see the nature of the historicity of the faith in the present period of the economy of salvation, one must not only examine it in terms of the economy of salvation, but within that context, one must examine the Church in its relationship to Christ and the Spirit.

Congar insists that Christology is essential to ecclesiology, for if Christ is the full revelation of the relationship between God and man, and the Church is somehow a continuation of this life, then the life of the Church should reflect the relationship between man and God found in the Incarnation.[728] In a sense one finds here the seeds of the idea of a "continued Incarnation." But Congar is careful in the use of this term

---

[726]Congar, *The Mystery of the Temple*, p. 246.

[727]Congar, *Sainte Eglise*, pp 52-53. Here Congar, like Cullmann, sees the decisive battle of the war as being won in Christ, yet the war continues. See Oscar Cullmann's *Christ and Time* for further discussion of this point.

[728]Congar, *Sainte Eglise*, pp 70, 74ff.

226

to avoid any monophysitic identity of Christ and the Church which the "one flesh" language might at first glance be thought to connote. There can be no monadic collapse of the relationship of Christ, the Church and the Eucharist into some single, personal entity, even if it is thought to be the Christ. The "one flesh" is not one person, but a covenantal and marital relationship between two.

According to Congar, the Incarnation is essentially an act, an act in which the definitive revelation of God is worked out in its entirety. "The *acta et passa Christi in carne* are included in this mystery."[729] This "event" is not simply a grace descending from heaven but the cause of salvation being introduced into the heart of the world. The Kingdom now enters the world precisely by the ecclesial institutions, the apostolic ministry and the sacraments.[730] The life of faith is formed by an event in space and time that simply cannot be reduced to a private "mental" experience.

> He did not effect this by disclosing this intended relationship to individual minds but by means of objective facts, words and actions, all public in character and intended for all men. This series of actions and words to which the Bible bears witness culminates in the Christ-event. In Jesus, God made flesh, and particularly in his paschal mystery, the final form of the religious relationship is revealed and established. It could not be more perfect. In his *transitus* Jesus reveals and establishes the new and eternal covenant in his blood.[731]

This event must have a public form of expression.

> Let us remark, finally, that God's purpose of grace has taken a sensible, visible, and we would say "public" form, in the strongest sense of the word. If the grace granted to our world in its universality and in a

---

[729]Congar, *The Revelation of God*, p. 74.

[730]Congar, *Le Christ, Marie et L'Eglise*, pp. 48-49.

[731]Congar, *Tradition and Traditions*, p. 257.

definitive way has come through Jesus Christ (Jn.
1:17), it has entered forever in the world in a bodily
form.[732]

It is this concrete event of Christ's offer of salvation which is important to the proper understanding of the historicity of the faith.

As has already been pointed out, the Church has a role, a function, in the unfolding of the economy of salvation. "The Church in her entirety is the actualization and the sacrament of Christ's unique mediation; she may be called - using the phrase with its utmost literal force - the great sacrament and sign of the cross. She presents the reality of the cross and applies it to mankind."[733] In this mediation the Church neither obscures or adds anything to the revelation of Christ.[734] As sacrament, the Church makes the whole process of salvation present now under the dimensions of time and space.[735] As a matter of fact, what is significant is that the Church possesses that of which she is a sacrament.[736]

It is essential for the faith and for our understanding of the Church in the present, that the Church's relationship with the Incarnation be understood. There is a real sense in which the Church has a character "parallel" to that of the incarnate Christ.[737] "The Church, sacramental and apostolic in its very nature, is, in every aspect, the expression of the sole mediation of Christ who came in the flesh for our sakes."[738] It is not accurate to see the Church as the continuation of the Incarnation in a rigorous

---

[732]Congar, *This Church that I Love*, p. 43.

[733]Ibid., p. 107. Also see *Le Christ, Marie et L'Eglise*, p. 75.

[734]Ibid., p. 108.

[735]Ibid., pp. 48-49.

[736]Congar, *The Revelation of God*, pp. 180-181.

[737]Ibid., p. 79. Also see *Le Christ, Marie et L'Eglise*, pp. 78ff.

[738]Congar, *The Mystery of the Church*, p. 80.

228

sense.[739] The Church is not absorbed into the person of Christ, for such an identity would not give proper consideration to the covenantal, marital structure of the Christ/Church relationship. If the Church were absorbed into the person of Christ, the Christ would then have to be considered a cosmic Logos. Perhaps the clearest expression of the nature of the Church comes in Congar's explanation of the relationship of the Church and the Holy Spirit.

According to Congar, the Church as the expansion of the life given in Christ[740] is not simply a human organization or simply a unity of people.[741] Nor is it simply the sum of all believers.[742] It is a body, a living being whose life is given by Christ in the sending of the Spirit.

The time of the Church is associated with the time of the Spirit. This is not to say that the Holy Spirit was not already operative in the economy of salvation prior to the Incarnation. Rather, this is simply to say that it is now operative in a new way.

> And all this because since the personal Mission of the
> Word, then since Easter and Pentecost (which means
> nothing more than the fiftieth day after Easter), the
> Holy Spirit exists for men in a new way, namely
> (through appropriation understood in the fullest, most
> authentic sense our minds can grasp) as the principle of
> divine efficacy linked to personal grace and to the
> operations of the Church, Christ's Body, who received
> first her body then her soul.[743]

---

[739]Congar, *Sainte Eglise,* p. 101. Also *Le Christ, Marie et L'Eglise,* p. 77.

[740]Congar, *Tradition and Traditions,* p. 279.

[741]Congar, *The Revelation of God,* p. 89. Also see *Sainte Eglise,* p. 13. "L' Église n'est pas l'instar d'une société humaine un ensemble résultant de l'addition de tous les croyants individuels, de leur efforts et de leur activités. Elle est en tout vivant, réalisée par le Saint-Espirit . . ."

[742]Congar, *Sainte Eglise,* pp. 44. "La Personalité de l'Église n'est rèductible de ses membres. Elle est le subject des promesses qui assurent l'indefectibilité des structures de l'Alliance, ou de principes formel de l' Église."

[743]Congar, *The Mystery of the Temple,* p. 289.

The activity of the Spirit is essential to the life of the Church, since the Church is the arena in which the Spirit brings to full effect the grace initiated by Christ.[744] The Spirit adds nothing new to the Church, but simply brings to life that which was given and instituted by Christ.[745] "The role thus vested in the Holy Spirit is the actualizing and interiorizing of what Christ said and did."[746] The activity of the Spirit has the role of actualizing in each believer the pattern of salvation given in the act of God in Christ by means of the indwelling of the Spirit in the Church.

Note, the nature of the Church must be understood in terms of the revelation of Christ and the sending of the Spirit. During the present time, the time of the Church, it is the operation of the Spirit that is in control, for the Holy Spirit brings the Church into being and causes "salvation and holiness wherever it is found."[747] The Church, as the mystical body of Christ, lives the full spiritual life of Christ. "Everything is already fulfilled in Christ; the Church is simply the manifestation of what is in him, the visible reality animated by his Spirit. Yet we have still to realize Christ and build up his body."[748] It is precisely in this working out of the process of salvation that the Spirit guards and guides the Church.

The presence of the Spirit in the Church is sometimes likened to the Incarnation, but this is not an adequate explanation. Congar is careful to note that the nature of the faith in the life of the Church is different from the unity of God and man as found in Christ. Unlike the hypostatic union, the presence of the Spirit in the Church allows the fallible in her to remain. "It leaves the Church conditioned by a genuine

---

[744]Ibid.

[745]Congar, *The Revelation of God*, p. 151.

[746]Congar, *Tradition and Traditions*, p. 342.

[747]Congar, *The Mystery of the Church*, p. 9.

[748]Ibid., p. 70.

230

historical development, a genuine dependence upon the conditions which space and time impose."[749]

> The Holy Ghost does not form a substantial and physical or concrete union between ourselves and God, any more than he does between us and our fellow believers; he creates a fellowship of persons . . . . For Christ really is God, as well as really being man. In him the union of the divine and the human natures is a substantial one, within his very being. This is true neither of any one of us, nor of the Church, although in her own right, she has received promises given to one of us. There is no "incarnation" of the Holy Ghost in the Church, like the incarnation of the Word of God in Jesus Christ; there is simply a covenant between them, guaranteed by God's absolute fidelity, as between two persons who do not form a single, physical, existing reality, but retain their liberty.[750]

The real essence of the Church, the historicity of the faith, is not a "continued incarnation," but a covenantal relationship that does not obscure the relations of the natural and the supernatural, the visible and invisible, the human and the divine.[751] "What we have here is only a union of alliance, based on the initiative, the institution and the promise of God."[752] In this new alliance of Christ and the Church, Christ remains present in history.

The covenantal relationship essential to the life of faith is the source of the offer of salvation given to man, and the Church itself, in the acceptance of this offer, is taken up into the life of Christ. But this does not destroy the historicity of the faith. As has

---

[749]Congar, *The Revelation of God*, pp. 151, 152.

[750]Congar, *The Meaning of Tradition*, pp. 55-56. Also see *Sainte Eglise*, p. 64 and the *Mystery of the Churc*, p. 171.

[751]Congar, *Tradition and Traditions*, p. 147.

[752]Congar, *The Church that I Love*, p. 82.

already been pointed out, according to Congar, the Spirit is at work in the Church as its soul.[753] In a real sense Pentecost is the beginning of the Church, for it is with the sending of the Spirit that the Church begins the final stage of its mission in the economy of salvation and the meaning of the New Covenant is revealed.[754] This mission is revealed in the dual agency of the Spirit and the apostles in the economy of salvation. The Spirit works internally, the apostolic ministry effects an external alliance.[755]

The New Dispensation, this new Israel, lives by its relationship to Christ by the presence of the Spirit: a covenantal relationship.

> With the traditional theology, the Church is, in a real sense, the Body of Christ, to which the Spirit is joined by a bond, not a substantial bond in the sense of an incarnation, but a covenant bond. The Word of God, with the sacrament of Christ, and the Spirit of Christ, form this Church unceasingly, according to the patterns given to it by the incarnate Word. There is no break between the apostolic and the historic moments of the Church; there is no arbitrary distinction between the apostolic period and texts, as obviously normative, and the full scope of the Church's life.[756]

The presence of the Spirit forms an alliance, or covenant; a union that is the permanent element established by God, the norm of salvation history, a history brought to an end in the full revelation of God in Christ, the New Covenant.

> This is why the Church through the gift of the Holy Spirit and through this indwelling in her - the supreme factor in the new and conclusive alliance - has a

[753]Congar, *The Mystery of the Church*, pp. 34-35. And *The Mystery of the Temple*, p. 290.

[754]Ibid., pp. 43-44, 119, 167.

[755]Ibid., p. 186.

[756]Congar, *Tradition and Traditions*, p. 173.

232

> stability and a real infallibility in matters which concern
> her existence as the New Eve, the Bride of Christ, his
> helpmeet in the work of the second creation, which is
> that of the redemption and communion between men
> and God in Jesus Christ.[757]

This is the situation of the order of redemption; a redemption active in the life of the Church and mediated by the Church.

According to the marital imagery of the New Testament, the partners in this covenant are Christ and the Church, but this is obscured at times by Congar's emphasis on the role of the Spirit in the life of the Church. Some might contend that for Congar the partners in this relationship are the Spirit and the Church. But Congar, against this, seems to believe that this covenant is founded in Christ, and that the Church thus has her source of life in Christ.

F. Church, historicity and the New Covenant

In Congar's theology the true meaning of history, the proper interpretation of time, is the Eucharistic actualization of the deposit of faith, the Christ-event.[758] The historicity of the faith is based upon the acceptance of the grace of the New Covenant. Sacred history is a succession of revelations from God to man, to which man must respond. The history of the Church, then, is the "achievement or consolidation of this relationship, already perfectly established, but not yet fully consummated."[759]

> This history retells Christians' responses to the calls of
> God and of time; it is made up of councils, acts of the
> magisterium, missionary endeavors and religious
> foundations, of conversions and decisions taken for

---

[757]Congar, *The Revelation of God*, p. 152.

[758]Congar, *Tradition and Traditions*, p. 21.

[759]Ibid., p. 263.

God, but also the more secret history, to be disclosed
only at the last judgement, of all the movements of faith
and love drawn from our human freedom by God's
grace.[760]

It is exactly in the light of this covenantal relationship that the historicity of Catholic
faith can best be understood.

As has been noted, the Church is not simply a spiritual - that is, non-historical -
reality; it also must be visible. Even though it is the Spirit that acts in the Church, this
activity is achieved through and by the mediation of the visible Church.[761] The nature
of the Church is best expressed as sacrament. "The Church is essentially visible, not
only "materially" because of the fact of men being members, but finally, in as much as
she is a suprapersonal institution administered by Christ. As such, she is the sign of the
appearance of God's Grace in Jesus Christ."[762] Since it is a means of extending the
grace given in Christ, the Church has both the visible aspect (the sign) and the efficacy
of a sacrament.[763] The very nature of the offer of salvation mediated by the Church,
like that of Christ, is covenantal; i.e., the offer of salvation to men.[764]

Because of the covenantal structure of the faith, salvation is not imposed by
God but offered to man and requires a free response. History, the history of the
Church, then, is a time which takes its meaning from the dynamic of God's free offer of
grace and our free human response to God's offer of salvation. "Each moment of this

---

[760]Ibid.

[761]Congar, *The Mystery of the Church*, p. 30.

[762]Congar, *The Church That I Love*, p. 48.

[763]Ibid., pp. 48-49.

[764]Congar, *Le Christ, Marie et L'Église*, p. 14. "Pour elle, en effet, L'Eglise est circonscrite objectivement par l'exercice des moyens ecclesiaux de grâce; elle existe, et d'hommes peuvent véritablement étre dits contitues en église là où ministére apostolique de la parole et des sacrements auquel a été promise l'assistance active du Saint-Esprit, réalise objectivement les conditions d'une communauté d'hommes fidéles."

234

time is thus the present reality of the relationship, the active presence of what brought it about once and for all, and at the same time the beginning of its final consummation."[765] Each moment in time is a stage in the development (or regression) of our relationship with God, a relationship that is marital in structure.[766] Consequently, it is free and it is this freedom which concretizes this economy and makes history.[767]

The Christian faith is a relationship that both includes and goes beyond any merely personal relationship to God. "The dialogue with the Word is realized in each Christian, but it is incomplete and only fully what God wishes it to be when realized in the whole body."[768] Faith is an ecclesial event, moving toward from the individual encounter towards the historical expression of the faith, which is essentially that of the covenant.[769] Thus the whole body, the Church, is the locus of the free acceptance of God's redemption.

In this process, men are not divinized or taken up into God, "Nevertheless, this life does not dissolve us in God: it is, indeed, a wonderful thing that, while living by the life of God, we are able to be and to remain personalities; it is genuinely we ourselves who live by this life."[770] The individual believer is not united to God in a way that extinguishes the identity of that person. Rather, the relationship is covenantal.

> In the first case all the actions of the Man - God may be
> predicated of God and thus be an absolute guarantee.
> In the second we have a "mystical" body, which is also

---

[765] Congar, *Tradition and Traditions*, p. 264.

[766] Congar, *Sainte Église*, pp. 94, 95,

[767] Ibid., pp. 91ff; also see *Le Christ, Marie et L'Église*, pp. 94-95.

[768] Congar, *Tradition and Traditions*, p. 264.

[769] Congar, *The Meaning of Tradition*, pp. 255ff.

[770] Congar, *The Mystery of the Church*, p. 101.

> the Bride and keeps its own individual subjectivity
> before Christ its Lord; the human subject is left to its
> own freedom and responsibility within a framework of
> weaknesses and graces, efforts and ups and downs in
> fidelity; only the ultimate decisions about the reality of
> the covenant are guaranteed.[771]

The Church is therefore the source of the life of faith because she is the Bride, mediating the life which is solely the gift of the Bridegroom.

Congar warns against giving into the temptation to reduce the faith to a "subjective," "immaterial" relationship.[772] The presence of Christ in the Church has a genuine historicity, because the covenant is worked out in time, in a visible institution. "The institution flowers in "events," which produce the fruits of the original institution throughout a time watched over by the Spirit who shares in eternity, who is, in fact, the eternal God coming to us and abiding with us in time."[773] Not only is it a presence in time, but a presence that gives meaning to time. "Now the work done by the Holy Spirit in an individual soul, as though it were the only one in the world, is also done by him in countless souls, harmonizing each and all in the development of a history, which amidst the history of the world in general, is a history of holiness in that world and of the world's salvation."[774] The presence of the Spirit in the Church is an event, a concrete presence in the economy of salvation.

Now, according to Congar, the concrete nature of the Church is more than simply a "religious experience" confined to the individual, but it is also communal. He admits that faith is personal, but insists that it must extend beyond the limits of the individual. "It finds its achievement by passing through a framework established

---

[771]Congar, *Tradition and Traditions,* pp. 312, 313. Also see *Sainte Église*, pp. 94-95.

[772]Congar, *The Mystery of the Church*, p. 18.

[773]Congar, *Tradition and Traditions*, p. 343.

[774]Congar, *The Revelation of God*, p. 159.

publicly, which is essentially that of the Covenant."[775]   "Faith, the element which generates the religious relationship, is received, then lived, in the Church in its concrete historical reality."[776] Faith, according to Congar, is an ecclesial event.

> She is the public and universal sacrament of salvation, whereas the encounter of another person is only a private, particular and occasional "sacrament." Catholic theology has always insisted on the importance of the public character and the universality of Revelation and of the institution of the Church, an importance so radically disregarded by purely existential interpretations, such as Bultmann. The Church is the universal sacrament of salvation instituted for all, and sufficient for all; the only one truly capable of gathering men together in a single and visible People of God, Body of Christ and Temple of the Holy Spirit. That is actually the will of God. Occasional encounters could, and by the grace of God, actually do save men. Only a public revelation, only a public sacrament of salvation, within universal reach, can gather a visible People of God and answer to God's design, which wishes it to be so. . . .[777]

Congar admits to salvation outside the Church, yet the fullness of salvation is mediated by God only in the Church.

Congar explains the necessity of this concrete historicity of the faith according to the plan of God, but he also sees it as necessary if salvation is to coincide with the nature of man. For if God wishes to save man then salvation must be made available in history, because man is essentially an historical being. The saving event, given once and for all, must actually be received by man in his present condition.[778] That is, not

---

[775]Congar, The Meaning of Tradition, p. 61.

[776]Congar, Tradition and Traditions, p. 256.

[777]Congar, The Church That I Love, p. 55.

[778]Congar, Tradition and Traditions, p. 256.

simply situated in time, but as having a history.[779] It is precisely in history that man encounters God in Christ as mediated by the Church.

The Church, then, as the Body of Christ, mystery and sacrament, is a historical event. The definitive event of the full revelation of the relationship of man and God is committed to the Church.

> These events are, as we have seen, public by their nature and destined to be made fully public. Words, divine interventions, the events of the life and *transitus* of Christ, the institutions he set up, are so many elements inaugurating the covenant relationship, and they will henceforth bring it to its universal consummation "through an unending succession of new beginnings."[780]

The Church is the public expression of the revelation of God, an expression which corresponds to the nature of man, yet is intrinsically linked by its worship to the revelation itself (a historical revelation). This historical character is not a secondary addition, but like the human nature of the Incarnate Christ, it is essential.[781]

If one accepts the fact that the Church is a sacrament, the time of the Church must be understood by Congar to be sacramental time. "The ontology of sacred history is related to that found in the sacramental order, itself a unique phenomenon."[782] The time of the Church is sacred time with the concrete unity of a sacrament.[783]

---

[779]Ibid., p. 256.

[780]Ibid., p. 258.

[781]Ibid., pp. 257-258. Also see *The Mystery of the Temple*, p. 186.

[782]Ibid., p. 259.

[783]Congar, *The Mystery of the Temple,* p. 241; also p. 89.

238

The historicity of the Church is linked to the sacramental nature of the life of faith because the Church lives by her relationship to Christ, the New Covenant. Her life is sacramental, for the sacraments are the primary means of the communication of the Paschal mystery, the mystery of the New Covenant. Within this context the liturgy re-presents to the Church the fullness of the revelation given in Christ. "The liturgy is itself completely centered upon the paschal mystery, which is its heart precisely because the Eucharist is its heart."[784] The Eucharist is from the very beginning of the Church the center of this sacramental life. "Wherever in the world the Eucharist is celebrated, the liturgy's spiritual location is the Jerusalem of Easter; it is, as it were, the permanent making present of that temporal situation."[785] The Eucharist, then, is the focal point of the continuity of the Church, the source and the guardian of its life.[786] Therefore Congar can assert that the reality of time, which is the real temporal unity and continuity of the Church, is sacramental; time as history is even Eucharistic time, the time of the New Covenant. "The ontology of sacred history is related to that found in the sacramental order, itself a unique phenomenon."[787]

> Sacramental time, the time of the Church, allows the
> sharing by men who follow each other through the
> centuries in an event which is historically unique and
> which took place at a distant time; this sharing is
> achieved not merely on the intellectual level, as I could
> commune with Plato's thought, or with the death of
> Socrates, but in the presence and action of the mystery
> of salvation.[788]

---

[784]Ibid., p. 431.

[785]Ibid., p. 431.

[786]Ibid., pp. 429ff.

[787]Ibid., p. 259.

[788]Ibid., p. 260.

The time of the Church, as sacramental time, is pregnant with the salvation of Christ.[789] It refers to an event in time in which God made himself known to us, an initiative truly human and divine.[790] The Church, then, like the sacraments which *ex opere operato*, mediating the presence of the fullness of redemption in concrete space and time.[791]

According to Congar, history is for the Christian a history of redemption, a history of the covenantal relationship between God and his people. "At the level of the ultimate purposes God has in mind, the history of the world is the history of the accomplishment of his divine plan to provide for himself a perfect dwelling place among his creatures."[792] "The fundamental history of creation is, therefore, that of those communications through which God establishes in creation his own increasingly intimate presence."[793] It is a history which unfolds in the economy of salvation. "Now the work done by the Holy Spirit in an individual soul, as though it were the only one in the world, is also done by him in countless souls, harmonizing each and all in the development of a history which amidst the history of the world in general, is a history of holiness in the world and of the world's salvation."[794]

Congar is careful not to identify the history of salvation with the history of the world or Church history in the modern empirical sense of history; that would be like identifying the *sacramentum tantum* with the *res et sacramentum*. These coincide, but in that coincidence they remain distinct.[795] For him, history is a deeper reality not

---

[789]Congar, *The Mystery of the Church*, p. 160.

[790]Congar, *Tradition and Traditions*, p. 220.

[791]Congar, *The Mystery of the Temple*, pp. 149, 182. Also see *Le Christ, Marie et L'Eglise*, pp. 68-69.

[792]Ibid., p. 192.

[793]Ibid., p. 238.

[794]Congar, *The Revelation of God*, p. 160.

[795]Congar, *The Mystery of the Temple*, pp. 298ff.

identical with secular history. On the other hand, it is not a perfectly hidden reality (as has already been stated). Rather, it coincides with the history of the world. "Keeping these things in mind we may be able to get a better grasp of the precise content of the history of the Church as the People of God or City of God, which unfolds at the heart of secular history as the gradual realization of man's covenant relationship with God."[796] The history of the Church is a history that is linked to the concrete reality of time and space and is affected by it, moving towards a total union with time and space.[797]

> On the one hand, there is reference to a model, given in the written Word, a model, entirely transcending history, to which, in the course of history the Christian Church seeks only to conform itself, criticizing by perpetual reforms her tendency to a synthesis, to a distorting syncretism. On the other hand, there is affirmation of the self-gift of God, truly entered into history, and consequently a logic of incarnation, of life, of assimilation.[798]

According to Congar, it is the latter which describes the Roman Catholic understanding of the faith. It is faith grounded in the sacramental life of the Church and the life of Church as sacrament, presently mediating the salvation of Christ. In this economy, the

---

[796] Congar, *Tradition and Traditions*, pp. 262, 263. Also see pp. 457ff.

[797] Congar, *Sainte Eglise*, p. 80. And *Le Christ, Marie et L'Eglise*, p. 73. Congar's work in the area of tradition reveals his concrete understanding of the historicity of the faith. In the varied richness of tradition, the essential dimensions of the Church have been handed down. This is a very tangible expression of the continuity and the historicity of the Church. See *Tradition and Traditions* and *The Meaning of Tradition*.

[798] Congar, *Tradition and Traditions*, p. 153. Congar does not fail to note the eschatological dimension of the Church. The Church is the "New Jerusalem" present in time. (See *The Mystery of the Temple* , pp. 226ff.) However, the Church will reach its final consummation only in the eschaton; in history it remains imperfect. Nonetheless, in its sacramental actuality, its Eucharistic worship, it possesses in history its own fullness as the gift of the Eucharistic Lord. As sacramental, this worship will be transcended, not annulled, by the eschatological consummation to which it points. In this sense, the Church is temporal and temporary, as history is.

fullness of the grace of Christ, in all its dimensions, is present now as in the past and as it will be in the future. It is by means of the sacramental quality of the life of faith (which means covenantal and marital) that the full historicity of the Church is revealed.

Perhaps the most precise articulation of this historicity is to be found in the Marian doctrine. According to Congar, Christology, ecclesiology and Mariology are inextricably related.[799] In the life of Mary, as in the Church, one finds the full acceptance of the offer of salvation. "She is this temple as is the whole Church and, in the Church, each one of our own souls, but she is this temple in the most pure and perfect way, for she is the supreme type of the Church, its perfect personal realization."[800] As free from sin, Mary is able to accept the offer of salvation in its completeness: an acceptance which is the center of the sacramental life of the Church.

> It (liturgy) places her in a relation to the whole plan of God and to the inspired texts by which that plan is communicated to us, and experiencing the Marian mystery in the fact of its celebration, as a way which words are unable to express adequately, the liturgy has stored up an understanding of this mystery which is irreducible to the understanding obtainable by theological study and investigation, no matter how great - but also how precarious - this grasp of the mystery may be.[801]

Through the free acceptance of the offer of redemptiom, the salvation of God for man becomes fully realized in history. So like Mary, the Church, as sacrament, becomes the *fiat* by which God reveals himself in the present. For both have their significance in

---

[799]Congar, *Le Christ, Marie et L'Eglise.*

[800]Congar, *The Mystery of the Temple*, p. 257. Also see *Tradition and Traditions*, p. 433.

[801]Congar, *Tradition and Traditions*, p. 433.

242

salvation history through their cooperation with Christ in this economy; i.e., an economy that realizes itself in space and time.[802]

G. Summary

In conclusion it may be said that Congar links the historicity of the Church to the sacramental concreteness of the faith, bringing together Christology, ecclesiology and Mariology. But within this context, sacramentology is the most pertinent to a discussion of the historicity of faith, and consequently of ecclesiology. According to Congar, liturgical worship is the *a priori* of the life of faith. To understand the faith, one must not simply look at formulated beliefs and dogmatic treatises; "we must add to this a concrete knowledge, and hence some sort of experience, of its life and liturgy."[803] "Made up as it is of both action and ritual, the liturgy is in the highest degree synthetic."[804] The liturgy is the prius of the life of the Church.

It is essential to understand the liturgy correctly if one wishes to truly understand the nature of the historicity of the Church. For Christians this means that it is essential that the Eucharistic symbols be interpreted properly. "I will simply remark that history as well as theology shows that a connection exists between a loss of a full understanding of the Mass and the Church, on the one hand, and consideration of the Eucharist and of the institution of the Church as things existing entirely for their own sakes, as terminal realities and objects, on the other."[805] The separation or the loss of

---

[802]Congar, *The Meaning of Tradition*, p. 105. Also see *Le Christ, Marie et L'Eglise*, pp. 22-23. Congar observes that if one wishes to see the true historicity of the salvation worked by Christ, which is presently at work in the Church, one must look to the Assumption of Mary. This indicates (along with the Cross and resurrection) the concrete full historicity of the economy of salvation. See *Le Christ, Marie et L'Eglise*, p. 82.

[803]Congar, *Tradition and Traditions*, p. 433.

[804]Ibid., p. 434. Also see *Communion and Diversity*, p. 84, and *The Church That I Love*, p. 97.

[805]Congar, *The Revelation of God*, pp. 183-184. Also see *Tradition and Traditions*, p. 153.

the full understanding of the Eucharist are detrimental to the life of faith and lead to inadequate ecclesiologies. It might be suggested here, that reflection on the faith, its nature and its role in space and time, must begin with a reflection on the nature of worship. This is a method that one finds at work, at least implicitly, throughout Congar's theology.

Much of what is said here refers to the early writings of Congar. In his later work he distinguishes between two principal ways of viewing the Church: the Church as sacrament and as the People of God. In these later writings, he tends to emphasize the "model" connoted by the title, The People of God. Here he is primarily concerned with ecumenical questions and a discussion of the place of the laity in the Church. The result is that the sacramental emphasis found in his early work is almost totally lacking. Instead, he emphasizes the historicity of the fait in terms of the life of the People of God in the economy of salvation.

It might also be noted that Congar's critique of Protestantism would now probably be dropped. In his more recent works, Congar points out that Protestantism did not destroy the unity of the the Church, for an original unity really never existed. He looks for an answer to question the nature of the unity of the Christian faith beyond their historical manifestations. Congar seems to hold that the present direction in ecumenism is not a return to an "original" unity, but is a movement toward the creation of something new, a new ecclesial plenitude. There seems to be a coincidence between his de-emphasis of the historicity of the Church and with the de-emphasis of the Eucharistic event.[806]

---

[806]Examples can be found in Congar's *Communion and Diversity* and "The Church: The People of God." Here one can find evidence of the corresponding de-emphasis of the historicity of the sacrament and the de-historicization of the Church.

Chapter VIII: Henri de Lubac - The Church and the Eucharist

Unlike Hans Urs von Balthasar, Henri de Lubac never wrote a theology of history. On the one hand, this makes it more difficult to discover his understanding of history, but, on the other hand, it is by reason of the absence of any direct treatment of the theology of history that de Lubac's theology will provide an especially clear illustration of the relationship between worship and history. As a Roman Catholic, his theological reflections presuppose a certain understanding of the eucharistic symbols and, consequently, of the manner in which Christ is present in the Church. The Church, according to de Lubac, reflects the fullness of this eucharistic presence. And, as a result, the only way in which one can truly understand the nature of the Church is to reflect upon it in relation to the Eucharist.[807]

A. The Nature of the Sacraments

The sacraments play a fundamental role in the life of the Church as the means by which the Church is built up. "Since the sacraments are the means of salvation they should be understood as instruments of unity. As they make real, renew or strengthen man's union with Christ, by that very fact they make real, renew or strengthen his union with the Christian community."[808] The sacraments do not simply "affect" the relationship between God and individuals, but bring the individual believers into the Church. They are esssential to the life of faith, for the sacraments are at the same time the source of the Church and the "context" in which the individual believer comes to faith.

---

[807]This is the central theme running through the ecclesiology of Henri de Lubac. His great work *Corpus Mysticum: L'Eucharistie et Eglise au moyen ages*. Étude historique. Deuxiéme Édition, revue et augmentée. Coll. Théologie, vol. 3 (Paris: Aubier; Editions Montaigne, 1949), is evidence of this tendency in his thought.

246

> Just as redemption and revelation, even though they
> reach every individual soul, are none the less
> fundamentally not individual but social, so grace which
> is produced and maintained by the sacraments does not
> set up a purely individual relationship between the soul
> and God or Christ; rather each individual receives such
> grace in proportion as he is joined, socially, to that one
> body whence flows this saving life-stream.[809]

The sacramental life of the Church plays an essential role in bringing man to a full encounter with the grace given Christ. It is the very nature of a sacrament, as event, to lead the individual beyond themselves into the great mystery of our salvation wrought by Christ.

So, it is by the grace of the sacraments that one is bound to the community. In Baptism one enters the Church. Penance, where the forgiveness of sins is given, is nothing other than a return to communion with the Church.[810] These are examples which indicate the social nature of the sacraments. They effect an entrance into the Church where it is alone possible to be united to Christ in a definitive manner. And of all the sacraments, the one which most poignantly focuses and reveals the nature of the Church is the Eucharist.[811]

---

[808]Henri de Lubac, *Catholicism*, tr. Lancelot Sheppard (New York: Mentor - Omega Books, 1964), p. 48.

[809]Ibid., p. 48.

[810]Henri de Lubac, *Henri de Lubac*, S.J. in "Theologians Today," ed. Martin Redfern (Westminster, MD: Christian Classics, 1972), pp. 37-39.

[811]According to de Lubac, the key to understanding the mystery of the Church involves perceiving a twofold relationship: one, between the doctrine of the Church and that of the Eucharist; two, between the church and the later addition of the word "mystical" to the Pauline expression: "Body of Christ." cf. Henri de Lubac, *The Splendour of the Church*, tr. Michael Mason (New York: Sheed and Ward, 1956), pp. 87ff. It is the former that will be the focus of this work.

If we were to place de Lubac in the framework of the previously discussed theologians, one should notice de Lubac' assertion that there should be no dichotomy or separation of the word and sacrament. He understands any such division to be the result of an incorrect view of the liturgical life of the Church.

> A few distinct accents are noticeable within the unanimity just observed in ancient tradition with regard to this motherhood, depending on whether the birth of the Christian by the Church is considered in the sacrament (above all of baptism, followed by the Eucharist), or in the proclamation of the word. But it is not necessary to see any opposition in that, or even a duality, properly speaking. In fact, as anyone with any religious instruction knows - the sacrament is never without the gift of the Word, and the Word itself is sacramental. It is the living Word announced by the Apostles, the Word of God himself, delivered, explained to men.[812]

It appears here that neither the word nor the Eucharist should be separated from each other. They are two privileged fields, containing the same mystery. But upon investigation, one finds in de Lubac's theology a primacy atttributed to the sacramental interpretation of the Eucharistic symbols.

As a Catholic theologian, de Lubac does not wish to diminish the importance of the Word of God. He preserves its importance in his theology by stating that the proclamation of the word of God has a sacramental function. Preaching leads and prepares the believer for the Eucharist, which consecrates all of Christian existence. Moreover, it finds its consummation in the Eucharist the "source and summit of all evangelization."[813] The proclamation of the Word of God finds it summit in the

---

[812]Henri de Lubac, *The Motherhood of the Church*, tr. Sr. Sergia Englund, O.C.D. (San Francisco: Ignatius Press, 1971), pp. 59-60.

[813]Ibid., p. 348. Here de Lubac understands himself to be following the documents of Vatican II, where the sacrifice of the Mass has a primary role in the life of the Church.

248

representation of the Cross of Christ given in the Eucharistic worship of the Church. Consequently, the Scripture can only be understood within the liturgical life of the Church. "We must follow the guidance of the liturgy and grasp the letter in a new Spirit, that is to say - let us repeat it - in the Spirit of the New Testament, the fruit of the Spirit of Jesus. "[814] It is in the Church, then, caused by the Eucharist, in which the living Christ is encountered, that the interpretation of scripture reaches its fullest expression.[815] Eucharistic worship, in its mediation of the full revelation of Christ, is the locus of the Church's interpretation of Scripture.[816] Nevertheless, the Scriptures must not be thought to play a secondary role.

In his discussion of the *corpus mysticum*, de Lubac points out that the relationship between the Eucharist and Scripture is best understood in terms of the economy of salvation. According to this interpretation of *corpus mysticum*, the Eucharist is the sacrament of the unique sacrifice of Christ accomplished by Christ in the days of his flesh. In the light of this complete sacrifice, the full revelation of God in history, all symbols find their norm. So that Scripture, which contains all of salvation history, must be interpreted in terms of this definitive revelation of God. In the sacrament of the Lord's Supper, that which the Old Dispensation announced symbolically is present in its entirety. The Eucharist is the fulfillment of salvation

---

[814]de Lubac, *The Sources of Revelation*, p. 75.

[815]In his discussion of the relationship of sacrament and word, de Lubac raises the central issue of this work. Note that he is careful not to equate the two, thereby avoiding the monphysitism so prevalent in many ecclesiologies today. He appears to give primacy to the Eucharist, thereby following the doctrinal tradition of the Roman Catholic Church which has always insisted that the Eucharist is both the source and summit of Christian worship. Consequently, only a believer, standing within a certain ecclesiological tradition, is able to more fully understand the meaning of scripture. This, of course, presupposes a certain theology of history where the worship of the Church is the a priori possibility for the unity of history. See *Corpus Mysticum* and *Exégése Médiévale* (Paris: Aubier, 1960).

[816]de Lubac, *Corpus Mysticum*, pp. 70ff.

history in the light of which the full meaning of salvation history and, therefore, the full meaning of the Scripture is made known.[817]

Within this perspective, the New Covenant is not to be understood simply as a New People displacing the children of Israel; moreover, the New Covenant is a new worship. The sacrifice of Christ fulfills and replaces the sacrifices of the Old Law. The Cross, which is represented in the Mass, is the unique historic sacrifice which the old rites prefigured.[818] (*In sacramento .... passio Christi promptu est.*) In the Lord's Supper the passage from the Old Covenant to New, from figure to fullness, from promise to fulfillment, is completed. For example, in Luke's gospel the two cups symbolize the two covenants, the transition from the Old to the New. De Lubac points out that for all the ancient tradition of the Church, the idea of the opposition and continuity of the two covenants was a fundamental category of their thought. They were two different dispensations, but they make up one history, one economy, composed of two different sacramental institutions.[819]

De Lubac finds his precedence for this approach to worship in the writings of the Church Fathers. Like the Fathers of the Church, De Lubac connects the Church's interpretation of the scriptures with its Eucharistic worship. The Fathers saw the Eucharist in terms of the economy of salvation which is revealed in Scripture and that the fullness of God's revelation to man continues to be present in the Eucharist. De Lubac accepts this, yet insists that the scriptures are essential to understanding the Eucharist in its many dimensions.[820] In particular, scripture plays the essential role of linking the faith to salvation history. By so doing, it affirms and reflects the historicity of the Christian faith as informed by its Eucharistic worship, since the whole of

---

[817]Ibid., pp. 70ff.

[818]Ibid., p. 71.

[819]Ibid., pp. 71ff. Also see *Exégése Médiévale*, II, 1, pp. 128-156. The Old Testament prepares for the New, the New transforms the Old by fulfilling it.

[820]Ibid., p. 78.

250

salvation history, past, present and future, finds it integration and unity in the Cross of Christ represented in the sacrifice of the Mass.

On a fundamental level, the primary focus of the exegesis of Scripture becomes the revelation of the sacramental nature of reality, wherein all of creation and all of history is shown to have it foundation in the Triune love of God. This approach to Scripture has a direct effect on Eucharistic theology and ecclesiology. Within this theology the spiritual understanding of Scripture is linked directly to the discussion of ecclesiology and Scripture.[821] Any methods of approaching scripture, especially the allegorical, tropological and anagogical interpretations discussed by de Lubac in his *Exégése Médiévale*, reveal not only the richness of Scripture itself, but the depth and richness of a reality created in Christ, a revelation essential to a complete understanding of the sacramental nature of the Eucharist and the Church.[822]

B. The Eucharist - the fullness of the proclamation

Despite the importance of Scripture in revealing to the faithful the process of salvation, the Eucharist holds the central position in de Lubac's theology. The Eucharist, as the fullest proclamation of the Church, is both the source and measure of the life of faith, an ecclesial life.

> The sacraments in the highest sense of the word - *sacramentum sacramentorum, quasi consummatio spiritualis vitae et omnium sacramentorum finis* - the sacrament "which contains the whole of the mystery of our salvation," the Eucharist, is also especially the sacrament of unity: *sacramentum unitatis ecclesiasticae.*[823]

---

[821] de Lubac, *The Sources of Revelation*, pp. 82ff.

[822] See Sr. Susan Wood, *The Church as the Social Embodiment of Grace in the Ecclesiology of Henri de Lubac*. Ann Arbor, MI: U.M.I. Dissertation Information Service, 1986.

[823] de Lubac, *Catholicism*, p. 51.

The Church is entirely concentrated in this sacrament. "In compensation, the Eucharist is fully, if sporadically, exploited (a happy legacy from the Fathers this) not only as the source and summit of the Christian life but as the inner force in the Church's make-up."[824] This worship takes one to the very heart of the Church and the life of the faith.[825]

From the earliest times one can trace in the prayerful reflection of the Church, a very "natural" relationship between the Church and the Eucharist. Concerning this de Lubac says:

> Thus everything points to a study of the relation between the Church and the Eucharist, which we may describe as standing as cause of each other. Each has been entrusted to the other, so to speak, by Christ; the Church produces the Eucharist, but the Eucharist also produces the Church. In the first instance the Church is involved in her active aspect - the exercise of her sanctifying power; in the second case she is involved in her passive aspect, as the Church of the sanctified. But in their last analysis it is the one Body which builds itself up through this mysterious interaction in and through the conditions of our present existence up to the day of its consummation.[826]

---

[824]Henri de Lubac, *The Church: Paradox and History*, trans. James R. Dunne (Staten Island, NY: Alba House, 1969), pp. 5, 36. From now on this will be referred to as *The Church*.

The quote emphasizes the centrality of the Eucharist in the Vatican II Roman Catholic understanding of the Church. The Church is a eucharistic community. He says that this emphasis on the Eucharist compensates for the lack of pneumatological development in the documents of Vatican II. Although, de Lubac is quick to point out that this understanding of the Eucharist has patristic roots.

[825] de Lubac, *The Motherhood of the Church*, pp. 348ff.

[826]de Lubac, *The Splendour of the Church*, pp. 92, 93. It should also be noted that it is at this point that de Lubac speaks of the priesthood. The priesthood is instituted for the sake of the Eucharist which exists for the sake of the Church, pp. 94ff. Also see *The Motherhood of the Churc*, pp. 96ff, 340ff.

The unity of the Church and the Eucharist are not distinct actions. Speaking of the relationship of the Church and the eucharistic body in *Corpus Mysticum*, de Lubac says: "Because the Body of Christ which is the Church, is not other than the body and blood of the mystery. Through the Eucharist each is inserted in all reality in the unique body. All members are invited in her as they are united to their same Head."[827] "And thus the social body of the Church, the *corpus christianorum*, united round its visible pastors for the Lord's Supper, really does become the Mystical Body of Christ; it is really Christ who assimilates it to Himself, so that the Church is then truly *Corpus Christi effecta*."[828] The total Christ is now united with the Church in the present amid space and time.

An important aspect of this discussion is not only that the Eucharist is the cause and heart of the Church, but that the Eucharist is the representation of the one Cross of Christ: the Mass is a sacrifice. It should be obvious by now that this unity of Christ and the Church, the New Covenant, is not a "natural" development, but it is linked to the revelation of God's grace in the world. "The unanimous life of the Church is not a natural growth; it is lived through faith; our unity is the fruit of Calvary, the result of the Mass's application to us of the merits of the Passion, with a view to our final redemption."[829] The Eucharist is the *act* by means of which the believer comes to participate in the *act* of redemption: the Cross. In the Eucharist the sacrament and the sacrifice are united.[830]

De Lubac insists that what is essential to the Eucharist is not the objective presence under the species, but the Eucharistic action. The Eucharistic activity is that of a sacrament and a sacrifice. The sacrifice informs the sacrament and the sacrament

---

[827] de Lubac, *Corpus Mysticum*, p. 33.

[828] de Lubac, *The Splendor of the Church*, p. 107.

[829] Ibid., p. 110.

[830] de Lubac, *Corpus Mysticum*, p. 70.

the sacrifice; they cannot be separated.[831] The Mass is the "Pasch of the Lord," where the sacrifice of the Church and the memorial of the passion are indissociable. They are rigorously one.[832] The act and the presence, sacrifice and sacrament, sensible object and profound reality, are all united by the Cross of Christ.[833]

The act of our redemption, accomplished in the sacrifice of Christ, is the sole means by which the believer receives the full offer of salvation. In Christian worship, the believer partakes of this salvific activity through the sacramental participation in the history of salvation. Only in such a worship can history be fully integrated and be given meaning. It is a liturgical enounter that is historical; i.e., eucharistic.

C. The Eucharist and the New Covenant

De Lubac's insistence that the Eucharist be understood as an act, reflects what he understands to be the nature of the sacramental life of the Church. The liturgy of the sacrament is a historical encounter with the Lord of history, where the faithful participate in the events by which the believer is saved, the life, death and resurrection of Christ. According to de Lubac, this liturgical participation in the events of salvation is not simply a participation in certain "happenings" which are to be abstracted from the flow of "secular" history; rather, it is a participation in the economy of salvation which is unfolding the midst of history. Faith is not a mere abstract remembrance of an event from which one is temporally separated. Rather, the event character of the sacraments means a participation in those very events by which we are saved. This means that the believers in each and every age are saved through the participation in the Cross, a participation offered in the representation of the Cross in the sacrifice of the Mass. Worship, as the participation in the Trinitarian life of God, mediates the revelation of

---

[831] Ibid., p. 70.

[832] Ibid., p. 71ff.

[833] Ibid., p. 78.

the divine life to man in history, but it does this in and through its participatation in those very divine acts which constitute the source of the Christian faith. This places the worship of the Church at the center of ecclesial life. Therefore, if one wishes to appreciate the full historicity of the worship of the Church, one must view it in the context of the relationship of worship and salvation history.

Contrary to this Christian insistence upon the importance of history, all the various non-Western religions, according to de Lubac, agree at least in this: that they press for an escape from time and space. "Yet running through all these many differences there is always agreement about the basic problem and presuppositions: the world from which escape must be sought is meaningless, and the humanity that must be outstripped is without history."[834] Christianity, on the other hand, is fundamentally social and historical.[835] That is, Christians understand salvation to unfold in space and time. "For if the salvation offered by God is in fact the salvation of the human race, since this human race lives and develops in time, any account of this salvation will be the history of penetration of humanity by Christ."[836] The Christian faith is based on the belief that God has entered history and continues to act in that history to save his creation. This salvation unfolds in the present in the process of salvation history. "From first creation to the last end, through material opposition and the more serious opposition of created freedom, a divine plan is in operation, accomplishing its successive stages among which the Incarnation stands out as its chief."[837]

Within the Christian tradition, the Eucharist is understood as a participation in history. In the Judeo-Christian tradition, history is indeed a reality. Consequently, Christian worship does not lock the believer into a cosmic dualism which demands a

---

[834] de Lubac, *Catholicism*, p. 78, 79.

[835] Ibid., p. 78.

[836] Ibid., pp. 78, 79.

[837] de Lubac, *Henri de Lubac, S.J.*, p. 14.

liturgical escape from material existence into some cosmic unity. Such comological views are drenched in a thorough pessimism that renders human history opaque to any salvific activity. Within this world view, life, amid the particularity of historical existence, is painful and meaningless. The only solution is to escape history. In the Judeo-Christian tradition, on the other hand, the understanding of time rests on the belief that it is here, in space and time, that man encounters God. "This conception of the history of the world, like the social conception with which it is allied, has its roots in Judaism. Jahweh is the living God, the God who speaks to man's heart, but also the God of history."[838] "Facts are no longer phenomena, but events, acts. Forthwith something new is wrought - birth, real growth; the universe grows to maturity."[839] "Henceforward the stages of history are important: they are in reality stages of an essentially collective salvation."[840] Within this metaphysical framework, the eternal and finite are not mutually exclusive. In fact, from its creation, the material order is open to the mediation of the divine. What happens in the Eucharist, then, is consistent with this metaphysical order. In this eucharistic worship the believer is brought into a full participation with this salvation history, wherein the divine is present to the human. The Eucharist takes the believer to the very heart and the summation of this whole process, the Christ-event.

The Eucharist as the New Covenant fulfills the Old just as Christ fulfills the promise of the Old Covenant. Like the manna, the *res mystica* in relation to the Eucharist, of which it was the promise and the sign, the eucharistic mystery stands as a figure to the future fullness in which it now participates.[841] In this movement from the

---

[838] de Lubac, *Catholicism*, p. 86.

[839] Ibid., p. 80.

[840] Ibid., p. 83.

[841] de Lubac, *Corpus Mysticum*, p. 81.

old economy to the new, there are both continuities and differences.[842]   The Old Testament prepares for and prefigures the New.[843]   In this history one can identify the lines of a single development, a single economy, a single plan of God, that culminates in the Christian revelation.[844]   "Thus, 'biblical images,' and the concrete facts behind them, furnish the thread, both historical and noetic, from which is woven the Christian mystery in all its newness and transcendence."[845]   One finds in the Bible the account of the revelation of God's plan of the history of salvation of the world.   The Old and the New Testaments are not simply books; they record the stages of the two-fold covenant.[846]

What is of course distinctive in the New Covenant is that in these events the fullness of the revelation of God is made known in the man Jesus Christ.   What is significant is that this revelation is not simply what Christ said, but it is the personal revelation of God in the incarnation of the second person of the Trinity.   For the very nature of this revelation manifests the truth about God and the manner in which God works in His creation.   The revelation has the character of an event and these events become the keys to understanding the meaning and purpose of the order of salvation. "The point is that the exegesis of Christ, in all its essential and decisive aspects, is not principally a matter of words: it is something in act. It is Act itself."[847]   In Christ the true meaning of salvation history is revealed, for in his incarnation is given the full revelation of God to man. "Jesus is Exegete of Scripture pre-eminently in the act in

---

[842]For the full elaboration of this see *The Sources of Revelation*.

[843]de Lubac, *Historie et Esprit*, pp. 171ff.

[844]de Lubac, *The Sources of Revelation*, p. 37. The liturgy makes us constantly aware of the biblical images which are used to link the two testaments.

[845]Ibid., p. 8.

[846]de Lubac, *Catholicism*, p. 95.

[847]de Lubac, *The Sources of Revelation*, p. 107.

which he fulfills his mission, at the solemn hour for which he came: in the act of sacrifice, at the hour of his death on the Cross."[848] The "act" of revelation has a priority over the message of Christ, revealing the meaning of the words. "The Cross is the key, unique and universal. By the sacrament of the Cross, he unites the two testaments into a single body of doctrine, blending the ancient precepts with the grace of the Gospel."[849] It is in this event, the center of all salvation history, that the true exegesis of Scripture can be found.[850]

The Eucharist as the New Covenant is the fulfillment of the worship of the Old Covenant. The sacrifices of the Old Law, that of Melchezidek, Abraham and Moses, are simply a figure of the true and full sacrifice of Christ.[851] This "new sacrament" has a new scope, far exceeding that of the Old Law, embracing all of reality and placing it in a new context.[852] In the light of faith and the mystery of the Cross, the real meaning of the Old Dispensation is now revealed.[853] But again, this liturgy is not simply a celestial, spiritual, non-historical ritual; rather, it takes one to the very heart of the faith, where its historicity is most stringently grounded: the Cross. "This points to the added responsibility incumbent on whoever has received the revelation of redemption in the

[848]Ibid., p. 109.

[849]Ibid., p. 109.

[850]One of the consequences of accepting the Christ-event as the key to interpreting Scripture is that the Eucharistic liturgy, as the participation in this central event, must play a role in the interpretation of Scripture. This consideration underlies the magisterial responsibility of the episcopacy in de Lubac's theology; the bishops are responsible for the Eucharistic worship as a worship which is not only in unity, but also in truth: both require historical manifestations.

[851]de Lubac, *Corpus Mysticum*, pp. 277ff.

[852]Ibid., p. 233.

[853]de Lubac, *Histoire et Esprit*, p. 173.

blood of Christ - the duty of fulfilling this role which has fallen to him, to share by grace in the salvation of the world."[854]

> In the primitive Church the word "sacrament" was used to indicate historical events, the words of Scripture and those of religious worship which make known the saving action of Christ and which therefore allow the Eternal to manifest himself in time and even to become present in it, as constituting its true inner reality.[855]

This historical character of the Eucharist and the sacraments informs the life of the Church. Therefore, to speak of the mystery of Christ is to speak of the Church, and to speak of the perfection of the Church is to speak of the holiness already inaugurated in Christ.[856] The life of the Church, the life of faith, is grounded by Christ's covenantal-historical immanence in the world, a world whose time is by that historical immanence and whose materiality thereby is sacramental. As Christ is the historical bond linking the Old Tesament to the New Testament, as sign to that which is signified, so the Church by its Eucharistic worship continually represents that event of the Cross amd makes the present significant with the significance of Christ's sacrifice. There can be no spiritual life divorced from the historical. "For there is no authentic spiritual life which does not depend on the historic fact of Christ and the Church's collective life."[857] The real problems of the faith arise when people begin to limit the historicity of the faith; those who hold such interpretations of the faith limit the Eucharist to a mere

---

[854]Henri de Lubac, *Nature and Grace,* tr. Br. Richard Arnandez, F.S.C. (San Francisco: Ignatius Press, 1984), p. 170.

[855]Ibid., p. 208. Here de Lubac is quoting Cardinal Jospeh Ratzinger, "Eglise signe de salut au milieu des hommes," ed. Msgr. Robert Coffey and Roger Varro (Reports presented to the plenary Assembly of the French Episcopate at Lourdes, 1971), p. 32.

[856]de Lubac, *Histoire et Esprit,* p. 173.

[857]de Lubac, *Catholicism,* p. 109.

edification.[858]   Such retreats from history ultimately affect the whole Church and limit the perception of the true fullness of grace present in the Church.

D. The New Covenant and historicity of the faith

In the Mass, the historical sacrifice of Christ is re-presented. So, the recitation of the Eucharist is an act of participation in the one sacrifice of Christ.[859] This personal participation in the event of redemption, then, is not a flight from history, but truly a concrete event. This makes the process of salvation something that is grounded in the concrete, giving meaning to the present. "As the notion of the supernatural would remain an abstraction unless it were made concrete in the reality of the Covenant communicated in the God-man, the idea of salvation would likewise remain an abstraction without the reality of the new Sacrifice: Incarnation and redemption are inescapable for us."[860] Because the incarnation and redemption of fallen creation are historical events, the Eucharist, as a participation in those events, must have the character of an event.[861]

According to de Lubac, this present participation in salvation is both visible and invisible, that is, sacramental. "Being as she is, a body which is at one and the same time mystical and visible, she frees us, by the very fact of her existence, from the illusions of a spiritual vocation conceived as solitary and dis-embodied."[862] Universal

---

[858]Ibid., p. 174.

[859]Ibid., pp. 70-80.

[860]de Lubac, *Nature and Grace*, p. 168.

[861]De Lubac does not label the Eucharist as an event, but its event character becomes obvious in that it is linked to the Incarnation and therefore to the full historicity of the Christ-event. One can see this when de Lubac links the Eucharist to the sacrifice of the Cross, and insists that the Mass is a sacrifice. As sacrifice, the worship has the event character of the sacrifice of Christ which it represents. This is the basis for the Catholic understanding of the Church's historicity.

[862]de Lubac, *The Splendour of the Church*, p. 131.

salvation, as personal salvation, is accomplished in the Church in concrete time and history. The spiritual life of the individual never evaporates into "illusory contemplation." Rather, it is always part of the larger process of salvation history. Therefore, the spiritual life is a process which is unfolded in time; "It is implanted in human history, but implanted without being engulfed."[863] While discussing the nature of human person, de Lubac similarly points out that within the Christian vocation is the summons to participate in the "Whole," playing, what he calls, an "eternal role."

> Now perhaps it will be understood how the historical character that we have found in Christianity, as well as the social, emphasizes the reality of this rôle: since the flow of time is irreversible nothing occurs in it more than once, so that every action takes on a special dignity and an awful gravity; and it is because the world is a history, a single history, that each individual life is a drama.[864]

Time and space are not destructive of reality in the process of salvation. "Thus, history does not resolve itself into 'the continuous and painful creation of an ultimate caste of inheritors' which is itself marked down for death. Time is not purely destructive; in proportion as decaying elements crumble away there emerges what is destined to live."[865] It is true that there is a sense in which the present time is a time of war and unrest, but it is not a cosmic battle (in the sense that one finds in most dualist philosophies), a war between the salvation of Christ and his own creation, an innate antagonism; rather it is the war between the fullness of God's redemption, the re-creation offered in Christ, and sin.[866] In this situation, man is not totally at home in

---

[863]Ibid., p. 132.

[864]de Lubac, *Catholicism*, p. 185.

[865]de Lubac, *The Splendour of the Church*, p. 132.

[866]Ibid., p. 127.

the created order. The Church and the Christian in the world communicate a certain unrest; the conflict within fallen creation."[867]

De Lubac notes that Christianity finds itself at war with the claims of the world. The individual finds himself in a situation where temporal institutions, purely human powers, make a total and, therefore, tyrannical claim upon the whole man, who, as a historically responsible person, cannot but transcend whatever is merely temporal. As a spiritual creature he cannot be made to be totally subservient to any human convention.[868] The whole man can only find salvation in Christ, and therefore in the Church. For it is in the worship of the Church that the believer participates in the event of his salvation, the sacrifice of Christ.

E. Church, Eucharist and history

Christians today more than ever are conscious of the need to realize the Church in the world in ever greater ways.[869] But before this can be done, one must come to some understanding of the nature of the Church. During much of this century, Christians have debated the question of the nature of the Church and its role in the process of salvation. Within Roman Catholicism, faith was always understood to be an ecclesial event; it took place within the Church. Consequently, the magisterium of the Roman Catholic Church insists that any change in the manner in which the Church is portrayed must be consistent with the faith and must in no way distort or reduce the essential nature of the faith.[870] Any understanding of the faith, then, especially any understanding of the the historicity of the faith, is essentially tied to the understanding

---

[867]Ibid., p. 133.

[868]Ibid., pp. 142ff.

[869]Ibid., p. 10.

[870]Ibid., p. 6.

262

of the Church. From the Catholic perspective, one should argue that if Christians want to better understand the relationship of the Church to the world, the question that first needs to be answered has to do with the nature of the Church. Only when this question is answered can changes in the Church be discussed. The primary problem in ecclesiology, then, is the problem of identifying and locating the essence of the Church.

In the Roman Catholic tradition, the essential nature of the Church is most often referred to as mystery, a fullness which transcends any full conceptualization or articulation. Nonetheless, it is intelligible to the eyes of faith. But there remains the need for a point at which the fullness of the Church, the fullness of Christ, manifests itself in space and time.

The problem of identifying and locating this presence is perhaps the central difficulty that Christians face today. For if one looks at the Church one sees varying degrees of perfection. "Throughout the whole body of the Church, this treasure is always a variable quantity. The effects of grace vary in intensity from age to age and soul to soul, and we can never judge of them with certainty."[871] On one hand, the Church in the world remains full of sinners, awaiting the realization of the fullness of Christ to be given in the future consummation.[872] On the other hand, the Catholic Church claims that the Church can mediate holiness which only finds its full articulation in the Church. Futhermore it teaches that this holiness is present in space and time[873] in the sacramental life of the Church, especially in the Eucharist.[874]

---

[871]Ibid., p. 77.

[872]Ibid., pp. 78-80.

[873]The idea of the Church as the plenitude and fullness of Christ has been made explicit in the earlier discussion of de Lubac's understanding of the Church as mystery and sacrament. For the texts which refer to the holiness of the Church see *The Splendour of the Church*, pp. 72-84; also see *The Church*, pp. 24ff.

[874]Lest confusion arise, it should be said that this does not suggest that Church causes the Eucharist in the sense that it can merely be a remembrance by a people, or the expression of their faith. This confusion, often prevalent today, confuses the *sacrificium laudis* for the *sacrificium crucis*. In such theologies the Eucharist is reduced to an expression of praise by the believer, an explanation typical of the *sola fide* theology of the Reformation. Rather, following the Roman

The tendency de Lubac finds prevalent among most modern ecclesiological studies is to mistake the Church for a simply human institution.

> There are the illusions, impatience and criticism which are nearly always bound up with some distortion of the faith; confusions of mode and an over-naturalistic type of thinking which modern apologetic has not always steered entirely clear of, in the light of which the Church appears as if founded on human principles and directed to human ends, or is explained by human analogies which have been insufficiently scrutinized.[875]

Modern thinkers have purged from their discussion all those dimensions of the Church which exceed the boundaries of modern science: viz., whatever is supernatural, whatever is free from the freedom of Christ.

> Every notion which tends to bring down the supernatural order to the level of nature tends, by that very fact, to mistake the Church for the world, to conceive of her after the model of human societies, to expect her to change even in her essential structures and her faith in order to suit the world's changes - and this is indeed what is taking place among a number of our contemporaries.[876]

Catholic tradition, de Lubac understands the *ex opere operato* character of the Eucharist to mean that it is an *a priori* which has no other prior ground. As such it causes the Church. De Lubac does note that the Church as the Body of Christ cannot be separated from the Holiness that she mediates. In her holiness, the Church does sanctify in the sacramental action and therefore "causes" the Eucharist. Yet this "active" aspect needs to be balanced by her "passive" aspect "as the Church sanctified." cf. de Lubac, *The Splendor of the Churc*, pp. 92, 93. De Lubac, as a representative of the Catholic tradition, articulates clearly the relationship of the Church and the Eucharist and its consequences for the life of the Church. See *Corpus Mysticum.* For a fuller discussion of de Lubac's importance to contemporary theology see Keefe, *Covenantal Theology: The Eucharistic Order of History.*

[875] de Lubac, *The Splendour of the Church*, p. 9.

[876] de Lubac, *Nature and Grace*, pp. 109-110.

264

"The Church, composed of men, was not made by the hands of men."[877] The Church is not simply a human organization, a social convention, or an instrument in the history of human liberation, but a living organism.[878]

According to de Lubac, the Church is not a secondary addition to the faith, not a product or a construct of human, even apostolic, hands. The Church is not an afterthought of the early believers created out of the organizational needs resulting from the delay of the parousia. The Church is prior to that. "They (the apostles) entered, we maintain, a Church which was calling them together; they did not create her by their arrival."[879] "Not that she is the result of our assembly: one becomes a Christian only through her: She is therefore a mother, she brings us forth to life in Christ."[880] The source of her life and her unity does not arise from the desire to live in common on the part of individuals who share the same faith.[881] Rather, the Church gathers them together; it is she who communicates the faith to them. She is not the object of worship, but she is the means to our redemption.[882] She calls all men to her.

> This "Jerusalem from on high, our mother," who makes
> us free men, is not envisaged by St. Paul as being
> merely in some far off heavenly future; he sees it rather
> on earth, in every city that has received the Gospel,
> already beginning its work of liberation; she it is who

---

[877]de Lubac, *The Motherhood of the Church*, p. 15.

[878]Ibid., p. 115. Also see *Corpus Mysticum*, pp. 103ff. Here he points out that the Church is more than a sociological institution. "Mais pour dépasser ainsi l'ordre sociologique et devenir en toute vérité ce «corpus Ecclesiae Spiritu vivicatum», le corps ecclesial doit devenir en toute réalité corps du Christ: «corpus Ecclesiae *conficiatur*», «Ecclesia, *corpus Christi effecta*»."

[879]Ibid., p. 15.

[880]de Lubac, *The Church*, p. 21.

[881]de Lubac, *The Motherhood of the Church*, p. 15.

[882]de Lubac, *The Splendour of the Church*, p. 20.

speaks by the mouths of the Apostles and of the heads
of the churches.[883]

The Church is the means, the instrument, of sanctification whose strength is not that of
a community of men, but is derived from the One who lives in her and gives her life.
There is no Christianity proir to or independent of the Church, for the salvation
of Christ is not found anywhere in its fullness except in her mediation: a Christian
cannot accept Christ and reject the Church. Because the Church is necessary for
salvation,[884] there is no such thing as a non-ecclesial Christianity.[885] The individual
Christian receives the plenitude of the salvation of Christ only by living a life in
conjunction with this Church where the fullness of salvation is accessible in space and
time.[886]

In a real sense, the Church is a mystery that does not fit into any of the
organizational patterns of human societies. The result of no merely human effort, she
gives life to man and molds his life. Especially since Vatican II, the nature of this
mystery has been a matter of controversy, and depending on the answer one arrrives at,
one might conclude to very different interpretations of the faith. This will have grave
significance for living the Christian faith.

---

[883] de Lubac, *Catholicism*, p. 38.

[884] Ibid., pp. 38–43.

[885] de Lubac, *The Motherhood of the Church*, p. 18. It should be noted that although de
Lubac believes that the whole Church (including the visible) is necessary for salvation, he also
recognizes that the visible Church, like the world itself, is passing away. "Insofar as she is
visible and temporal, the Church is destined to pass away. She is a sign and a sacrament, and it
is the peculiar quality of signs and sacraments to be re-absorbed in the reality they signify. She is
a means - divine and necessary - but like all means, provisional." See *The Church*, p. 53. The
sacraments and the Church as sacrament will no longer exist in the Kingdom of God. That
which the sacraments mediate will be immediately present. The mediation of the Church and the
sacraments will no longer be necessary. Also see *The Splendour of the Church*, pp. 41-47.

[886] de Lubac, *The Splendour of the Church*, pp. 22-24. De Lubac goes so far as to say that
personal spiritual advancement is a participation in the spiritual perfection which is the Church's
alone. See pp. 27ff.

266

In the past, it was this very mystery of the Church which lead to a certain caution when discussing the nature of the Church. Even today the Church as "mystery" still guides contemporary ecclesiological discussions. Today, most theologains accept the fact that the Church is both a mystery whose fullness transcends human comprehension and a scandal in her claims to mediate the grace of Christ.[887]

> The Church is a mystery for all time out of man's grasp because, qualitatively, it is totally removed from all other aspects of man's knowledge that might be mentioned. And yet, at the same time, it concerns us, touches us, acts in us, reveals us to ourselves. To this end, it must have a tangible aspect, the incarnate Word of God, the expression of the Inexpressible, the efficacious sign to realize the plan of salvation.[888]

The mystery of the Church finds its source in the mystery of Christ, the revelation *par excellence* of mystery. He is *the* mystery.[889] "The Church is a mystery because, coming from God and entirely at the service of his plan, she is an organism of salvation, precisely because she relates wholly to Christ and apart from him has no existence, value or efficacy."[890] The Church, then, is a mysterious extension of trinitarian life into time. She alone mediates this salvific mystery.

As mystery, the Church plays an integral role in the living out of salvation and must be understood in terms of the role that she plays in the economy of salvation, a universal salvation, which is unfolding in her life. She is a universal and holy Church.

> Following in the footsteps of St. Thomas, we can give the name "Church" to the gigantic organism which

---

[887] de Lubac, *The Splendour of the Church*, p. 4.

[888] de Lubac, *The Church*, p. 14. Here de Lubac is making reference to Yves de Montcheuil, *Problèmes de vie spirituelle* (Ed. de Epi, Paris, 7th ed., 1959), pp. 185-92.

[889] Ibid., p. 14.

[890] Ibid., p. 15.

includes all the hosts of angels as well as men, and even
extends to the whole cosmos as well. But even if we
take it in a sense less wide than this, "the Church of
God" still knows, in principle, no limit of place or time.
She is open to all; she draws her recruits from
anywhere and everywhere, and "embraces the whole of
humanity."[891]

De Lubac affirms that "*Ecclesia catholica, id est universalis.*" Yet, speaking of the "*sancta ecclesia, catholica,*" de Lubac points out, the catholicity of the Church transcends it geographical or statistical development. He says, "Like sanctity, Catholocity is primarily an intrinsic feature of the Church. . . . The Church in each individual calls on the whole man, embracing him as he is in his whole nature. [892] Catholicity means the comprehensive nature of the call to faith. It includes the whole of the created order, all people and the totality of human life. Here one begins to see the depths of this mystery as it is applied to all of creation. The Church is the mysterious presence of Christ, on the one hand, and on the other, it is a fullness that includes all of men and all of creation.

According to de Lubac, the nature of the mystery of the Church is beyond natural intelligence. One needs a proper "insight" to see the essence of the Church, an insight that de Lubac finds at work in the writings of St. Paul, St. John and many of the Church Fathers when they link the Church and the Eucharist.[893]

---

[891] Ibid., pp. 29-30. One aspect that again affirms the trans-temporal character of the Church is that it is "pre-existent." "For though Christ was not to appear in the humility of our flesh until long after these things, he is nonetheless 'the first-born of every creature,' as St Paul teaches; so whatever is true of Him is also true of his Bride the Church." See pp. 38ff. The Church does not come into existence as an afterthought, but the world is made for her.

[892] de Lubac, *The Splendour of the Church*, p. 29.

[893] Ibid., pp. 90ff. De Lubac discusses at length the importance of this type of knowledge for understanding Scripture. It is a *sensus fidelium* of sorts, an understanding of the faith that results, not from speculation, but from the practice of the faith. The act of understanding becomes one of conversion. Conversion, then, leads to better understanding. See de Lubac, *The Sources of Revelation*, tr. Luke O'Neill (New York: Herder and Herder, 1968), pp. 14-23. He

> St. Paul, as it happens, formulates in theory what
> emerges clearly from primitive Christian practice, and
> he does so by uniting in one the eucharistic mystery and
> that of the Church community: "Is not the bread we
> break a participation in Christ's body? The one bread
> makes us one body, though we are many in number;
> the same bread is shared by all." (I Cor. 10:16-17)[894]

For St. Paul, the evangelists and the Church Fathers, the "Body of Christ" was the
Church, the mystical, perfect body.[895] Likewise, in the thought of Augustine, the
Eucharist corresponds to the Church as cause to effect, as means to an end, as sign to
reality.[896]

In effect, the terminology used to define the Church as the mystical body points
directly to a link between the Church and the Eucharist. To discuss the Church in this
manner is to place the Church in the context of the Eucharist. Referring to the
Tradition, "the first theologians to speak of the Church as the Body of Christ," de
Lubac says:

> By "the Mystical Body" they mean neither an invisible
> body nor a ghostly image of the real one; they mean the
> *corpus in mysterio*, the body mystically signified and
> realized by the Eucharist - in other words, the unity of
> the Christian community which is made real by the
> "holy mysteries" in an effective symbol (in the strict
> sense of the word "effective"). . . . In different terms, it
> is "the union, indissolubly both spiritual and corporate,
> of the Church's members with Christ present in the

---

uses the work of Origen as an example. Also see *Histoire et Esprit*. In this work, de Lubac
reveals the fuller meaning of this "spiritual sensibility" in his discussion of Origen.

[894] de Lubac, *The Splendour of the Church*, pp. 91-92.

[895] de Lubac, *Corpus Mysticum*, pp. 14, 23. As a matter of fact, in Church antiquity
references to the Body of Christ rarely refer to the Eucharist. It is usually used to refer to the
Church.

[896] Ibid., p. 23.

sacrament." Thus, the Mystical Body is the Body *par
excellence*, that with the greatest degree of reality and
truth; it is the definitive body, and in relation to it the
individual body of Christ Himself may be called a
figurative body, without any detraction from its reality.
In scholastic terms, it is of the same order as the *res of*
a sacrament, *res sacramenti*; behind the *signum
tantum*, or *sacramenti species*, and the *res-et-
sacramentum*, there lies the *res tantum* - that which is
no longer the sign of anything else, since it is the final
effect of the sacrament, *res ultima*.[897]

In this analysis, the Eucharist is not simply an objective "real Presence," but an
efficacious presence that effects the unity of the Church, wherein the *totus Christus* is
present; i.e., the presence of Christ in union with his body the Church.[898] The
Eucharist, then, is the locus of the real presence of the grace of Christ and the source of
unity in the Church of Christ.[899] And because of the comprehensive nature of the
sacramental life, one might say that it is here that the catholicity of the Church is most
evident.

---

[897]de Lubac, *The Splendour of the Church*, p. 92. De Lubac also affirms this is *Corpus Mysticum*, pp. 217ff. The Eucharist is the mystery of Christ in which one finds the continued evangelical fullness (plénitude évangelique).

[898]de Lubac, *Corpus Mysticum*,, pp. 24ff. One finds this understanding of the *totus Christus* in Augustine. Here the *totus Christus* has an ecclesial sense, referring to the unity of the Head and the Body in the plenitude of the Church. See Franciscus Mariones, *Enchiridion Theologica Sancti Augustini* (Matriti: Biblioteca de Autores Christianos, 1961).

[899]de Lubac, *Corpus Mysticum*, pp. 25-32, 191, 192. Here de Lubac can speak of a double effect. On the one hand, the food and drink relate to eternal life. On the other hand, the bread and wine signify the unity of the ecclesiastical body. "D'une part, on a une réalité objective et sociale, quoique également intérieure: l'unitéde la communauté chrétienne: *panis iste indicat unitatem*; tote l'Église se préparant et s'achevant dans ce Pain. D'autre part, une réalité «subjective», inhérente à chaque communiant: la vie, ou plutôt la vivification, la réflection de l'homme spirituel: *virtus et plenitudo spiritualis refectionis, - virtute sacramenti interior homo satiatur.*

F. The Church as sacrament

As has been remarked, the source of the unity of the Church is in her sacramental life, especially in the Eucharist.

> The great assembly never ceases to be united, really united; but in accordance with the law of its sacramental essence, the invisible unity must be visibly signified and visibly brought about. And thus it can be said that its continuing existence does none the less have certain focal moments of intensity; and in point of fact is never worthier of its name than when the People of God gather around its Shepherd for the eucharistic ceremony. Though only one cell of the whole body is actually present, the whole body is vitally there."[900]

Since in the Eucharist the full unity of the Church is achieved, so it is the source that informs the life of the Church.

Another way to state this would be to say that the Eucharist is the full participation in the life of Christ, an event in time and space in which the Church participates continually. It is this Eucharist which becomes the source of life for the Church, that is, a concrete and continuous presence of Christ . . . a presence that brings unity and meaning to fallen creation.

De Lubac points to the unity of the sacrifice for the whole Church by giving an example from the liturgical practice of the early Church. In Rome, there was the custom of *fermentum*, where consecrated bread would be sent from the bishop's Mass to that of the priest celebrating the *Tituli*. This aspect of the Pontifical Mass clearly expressed ecclesiastical union.

---

[900] de Lubac, *The Splendour of the Church*, p. 105.

> Thus, in all the Churches of Rome, and at every assembly there for liturgical worship past and present, there was always the same Sacrifice, the same Eucharist, the same Communion. Thus, in order to show clearly that the bread broken and distributed away from the altar was the same as that which had been consecrated on the altar, a fragment of it was allowed to remain on the holy table.[901]

Since in the Eucharist the full unity of the Church is achieved, it is the source of the continuity of the Church. The historical continuity of the Church is not guaranteed by a mere sequence of events, but by the continuous Eucharistic worship of the Church, which is inseparably the covenantal one flesh of the Church's union with her Lord.

If the Eucharist is the cause of the Church, the Church, then, whose life reflects this Eucharistic event, must mirror the historicity of the Eucharist in its own life. De Lubac points out that the sacramental realism (the historicity) of the Eucharist and that of the Church are the pledge and measure of one another.[902] The historicity of the faith is informed by this realism. The Church is not simply a spiritual reality; rather, as the liturgy of the sacrament expresses the full historicity of the faith, so in this liturgy the unity of the sacrament, salvation history and the Church is actual.

The Christian faith lives by its relation to the central event of all history, the Christ-event, the decisive historical event of God's intervention in his creation.[903] It is this act which the Eucharist re-presents, the center of biblical history, which informs temporality, making it the history of salvation. When speaking of the Cross and resurrection de Lubac points out that

[901]de Lubac, *Catholicism*, p. 59. Here de Lubac is quoting Duchesne, *Christian Worship: its Origin and Evolution*, tr. M.L. McClure (London, 1903), p. 185.

[902]de Lubac, *Corpus Mysticum*, pp. 283ff.

[903]de Lubac, *The Splendour of the Church*, p. 119.

> The Act of Christ in fulfilling the Scriptures and
> simultaneously bestowing the fullness of their meaning
> upon them is also compared by Christian tradition to
> the act of Eucharistic consecration. For a truth
> Scripture is bread, but bread which becomes for the
> Christian the life-giving food which it must be only
> after it has been consecrated by Jesus: "Then the Lord
> Jesus took into his hands the bread of the Scriptures,
> when, incarnate according to the Scriptures, he
> underwent his passion and rose again; then, I say,
> having taken the bread into his hands, he gave thanks,
> when thus fulfilling the Scriptures, he offered himself to
> the Father as a sacrifice of grace and truth.[904]

Like the union with its Head, the Church, as the Body of Christ, becomes the extension of the life of Christ into the world and comes to be associated with and informed by the sacramental nature of God's revelation. The Church is not simply the *res tantum* of the sacraments; rather she is also the the sacrament of Christ's presence in the present age, as well as the *res tantum sacramenti*: the eschatological fulfillment of her sacramental historicity, since it is in the Church that one becomes holy and receives grace, and the *res et sacramentum* of the Eucharist: the utterly reliable and unambiguous efffective sign.

In a sense the historicity of the Eucharist becomes evident at this point, not because the Eucharist is simply an event in time and space, not simply because is it the source of a present, historical unity in the Church, and not because the eucharistic worship is continuous in the life of the Church, but because now, as always, the Eucharist is the event which involves the believer in the Christ-event which is at the center of the economy of salvation.

Since the Eucharistic fullness, understood as an event, brings the believer into the heart of salvation history, the Church represents and mediates the salvation of

---

[904]de Lubac, *The Sources of Revelation*, p. 112. Here de Lubac is quoting Rupert of Deitz. (Pl 169, 443B-D).

Christ from now until the end of the world. "The new city, the sheltering womb and matrix of the new world, is the Church - the new universe already active at the very heart of our earthly and mortal existence; it is through her that God re-creates and re-forms the human race."[905] In the present time, the Church mediates this concrete fullness bringing about of the salvation wrought by Christ.

Here the Church, acting as a sacrament, lives out the grace of Christ in the present time. Like the Eucharist, it is not only oriented toward the past, but also toward the future.[906] Yet this eschatological orientation does not undercut the present mediatory capacity of the Church[907] in which the Church acts something "like a sacrament."[908] "The Church is a mystery; that is to say that she is also a sacrament. She is 'the total locus of the Christian sacraments,' and she is herself the great sacrament which contains and vitalizes all others. In the world she is the sacrament of Christ, as Christ himself, in His humanity, is for us the sacrament of God."[909] The entire existence of the Church, as sign (visible) and signified (invisible) which makes Christ present, is oriented to bringing man into a relationship with God. "The Church is the sacrament of Christ; which means, to put it another way, that there is between her and Him a certain relationship of mystical identity."[910] Again, speaking of the Church, de Lubac says, "The Spirit of Christ has reposed in her a 'unique power of divinization.' She is the sacrament of Christ, the channel through which the light and

[905] de Lubac, *The Splendour of the Church*, pp.119-120.

[906] de Lubac, *Corpus Mysticum*, pp. 79, 80.

[907] de Lubac, *The Splendour of the Church*, p. 129. As previously noted within the Protestant theologies, the focus on the future fullness reflected their sense of doubt about the ability of fallen creation to mediate the grace of Christ. Within Catholicism, this doubt vanishes in the light of sacramental realism, where the full grace of Christ is offered to the believer.

[908] *Lumen Gentium*, para. 1.

[909] de Lubac, *The Splendour of the Church*, p. 147.

[910] Ibid., p. 152.

274

strength of the gospel is communicated to us. In our times she is the axis round which the great mystical re-assembly must group itself."[911]

As the efficacious sign of the presence of Christ, the Church unites and mediates.[912] This, of course, is consistent with the thought of *Lumen Gentium*. There the Church is described as the "visible and mystical body of Christ." She is the "instrument, sign and sacrament of union with God and of the unity of all human kind."[913] She is a sign that cannot be discarded. For to lose the Church would be to lose access to Christ and therefore to lose the possibility of redemption.[914] It should be remembered that de Lubac understands the Eucharist to be not simply a presence, but an action, a sacrifice. The Eucharistic worship that causes the Church has an event character that the Church in her sacramental nature mirrors. Accordingly, the historicity of the Church must reflect this sacrificial event of Christ which is continually re-presented in the Eucharist.

This sacramental character of the Church is consistent with the important role that the Church plays in the process of salvation. In this dynamic approach to salvation history, the Church's whole being is linked to its sacramental function. She would be no more than a human organization without the presence of Christ who through the Church is mediated here and now. The Church is really an extension of the trinitarian life which began in the Old Dispensation and is fulfilled in Christ, the New Covenant, and is continued in the Church, in her mediation of the forgiveness of sins. It is in her

---

[911]de Lubac, *The Church*, pp. 7-8.

[912]de Lubac, *The Splendour of the Church*, p. 148.

[913]*Lumen Gentium*, para. 1.

[914]In his discusssion of the necessary role of the Church in the process of salvation, de Lubac cites Irenaeus. "Where the Church is, there is the Spirit of God, where the Spirit of God is there is the Church and all grace, the Spirit is Truth; to sever ourselves from the Church is to reject the Spirit" - and in virtue of that "to shut ourselves out of life." *The Splendour of the Church*, p. 154.

role in the process of redemption, the forgiveness of sin, that the authority and nature of the Church is most evident today.

Sin, as the separation of man from God, implies a personal relationship between man and God. Sin is not merely a guilty "feeling," a psychological flaw or an "error" in human judgement. "The basic sin; of which the thoughtful man seeks in this way to justify himself in atheism, is 'believing himself to be innocent.'"[915] It is this hubris which places man at odds with his Lord, creating a division, a gap, that is only overcome in the Incarnation. Here God enters his creation to restore all things to their proper order. "He incorporated himself in our humanity, and incorporated it in himself."[916] The Church, in its life in the world, is an extension of this restoration process. "The Church which is 'Jesus Christ spread abroad and communicated' completes - so far as it can be completed here below - the spiritual work of reunion which was made necesssary by sin; that work that was begun at the Incarnation and was carried on up to Calvary."[917] The Church, then, mediates a salvation that transcends human societies, yet it remains a salvation that is mediated in the world.[918]

As a representative of Roman Catholic ecclesiology, Henri de Lubac understands that the essence of the Church exceeds the visible Church, yet, it can never be totally separated from her.[919] "What we shall affirm is that the Church mysteriously transcends the limits of her visibility, that by her very essence she carries herself, as it

---

[915] de Lubac, *Nature and Grace*, p. 140.

[916] de Lubac, *Catholicism*, p. 22.

[917] Ibid., p. 31.

[918] According to de Lubac, it is precisely on this point that the Protestants separate themselves from Catholic ecclesiology. Protestants have the tendency to ignore the fullness and depth of the Church. "Having stripped it of all its mystical attributes, it (Protestantism) acknowledged in the visible Church a mere secular institution; as a matter of course it abandoned it to the patronage of the state and sought refuge for spiritual life in the invisible Church, its concept of which had been equated with an abstract ideal."(*Catholicism*, p. 42.) Also see *Catholicism*, p. 37. The inability to hold together the visible and invisible dimensions of the faith creates this problem.

[919] de Lubac, *Catholicism*, p. 38.

276

were above herself."[920] Nevertheless, de Lubac defends the visibility of the Church as constitutive of the Christian experience of faith.[921] "The mystery, the efficacious sign, is not separated from that which it signifies and, on the other hand, what is signified can only be grasped through the mediation in the sign."[922] To either identify or to separate the visible and the invisible aspects of the Church results in error.[923]

De Lubac uses the analogy of the incarnation to best demonstrate this tension of the visible and invisible, the human and divine, in the Church.[924] "There, then, is the Church - human and divine at one even in her visibility, 'without division and without confusion,' just like Christ Himself, whose body she mystically is."[925] Just as a human lives in time with a visible continuity and history, the same is true for the Church. "Jesus lives for us. But without the visible continuity of the Church, the desert sands would have long since swallowed up, if not perhaps his name and memory, certainly the influence of his gospel and faith in his divinity."[926] The Church has a visible dimension and a continuity in time, a "history," both essential characteristics of a historical reality.

---

[920] de Lubac, *The Church*, p. 27.

[921] Ibid., pp. 27, 35.

[922] Ibid., p. 26.

[923] de Lubac, *Catholicism*, p. 42. This can be seen in the distinction between the militant Church and the Church triumphant. The history of ecclesiology is full of errors caused by over-emphasizing either of these. See *Church*, pp. 51ff.

[924] de Lubac, *The Splendour of the Church*, p. 58.

[925] Ibid., p. 69.

[926] de Lubac, *The Church*, p. 6.

G. The Church and the redemption of the world

Since the fullness of salvation is present in the Church, she is the most pregnant witness to the fullness of her historicity. "As she is the only ark of salvation, within her immense name she must give shelter to all varieties of humanity. She is the only banquet hall, and the dishes she serves are the product of the whole creation. She is Christ's seamless coat, but she is too - and it is the same thing - Joseph's coat of many colours."[927] The power of the Church is a spiritual power which extends to all creation, just as the grace of God extends to and transforms every individual now under the power of sin.[928]

Since the Church is the locus of salvation during the present age, the redemptive nature of the Church is best understood in terms of the Eucharist, because in the Eucharist this redemptive sacrifice of Christ is actual in history, and actualizes history.[929] "And the purpose again is unity, for it is for the Church once more that it is offered, for a greater, more united Church: *pro totius mundi salute*."[930] Creation was the first stage of this process. "The work of Creation, however spoilt by man, yet remains the natural and the necessary preparation for the work of the Redeemer, and

---

[927]de Lubac, *Catholicism*, p. 159. Also see pp. 194ff.

[928]Henri de Lubac, *Surnaturel: Ètudes Historiques* (Paris: Aubier, 1946). Also see *The Mystery of the Supernatural*, tr. Rosemary Sheed (New York: Herder and Herder, 1967). At this point de Lubac's extensive work on the relationship between nature and grace becomes relevant.

[929]If history is the interpretation of time, it requires a definitive event by which such an interpretation can be made. Accordingly, since the Eucharist is the representation of the sacrifice of the Cross, the definitive event in history, one might say that history is eucharistic, or that the Eucharist, as event, actualizes history.

[930]de Lubac, *Henri de Lubac, S.J.*, p. 53.

the better the history of Christian origins becomes known the more we realize it."[931] The object of this salvation is to restore the created order to its fullness.[932]

The Church does not mediate some abstract, non-historical grace, but rather she mediates the grace of Christ which saves all of creation: the grace of Christ, the second person of the Trinity, the Creator become incarnate. Speaking of the dynamics of the faith that unites all believers, de Lubac says, "It is neither the 'idea of Christianity' nor 'Christianity' itself. It is a reality, an existence, a personal force: it is the very person of Christ. *Ego sum via, veritas et vita.*"[933] It is this concrete historical person, as incarnate and as continually present in the Church, who is the key to the historicity of the salvation of all of creation - a salvation not simply spiritual, but one that includes the whole person, body and soul. The Eucharist which is the incarnate presence of God in the world is the historical locus, the event of the substantial and continuous presence of Christ in time.[934]

Note that de Lubac recognizes the eschatological dimension of the life of the Church. The Eucharist sanctifies, causes, builds up the Church, but she still looks forward to her completion.[935] The Eucharist both edifies the Chruch and is the advent of the consummation of all things in Christ, a future consummation not yet completed. The "Body of Christ" signifies a process that is no longer retrospective, but prospective.[936] The Eucharist is not only the sacrament of memory that simply

---

[931] de Lubac, Catholicism, p. 153.

[932] de Lubac, *The Church*, pp. 72ff.

[933] Ibid, pp. 76ff.

[934] It is both beyond the scope of this study and the ability of the author, at present, to take up the study of nature and grace in de Lubac. It should be noted though, that by arguing that Eucharist is the "substantial" and continuous presence of Christ in history, I understand grace to be substantial. For the best study of this problem see Donald Keefe, S.J. *Covenantal Theology*. Keefe's work is heavily influenced by de Lubac.

[935] de Lubac, *Corpus Mysticum*, pp. 78ff.

[936] Ibid., p. 76ff.

reproduces the past, but as sacrament of hope it anticipates the future. This eschatological tension destroys neither the continuity of the Eucharistic worship nor the continuity of the Church, but it does point to a future in which the fullness that is already present in the Church will result in the final redemption of all creation.

H. Mary and the Church

The Eucharist, the mystery which constitutes the essence of the Church, has been discussed in terms of the concrete event of Christ, salvation history, the redemption of the individual and the redemption of all of creation. In all of these dimensions, de Lubac is careful to reaffirm the fullness and the concreteness of the salvation of Christ in the Church. It is important for de Lubac that this "realism", this historicity, of the Church reflect the realism and the historicity of the Eucharist, which in turn reflects the realism of the historicity of the Christ-event. In each instance there is a definite concreteness, a notion of history, that is definitely Catholic.

Moreover, like von Balthasar, de Lubac uses the Marian imagery to speak of the Church. "When the Christian who knows what he is saying speaks of the Church as his mother, he is not giving way to some sentimental impulse; he is expressing a reality."[937] This attribution of motherhood is not extrinsic, nor simply a metaphor finally dispensible to the understanding of the Church, but is a rather strict title, pointing to her internal reality. "From one end of the Bible to the other there is scarcely a woman of prominence who is not in some way a figure of that Church."[938] From the Old Law to the New Covenant this feminine imagery permeates the Bible.

In the symbolism of the Old Eve and the New Eve, like the Old Adam and New Adam, is contained an understanding of the whole economy of creation and salvation. Her role centers on her perfect freedom to accept God's offer of grace

---

[937]de Lubac, *The Motherhood of the Church*, p. 39.

[938]de Lubac, *Catholicism*, p. 102.

280

wherin the whole economy of salvation is involved. This means that Mary's acceptance of God's offer of salvation, the summit of the doctrine of human freedom, is an intregal part of the whole process of redemption.[939]

Marian doctrine is therefore helpful for understanding the nature of the Church: what is said of Mary can be said of the Church. "These two mysteries of the faith are not just interdependent: we might say that they are 'one single and unique mystery.'"[940] "As far as the Christian mind is concerned, Mary is the 'deal figure of the Church,' the 'acrament' of it and the 'ision in which the whole Church is reflected.'"

> Our Lady speaks and acts in the name of the Church at every moment of her existence - "she shows forth in herself the figure of the holy Church" - not, of course, in virtue of some decision which is an afterthought nor, obviously, because of an explicit intention on her part, but because she already carries the Church within her, so to speak, and contains it, in its wholeness, in her own person.[941]

She is the summation of the Church. "Mary, full of grace, proto-type of all perfection, is the eschatological figure of the Church, that is, of the entire people of God."[942] "Mary - and she alone - appears by anticipation, as the perfect Church, the final communion of all the faithful. It is in the mystery of the assumption, therefore, that the theme finds its full flowering."[943] Mary, like the Church, can be understood only in terms of the economy of salvation.

---

[939] de Lubac, *The Splendour of the Church*, p. 239.

[940] Ibid., p. 240.

[941] Ibid., pp. 242-243.

[942] de Lubac, *The Church*, p. 58.

[943] Ibid., pp. 58-59.

Mary plays an essential role in the economy of salvation as the means by which the redemption of Christ can enter the world. Her sinlessness reflects a human freedom not bound by the strands of fallen creation, a freedom which on the part of all of humanity opens history to the full redemption of God. It is the sinless Church, like Mary, who was made sinless by the bridegroom Christ, that shares in the redemptive mediation of Mary.

Within this view of the economy of salvation, the *fiat* of Mary is the key to understanding the presence of the salvation of Christ in space and time. "For it was in her - that is, in her womb - 'that the whole Church was bethrothed to the Word and united to God by an eternal alliance.'"[944]

> In short, Our Lady "comprises in an eminent degree all the graces and all the perfections" of the Church; all the graces of the saints flow into her, as all the rivers flow into the sea. "It is from her, forever in place before his gaze, that the Eternal takes the measure of all things"; in her the whole Church is outlined, and at the same time already completed; she is simultaneously the "seed" and the "pleroma" of it.[945]

Since she is the fullness of the Church, she is the mother of the Church. But Mary is also a member of the Church. And the Church in its fullness, in its holiness, is Marian.

Like Mary, the Church appears as both sanctifying and sanctified. Both utter the *fiat* by means of which the grace of Christ entered and remains in the world as fully historical and concrete. "The one carried Life in her womb, while the other carries Him in the wellspring of the Sacrament. What was once granted in the flesh to Mary is now granted spiritually to the Church; she conceives the Word in her unfaltering faith, bears Him in a spirit freed from all corruption and contains Him in a soul overshadowed by

---

[944]de Lubac, *The Splendor of the Church*, p. 254.

[945]Ibid., p. 259.

the power of the most High."[946] Just as Mary was the Mother of Christ, the Church is the mother of a New People of God. The maternity of Mary is literally transferred to the Church.[947]

> And yet I (de Lubac) do have something to show for my pains, something obviously, literally childlike; something I knew before I began and which every reflection confirmed. I can tell it in one word, the first of all words: the Church is my mother. Yes, the Church, the whole Church, that of generations past who transmitted her life, her teachings, her witness, her culture, her love to me; and the Church of today. The whole Church, I say, not only the institutional Church, or the Church teaching, or, as we still say, the hierarchical Church that holds the keys confided to her by the Lord. No, more broadly and simply, I mean the "living Church"; working, praying, active and contemplative, remembering and searching, believing, hoping, loving . . . . Much more, the entire Church, without distinction, that immense flock of Christians, so many of whom are unaware of their royal priesthood and of the fraternal community they constitute, all this is my mother too.[948]

The Church, as mother by the sacrament of baptism, gives birth to the faith in the individual believer: to new life, of the new man born in Christ.[949]

This relationship between Christ, Mary and the Church is the focus of de Lubac's ecclesiology. Just as in the economy of salvation the fullness of the grace of Christ becomes incarnate through the *fiat* of Mary, so too the worship of the Church mediates the fullness of Christ into the world. The Church, in its holy splendor made

---

[946]Ibid., p. 244.

[947]de Lubac, *The Church*, p. 59.

[948]Ibid., pp. 3-4.

possible by the grace of Christ, is able to build up the Body of Christ. The motherhood extended from Mary to the Church is later extended to the individual believer born in the spirit of Christ.

> The Word is born in each one of us faithful, as in the Church as a whole, but this is in the likeness of His birth in the soul of Our Lady, and in addition, if faith is to bear its fruit, there must be in each of us the soul of Our Lady, who magnified the Lord, and the Spirit of Our Lady, who rejoiced in God.[950]

There is one mystery and the key to understanding the mystery of the Church and of our life of faith is Mary.[951]

In his discussion of Mary, it becomes evident that the Church, like Mary, can best be understood in terms of the economy of salvation: salvation history. As with Mary, the nature of the Church is clearly reflected in what it does. The fullness of the mystery of Christ is given in the Incarnation in which the *fiat* of Mary played an important role, and continues to be present in the Church through her free Eucharistic *fiat*, her responsive sacrifice of praise, the worship of the Bride of Christ sanctified by the blood of the New Covenant.

I. Summary

Against modern tendencies in ecclesiology which reduce the Church to a simply human institution or to an invisible society, de Lubac accepts what is positive in these tendencies while attempting to avoid their exaggerations. By rooting the

---

[949] de Lubac, *The Motherhood of the Church*, p. 120. It is in the light of the motherhood of the Church that the fatherhood of the priesthood can best be understood. See pp. 92-104, 120ff.

[950] de Lubac, *The Splendour of the Church*, p. 267.

[951] Ibid., p. 283.

sacramentality of the Church in the realism of her Eucharistic worship, de Lubac's
Eucharistic theology, which integrates he exegesis, his understanding of history and of
the Church in a single dialectical insight, provides a Catholic corroboration of Ebeling's
hypothesis.

Like Ebeling, de Lubac believes that eucharistic presence of the Cross of Christ
informs the Church as the source of the life of the Church. It causes and unifies the
Church. So that to break the link between the Church and the Eucharist is to endanger
the very life of the Church.

> The Church, like the Eucharist, is a mystery of unity -
> the same mystery, and one with inexhaustible riches.
> Both are the body of Christ - the same body. If we are
> to be faithful to the teaching of Scripture, as Tradition
> interprets it, and wish not to lose anything of its
> essential riches, we must be careful not to make the
> smallest break between the the Mystical Body and the
> Eucharist . . . The two mysteries must be understood
> by one another and their point of unity grasped at
> depth.[952]

Only in this tension, in this essential relationship, can the fullness of the life of the
Church be preserved. So like Ebeling, de Lubac holds that the interpretation of the
Eucharistic symbols is essential to the historicity of the life of the Church. To change
or to minimalize the Eucharist has important results for the life of faith.

De Lubac, as a Roman Catholiclike von Balthasar and Congar, understands the
historicity of the faith to reflect the *ex opere operato* presence of Christ in the
Eucharist. (De Lubac is closer to Congar in his understanding of the Eucharistic
symbols. Von Balthasar is sometimes unwilling to commit himself fully to the use of *ex
opere operato* to articulate the Eucharistic presence.) For him, the Church and the
Eucharist are inextricably linked. In the Eucharist the believing Church encounters
Christ, is purified by Christ and realizes (as Mary) the salvation of Christ in the midst of

---

[952]Ibid., p. 110. Also see pp. 206ff.

space and time. As a sacrament, the Eucharist both mediates and embodies the reality of salvation given in Christ, and provides the continuity between the Christ-event and the present life of the Church. Consequently, in this interpretetation of the Church and the Eucharist, de Lubac's view of the historicity of the faith, reflects a Catholic "realism," a realism which insists upon the the fullness of the salvation of Christ as present, here and now in the Church.

Chapter IX: Conclusion: Worship, Ecclesiology and a Theology of History

This study began with the belief that a great deal of the confusion in the Christian theological world is related to the problem of the historicity of the faith. One sees evidence of this confusion in the inter-confessional disputes that have plagued Christianity for more than four centuries, but this is not the only instance where the present turmoil can be seen. In general, there is even confusion amid most confessional ranks. One can see these divisions most clearly within Lutheranism, Anglicanism and Roman Catholicism, but they also exist within the host of other Christian confessions. Many of these disputes stem from a fundamental disagreement over the nature of the historicity of the faith which is reflected in their different views of the way in which Chrisitniaty "works;" i.e., how God reveals himself and how he acts to save his people in Fallen creation. This study has been written to lend clarity to the problem of the historicity of the faith, an issue central to the continued possibility of living a Christian life in a continually secularized world, as well as the basis for any hope for the possible restoration of Christian unity.

Once again it appears, that just as in the sixteenth century, modern confessional divisions and ecclesiological discussion find their focus on the "altar." In this work the question of the historicity of faith has been examined in relation to the worship of the Church. Evidence has been discovered that implicit in the different confessional interpretations of the Eucharistic symbols are different understandings of the manner in which God is present in his Church. The historicity of faith is thus central to the life of faith and perhaps theologians concerned with questions of ecclesiology and ecumenism might benefit from theological reflection on the worship of the Church.

This work has explored the hypothesis that the historicity of the Eucharist is linked to the historicity of the Church and the life of faith. This is a hypothesis operative in both Protestant and Roman Catholic theologies and has consequences for their ecclesiologies. To accept this hypothesis is to make history a fundamental theological category, one that is important to those ecumenically-minded theologians concerned with the widely differing confessional stances.

Pursuing the hypothesis of Ebeling which states that the position taken with respect to the historicity of the faith is linked to the interpretation of the Eucharistic symbols, it was discovered that among a number of contemporary Protestant theologians there is a real problem with locating a concrete continuity or presence of the salvation offered by Christ in fallen history. This was especially true for Ebeling and Fuchs, who reduce theology to the always ambiguous interpretation of the promises of Christ given in Scripture. Faith is a linguistic participation in the Word of God who became incarnate and to whom we have access by the proclamation of the word of God. In such a view of the liturgy, as the liturgy of the word, the word is fragmented by fallen creation and cannot mediate the full redemption of Christ in the present. All mediations of the word in fallen creation can only take place in the individual conscience and are devoid of any public historical expression. The concreteness of this faith event corresponds to its effect in the life of the believer, an effect that is never complete and therefore always tentative and ambiguous.

One of the difficulties of this theological interpretation of the Eucharistic symbols is the failure to adequately distinguish between the incarnate Word, the second person of the Trinity, and the proclamation of the Church. The strength of Ebeling and Fuch's position is their emphasis on the personal nature of the call to faith. Each proclamation is understood to be a call to which the faithful is to respond. They insist that the proclamation of the word of God is the real source of ecclesial history, since it is in the proclamation that the believer encounters the salvation of Christ. But they are also aware of the fragmentariness that plagues all human witnesses to the Christ-event (even the Scriptures are to some extent partial). Therefore, this proclamation has no public discernible continuity, for it collapses the historical proclamation into the eschatological event wherein the salvation of Christ will be encountered in its fullness. There is the tendency not to save man in the present, but to save him from his present fallen condition into the future of God.

Cullmann and Moltmann, on the other hand, insist upon the working of God in history and that faith must reflect the historical nature of the revelation of God. In Moltmann this historical character manifests itself in the praxis of the believer; i.e., solidarity with the victims of oppression. In such acts of faith, the believer makes present and lives out the dangerous memory of the cross under the present conditions of fallen creation. But much like Ebeling and Fuchs who collapse the event of faith into an eschatological future, Moltmann empties fallen creation of the full presence of Christ by his insistence that redemption is the process of being taken up into the history of God. I find little difference between this history of God and the eschatological future of Fuchs and Ebeling. They tend to empty the present time, now under the reign of sin, of the redemptive presence of Christ.

Of all the Protestant theologians discussed, Cullmann's theology appears to illustrate best the problem of the historicity of the faith in Protestantism. Against the other contemporary Protestant theologians discussed here who, affected by modern philosophical presuppositions, are unable to accept the full historical claims of Christianity, Cullmann insists that God reveals himself through events in history. Although to clearly see these events and to understand their ramifications requires faith, they are events that are public. There is a salvation history through which God reveals his purpose to man in space and time. Furthermore, Cullmann insists that these past events are essential for Christian faith and salvation. But like his fellow Protestant theologians discussed here, in Cullmann's description of the worship of the believer it is difficult to locate any unambiguous presence of Christ in fallen creation. The Eucharist becomes a memory, a mystical participation with the Christ, but it lacks the concrete public expression found in the Roman Catholic interpretation of the Eucharistic symbols. The result is that the full effects of the redemptive activity are not present to the believer in history.

Despite the diversity between these positions, they share a common belief about the Christian faith: there can be no unambiguous mediation of the redemption of Christ under the present conditions of fallen creation. The *sola fide* principle of the

Reformation presupposes that because of the Fall the original good creation is under the power of sin and is totally corrupt. As a result of this interpretation of Christianity, nothing in fallen creation is able to mediate the fullness of the divine. The Father sends the Son, but since we are saved by Christ alone, with the departure of the Son, fallen creation is left without any unambiguous presence of Christ. Consequently, all human activity is bound by sin and unable to even accept God's offer of grace. Left to our own devices, we will all be condemned to eternal damnation. But Christ so loved his chosen that he came to save them and left them with a promise of salvation, a salvation which will take place only in the future, a salvation not operative under the present conditions of fallen creation. Worship, then, cannot mediate the full redemption of Christ *ex opere operato* under the present conditions of fallen creation. Instead, it encourages the believer with the promise of future salvation at the second coming of Christ.

Using the traditional Roman Catholic language, this represents a collapse of the *res et sacramentum* into the *res sacramenti tantum*: the collapse of history into the eschaton, and consequently, of the historical community into subjectivity. In this instance (as is also the case with certain Roman Catholic theologies) the effect (*res*) of the sacrament is a private event, it has no real communal or public component, creating a gap between the grace of Christ and any concrete historical mediation. Without the *ex opere operato* interpretation of Roman Catholicism, the very nature of the historicity of the faith becomes a matter difficult to discern.

This is not to say that among Roman Catholic theologians the issue of the historicity is not a matter of dispute. For a variety of reasons, today more than ever, Roman Catholics find themselves at odds over the true meaning of the historicity of the faith. Reasons for this lack of agreement may stem from the influence of Protestantism in Catholic theology and the rise of modern historical consciousness, especially the historicism that stems from it. From this perspective, the heart of the problem is always the *ex opere operato* efficacy of the *sacramentum tantum* in causing the *res et sacramentum*. In the sacramental life of the Church this means that the Eucharist is the actual presence of the sacrificed and risen Christ as the "whole Christ," i.e., as the New Covenant. This New Covenant, the eschatological perfection, the Kingdom, is sacramentally present where Christ is present. This means that the Church acts as a sacrament in the economy of redemption. As historical, she is the *res et sacramentum* of the eucharistic "one flesh" which is the New Covenant sacramentally actual in the eucharistic action, the *res sacramenti* as the eucharistic community identified with the Kingdom, the eschatological Church in union with the eschatological Christ. This sacramentally objective event of the eucharistic action is at once the historicity of the eucharistic Christ and the equally eucharistic Church. Any theology in which the event character of the sacramental life is downplayed or denied (e.g., by a denial of transubstantiation, the sacrifice of the Mass or the working of the sacrament *ex opere operato)*, then the historicity of the revelation and the Church are eventually called into question.[953]

Within the Church documents of this century and those of earlier centuries, there is evidence of this sacramental dimension of the Church which insists upon the very sacramentality of reality itself. The link between the Christ-event, the Eucharist and the Church is of the greatest importance to the life of faith. This is precisely why there is a fundamental difficulty with von Balthasar's theology. Perhaps because of his Augustinian orientation, he is profoundly distrustful of the Catholic use of the terms transubstantiation and *ex opere operato*. Although loyal to Roman Catholicism, in his work, *The Glory of the Lord*, he is highly critical of metaphysics and possibility of systematic theology, and has the tendency, like the theologians of the Reformation, to collapse the *res et sacramentum* into the *res sacramenti*. This results in a distrust of

---

[953]The effects of such an abandonment of the sacrametnality of the faith are legion. As a matter of fact most ecclesiologies are filled with those ideas. Such issues as women's ordination, the democratization of the Church, magisterial authority, all reflect a rejection of the proper Roman Catholic understanding of the sacramental nature of creation and redemption. For an analysis of this see Joyce Little, *The and Culture War: Secular Anarchy or Sacred Order*, San Francisco: Ignatius Press, 1995.

any historical mediation of the grace of Christ, whether doctrine, morality or sacraments.

An example of von Balthasar's reluctance to accept the *ex opere operato* working of the sacrament is his hesitation to accept infant baptism. In this instance, like his Protestant counterparts, he desires to free the working of faith from what he sees as a mechanical model which falsely identifies the grace of Christ with its historical mediation. But in freeing the activity of the grace of Christ, which is the exact purpose of his theological aesthetics, he tends to deny or at least call into question the sacramentality of the life of faith.

Yet in his later work, *Theo-drama*, he seems to balance the earlier tendencies by focussing on revelation and redemption as primarily an "act." Here, the act of Christ becomes the norm, the concrete basis for the faith, by which and through which the redemptive activity of Christ is present. Sacraments, then, as acts are representations, a participation in those original events by which we are saved. Here is a sacramental real presence, not so much focused on a particular location of Christ in the present, but an understanding of real presence that is consistent with the event character of the revelation and the *ex opere operato* interpretation of the sacraments characteristic of Roman Catholicism. Not surprisingly, this interpretation of the eucharistic symbols is consistent with the Roman Catholic understanding of the Mass as event, a dimension preserved by the Church's doctrine that the Mass is a sacrifice. Von Balthasar's theology, in the end, affirms an understanding of the historicity of the faith consistent with that tradition.

Unlike von Balthsar's ecclesiology which shows a consistent development, Congar's theology can be divided between his earlier and later work. He emphasized the importance of the historicity of the Catholic articulation of the faith in his early work on tradition and sacraments. Like de Lubac, he then linked the life of the Church to the concrete presence of Christ in the sacraments, insisting that the historical presence of Christ under the conditions of fallen creation is like that of the presence of Christ in the Eucharist understood in terms of transubstantiation. The historicity of the

Church in the present was thought to reflect this sacramental presence wherein the bread and wine become the actual Body and Blood of Christ in a distinct place, in the present. Although Congar did not work out the full ramifications of this historical presence, there can be no doubt from his work in the area of tradition that he then understood the plan of God, his redemptive activity, to be essentially linked to the historical life of the Church.

In Congar's later work a significant change takes place.[954] The emphasis is shifted away from a definitive presence of the risen Christ in the Roman Catholic Church, which is now seen to exist in space and time, toward an eschatological fullness which has no sacramental re-presentation under the present conditions of fallen creation. According to his later position, the present ecclesiological divisions within Christianity reflect the possibility of faith in the fallen world. That is, like many of the Protestant theologians, he believes that the unambiguous or full mediation of the redemption of Christ is not possible in fallen history.

De Lubac, on the other hand, throughout his life has been the pillar of Catholic orthodoxy. Like Congar and von Balthasar, de Lubac situates the question of the historicity of the Church within his discussion of the Eucharist. In his theology, all historical salvation has its source in the Eucharistic action in which the Sacrifice of the Cross is re-presented under the present conditions of fallen creation. This is the presence of Christ to his people during this final period of the Church and the cause of the Church. As the cause of the Church, the Eucharist is also the source of the historicity of the faith during the present age.

Unlike those who tend to reduce the Christ-Church union to a monophysitical "one person" identity, de Lubac insists that this union is fundamentally marital. In this union of Christ and creation, the "whole Christ" or *totus Christus* of Augustine is interpreted in terms of the second Adam and the second Eve. This permits the unique

---

[954] Congar, *Communion and Diversity*. In this work he seems to move from being based strongly in the tradition to the kind of historical thinking that relativizes the importance of the past.

full historical actuality of the Church to be retained. He emphasizes this in his theology by making explicit the parallel between the interpretation of economy of salvation and the sacramental mediation. Within this analogy, the Old Testament is the *sacramentum tantum*, the New Testament, including the history of the Church, is the *res et sacramentum* and the the eschatological kingdom the *res sacramenti*. The Eucharisitic sacrifice, as the bond between Old Testament and New Testament, at once the communion in the holy elements of the Eucharist and the sanctified, is the continuous offer of God's grace to man in fallen creation. In this Eucharistic event, as in the Christ-event, the Old Covenant, the Church and the eschaton are brought together in the Eucharistic Lord, who is the cause of the Church and so the cause of the historicity of the faithful. The historicity of the faithful is their historical (sacramental) unity in their communion in the Eucharistic sacrifice and its effects.[955] Among the Roman Catholic theologians discussed in this paper, de Lubac most clearly represents the Roman Catholic counterpart of Ebeling's hypothesis.

The central problem of our discussion, of course, is the difficulty of interpreting the nature of the sacraments. If the *res et sacamentum* of the Eucharist can be reduced to the *res sacramenti tantum* as the collapse of history into the eschaton, of community into subjectivity, then, from a Roman Catholic perspective, the historicity of the faith becomes endangered. Such a reductionism excludes the *ex opere operato* interpretation of the Eucharistic worship, thereby denying the communal or public component of the actual mediation of the risen Lord in the historical order. Within Catholicism this tendency results in a dehistoricization that destroys the sacramental character of the faith, reduces the Church to one among many possible alternatives and denies the possibility of any definitive teaching authority in fallen creation.

Within Protestantism, this problem has manifest itself most clearly in its battle over the interpretation of the eucharistic symbols: e.g., in Luther's debate with the Zwinglians and others over the *manducatio impiorum* which asked whether the person

---

[955] de Lubac, *Corpus Mysticum*, pp. 90-130. Also see *The Church: Paradox and Mystery*, pp. 36ff.

without saving faith does or does not receive the Body and Blood of Christ. The answer that one gives to this question determines the character of the faith and the life of the Church. Consequently, it has been the source of division within Protestant Christianity.

The reader of this study finds here further evidence for a hypothesis concerning the link between the interpretation of the Eucharistic symbols and the understanding of the historicity of the Christian faith explicitly held by Ebeling and implicitly at work in most Protestant and Roman Catholic theologians. This is a discussion of interest to those ecumenically-minded theologians who wish to surpass the old polemics between Protestants and Roman Catholics. Since the Christ-event is the point from which all time takes its meaning, history is a theological category of fundamental importance; a category that is essential to present theological and ecumenical discussion.

BIBLIOGRAPHY

A. Primary Sources

Abbott, Walter M. and Joseph Gallagher, eds. *The Documents of Vatican II.* New York: Guild Press, 1966.

Balthasar, Hans Urs von. *Church and the World.* Translated by A.V. Littledale. New York: Herder and Herder, 1967.

_____. *The Glory of the Lord:* A Theological Aesthetics. Vol. I :*Seeing the Form.* Translated by Erasmo-Leiva-Merikakis. Edited by Joseph Fessio and John Riches. San Francisco: Ignatius Press, 1982.

_____. *The God Question and Modern Man.* Forward by John MacQuarrie. Translated by Hilda Graef. New York: Sheed and Ward, 1958.

_____. *Hans Urs von Balthasar.* In *Theologians Today.* Westminster, MD: Sheed and Ward, 1972.

_____. *Man in History.* London: Sheed and Ward, 1968.

_____. *The Office of St. Peter and the Structure of the Church.* Translated by Andre Emery. San Francisco: Ignatius Press, 1986.

_____. *A Short Primer for Unsettled Laymen.* Translated by Sister Mary Thereselde Sherry. San Francisco: Ignatius Press, 1980.

_____. *Theo-drama: The Action.* Translated by Graham Harrison. San Francisco: Ignatius Press, 1994.

_____. *Theo-drama: Dramatis Personae: Man in God.* Translated by Graham Harrison. San Francisco: Ignatius Press, 1990.

_____. *Theo-drama: Dramatis Personae: Persons in Christ.* Translated by Graham Harrison. San Francisco: Ignatius Press, 1992.

_____. *Theo-drama: Prolegomena.* Translated by Graham Harrison. San Francisco: Ignatius Press, 1988.

_____. *A Theological Anthropology.* New York: Sheed and Ward, 1967.

_____. *A Theology of History.* New York: Sheed and Ward, 1963.

_____. *The von Balthasar Reader.* Edited by Medard Kehl, S. J. and Werner Löser, S.J. Translated by Robert Daly, S.J. and Fred Lawrence. New York: Crossroad, 1982.

_____. *Who is a Christian?* Translated by John Cumming. New York: Newman Press, 1965.

_____. *Word and Revelation: Essays in Theology I.* Translated by A.V. Littledale. New York: Herder and Herder, 1964.

Congar, Yves, M.J. *Le Christ, Marie et L'Église.* Brower: Descleé, 1952.

_____. *This Church that I Love.* Translated by Lucien Delafuente. Denville, N.J.: Dimmension Books, 1969.

_____. *Diversity and Communion*. Translated by John Bowden. London: SCM Press LTD, 1984.

_____. *Laity, Church and World*. Translated by Donald Attwater. Baltimore: Helicon Press, 1960.

_____. *The Meaning of Tra dition*. Translated by A.N. Woodrow. New York: Hawthorn Books, 1964.

_____. *The Mystery of the Church*. Translated by A.V. Littledale. Baltimore: Helicon Press, 1960.

_____. *The Mystery of the Temple*. Translated by Regnold F. Trevett. Westminster, MD.: The Newman Press, 1962.

_____. "The People of God." *Concilium*. January 1965, Vol. 1: No. 1, pp. 7-19.

_____. *The Revelation of God*. Translated by A. Manson and L.C. Sheppard. New York: Herder and Herder, 1968.

_____. *Sainte Église: Études etEcclésologique*. Paris: Les Éditions du Cerf, 1963.

_____. *Tradition and Traditions*. Translated by Michael Naseby and Thomas Rainborough. London: Burns & Oates, LTD, 1966.

_____. *The Wide World My Parish*. Translated by Donald Attwater. Baltimore: Helicon Press, 1961.

Cullmann, Oscar. *Christ and Time*. Translated by Floyd V. Filson. Philadelphia: Westminster Press, 1964.

_____. *The Christology of the New Testament*. Translated by Shirley C. Gutherie and Charles A.M. Hall. London: SCM Press Ltd, 1959.

_____. *Early Christian Worship*. Translated by A. Stewart Todd and James B. Torrance. London: SCM Press LTD, 1953.

_____. *The Early Church: Studies in Early Christian History and Theology*. Edited by A.J.B. Higgins. Philadelphia: Westminster Press, 1956.

_____. and F..J. Leenhardt. *Essays on the Lord's Supper*. Translated by J.G. Davies. London: Lutterworth Press, 1958.

_____. *Heils als Geschichte*. Tübingen: J.C.B. Mohr, 1965.

_____. *Message to Catholics and Protestants*. Translated by Joseph A. Burgess. Grand Rapids, MI: Eerdmans Publishing Company, 1959.

_____. "Out of Season Remarks on the Historical Jesus of the Bultmann School." *Union Seminary Quarterly Review*, January 1961, pp. 131ff.

_____. *Salvation in History*. Translated by Sidney G. Sowers. New York: Harper & Row, Publishers, 1964.

_____. "The Tradition." *The Early Church*, 1956, pp. 55ff.

Ebeling, Gerhard. *Introduction to a Theological Theory of Language*. Translated by R.A. Wilson. Philadelphia: Fortress Press, 1973.

_____. *Luther*. Translated by R.A. Wilson. Philadelphia: Fortress Press, 1970.

_____. *The Nature of Faith*. Translated by R. G. Smith. Philadelphia: Fortress Press, 1967.

_____. *The Problem of Historicity*. Translated by Grover Foley. Philadelphia: Fortress Press, 1961.

_____. *Word and Faith*. Translated by James W. Leitch. Philadelphia: Fortress Press, 1963.

_____. "Word of God and Hermeneutics." In *The New Hermeneutics*. Edited by James M. Robinson and John B. Cobb, Jr.. New York: Harper & Row, Publishers, 1964.

_____. *The Word of God and Tradition*. Translated by S.H. Hooke. Philadelphia: Fortress Press, 1968.

Fuchs, Ernst. "Kanon und Kerygma." *Zeitschrift für Theologie und Kirche*. 1966, Vol. 63, pp. 410-433.

_____. "The New Testament and the Hermeneutical Problem." In *The New Hermeneutics*. Edited by James M. Robinson and John B. Cobb, Jr. New York: Harper & Row, Publishers, 1964, pp. 111-146.

_____. "Proclamation and Speech-event." *Theology Today*. January 1963, Vol. 19: No. 1, pp. 341-354.

_____. "Die sakramentale Einheit von Wort und Tat." *Zeitschrift für Theologie und Kirche*. 1971, Vol. 68: No. 2, pp. 213-226.

_____. "Sola Fide." *Zeitschrift für Theologie und Kirche*. 1976, Vol. 73: No. 3, pp. 306-314.

_____. Studies of the Historical Jesus. Translated by Andrew Scobie. Naperville, IL: Alec R. Allenson, Inc., 1964.

de Lubac, Henri. *A Brief Catechism on Nature and Grace*. Translated by Bro. Richard Arnandez, F.S.C. San Francisco: Ignatius Press, 1984.

_____. *Catholicism: A Study of Dogma in Relation to the Corporate Destiny of Mankind*. Translated by Lancelot C. Sheppard. New York: Mentor-Omega Book, 1964.

_____. *The Church: Paradox and Mystery*. Translated by James R. Dunne. Staten Island, NY: Abba House, 1969.

_____. *Corpus Mysticum: L'Eucharistie et L'Église au Moyen Age*. Paris: Aubier, 1949.

_____. *Dieu se dit dans l'histoire de la Revelation Divine*. Paris: Editions du Cerf, 1974.

_____. *Henri de Lubac, S.J.*. In *Theologians Today*. New York: Sheed and Ward, 1972.

_____. *Histoire et Esprit*. Paris: Aubier, 1950.

_____. *The Motherhood of the Church*. Translated by Sr. Sergia Englund, O.C.D. San Francisco: Ignatius Press, 1971.

_____. *The Mystery of the Supernatural*. Translated by Rosemary Sheed. New York: Herder and Herder, 1967.

_____. *The Sources of Revelation*. Translated by Luke O'Neill. New York: Herder and Herder, 1968.

_____. *The Splendour of the Church*. Translated by Michael Mason. New York: Sheed and Ward, 1956.

_____. *Surnaturel: Etudes Historique*. Paris: Aubier, 1946.

Moltmann, Jürgen. *The Beginnings of Dialectic Theology*. Translated by James M. Robinson. Richmond: John Knox Press, 1968.

_____ . *The Church in the Power of the Spirit*. Translated by Margret Kohl. London: SCM Press LTD, 1977.

_____ . *The Crucified God*. New York: Harper & Row, Publishers, 1967.

_____ . *An Ecumenical Confession of Faith*. New York: Seabury Press, 1979.

_____ . *The Experiment Hope*. Translated by M. Douglas Meeks. Philadelphia: Fortress Press, 1975.

_____ . "Exegesis und Eschatologie der Geschichte." *Evangelische Theologie*. 1962, Vol. 22, pp. 31-66.

_____ . *The Future of Creation*. Translated by Margret Kohl. Philadelphia: Fortress Press, 1979.

_____ . *Theology of Hope*. New York: Harper & Row, Publishers, 1967.

_____ . "Toward the Waiting God." In *The Future of Hope*. Edited by Frederick Herzog. New York: Herder and Herder, 1970.

_____ . *The Trinity and the Kingdom*. Translated by Margret Kohl. San Francisco: Harper & Row, Publisher, 1981.

Pope Paul VI. "The Eucharist: Summit of Christian Life." *Origins*, June 27, 1978, Vol. 8: No. 6, pp. 89-91.

_____ . *Mysterium Fidei*. AAS,57; (1965).

Pope Pius XII. *Mediator Dei*. AAS, 37; (1947).

_____ . *Mystici Corporis*. AAS, 35; (1943).

B. Secondary Sources

Achtemeier, Paul J. *An Introduction to the New Hermeneutic*. Philadelphia: Westminster Press, 1969.

_____ . "How Adequate a New Hermeneutic." *Theology Today*. April 1966, Vol. 23: No. 1, pp. 101-119.

Althaus, Paul. *The Theology of Martin Luther*. Translated by Robert C. Schultz. Philadelphia: Fortress Press, 1966.

Aubert, Roger, ed.. *Church History in Future Perspective*. New York: Herder and Herder, 1970.

Augustine of Hippo, *The City of God against the Pagans*. Translated by Henry Bettenson. Edited by David Knowles. Baltimore: Penguin Books,1972.

Bainton, Roland H.. *The Reformation of the Sixteenth Century*. Boston: Beacon Press, 1952.

Barth, Karl. "The Doctrine of Creation." Vol. III, *Church Dogmatics*. Edited by G.W. Bromiley and T.F. Torrance. Edinburgh: T. & T. Clark, 1958.

_____. *From Rousseau to Ritschl.* Translated by Brian Cozens. London: SCM Press LTD, 1969.

van Beeck, Franz Josef, S.J. "Sacraments and Church Order." *Theological Studies,* Vol. 30: No. 4, 1969, pp. 613-634.

Bultmann, Rudolf. *Essays, Philosophical and Theological.* London: SCM Press LTD, 1955.

_____. *Existence and Faith.* Translated and forward by Schubert Ogden. Meridian Books, Inc., 1960.

_____ and Arthur Weiser. *Faith.* London: Adams & Charles Black, 1961.

_____. *History and Eschatology.* Edinburgh: The University Press, 1957.

_____. *The Presence of Eternity.* New York: Harper & Row, Publishers, 1957.

_____. *The Theology of the New Testament.* Translated by Kendrick Grobel. London: SCM Press LTD, 1959.

Burgess, Joseph A., ed. *The Role of the Augsburg Confession.* Philadelphia: Fortress Press, 1980.

Butterfield, Herbert. *The Origins of History.* Edited with introduction by Alan Watson. New York: Basic Books, Inc., Publishers, 1981.

Chifflot, T.G., O.P. *Approaches to a Theology of History.* Translated by Mary Perkins Ryan. New York: Descleé Company, 1965.

Clark, Francis S.J. *The Eucharistic Sacrifice and the Reformation.* Westminster, MD: The Newman Press, 1960.

Collingwood, R.G. *Essays in the Philosophy of History.* Edited, with introduction by William Debbins. New York: McGraw-Hill Book Company, 1965.

_____. *The Idea of History.* Oxford: Clarendon Press, 1946.

Connolly, James M. *Human History and the Word of God.* Preface by Louis Bouyer. New York: Macmillan Company, 1965.

Daly, Robert J., S.J. *The Origin of the Christian Doctrine of Sacrifice.* Philadelphia: Fortress Press, 1978.

Danielou, Jean. *Essai sur Le Mystére de L'Histoire.* Paris: Editions du Seuil, 1953.

_____. "The Heart of the Problem." In *Catholic Protestant Dialogue.* Baltimore: Helicon Press, 1960.

Dulles, Avery, S.J. *Models of the Church.* Garden City, NY: Doubleday & Company, Inc., 1974.

Eichrodt, Walter. *Theology of the Old Testament.* Vols. I-II. Translated by J.A. Baker. Philadelphia: Fortress Press, 1961.

Eliade, Mircea. *From the Stone Age to the Eleusinian Mysteries.* Vol. I: *A History of Religious Ideas.* Translated by Willard R. Trask. Chicago: The University of Chicago Press, 1978.

_____. *Images and Symbols.* Translated by Philip Mairet. New York: Sheed and Ward, 1969.

_____. "Methodological Remarks on the Study of Religious Symbolism." In *The History of Religions.* Edited by Mircea Eliade and Joseph Kitagawa. Chicago: The University of Chicago Press, 1959.

_____. *Myth and Reality*. Translated by Willard R. Trask. New York: Harper & Row, Publishers, 1963.

_____. *The Myth of the Eternal Return*. Translated by Willard R. Trask. New York: Pantheon Books, 1949.

Empie, Paul C.. and T. Austin Murphy, eds. *Lutherans and Catholics in Dialogue I-III*. Minneapolis: Augsburg Press, 1965.

Florovsky, George. *Christianity and Culture*. Vol. II: _Collected Works of George Florovsky*. Belmont, MA: Nordland Publishing Company, 1974.

_____. "The Predicament of the Christian Historian." In *God, History, andHistorians*. Edited by C.T. McIntire. New York: Oxford University Press, 1977.

Gadamer, Hans-Georg. "Die Kontinuität der Geschichte und der Augenblick der Existenz." In *Geschichte - Element der Zukunft*. Tübingen: J.C.B. Mohr, 1965.

_____. *Philosophical Hermeneutics*. Translated and edited by David Linge. Berkeley: University of California Press, 1976.

_____. *Reason in the Age of Science*. Translated by Fredrick G. Lawrence. Cambridge, MA: M.I.T. Press, 1981.

_____. "Rhetorik, Hermeneutik und Ideologiekritik." In *Hermeneutik und Ideologiekritik*, 1971, pp. 73ff.

_____. *Truth and Method*. New York: Crossroad Press, 1982.

Harvey, Van Austin. *The Historian and the Believer*. New York: Macmillan Company, 1966.

Herrmann, Siegfried. *Time and History*. Translated by James L.Blevins.Nashville: Abingdon Press, 1981.

Hickey, James. "Catholic Worship: Challenge in the 80's." *Origins*, November 20, 1980, Vol. 10: No. 23, pp. 357-363.

Irwin, Kevin W. *American Lutheran and Roman Catholics in Dialogue on the Eucharist: A Methodological Critique and Proposal*. Rome: Editrice Anselmiana, 1979.

Joint International Commision for Theological Dialogue between the Roman Catholic Church and the Orthodox Church. "The Church, the Eucharist and the Trinity." *Origins*, August 12, 1982, Vol. 12: No. 10, pp. 157-160.

Pope John Paul II. "The Meaning of the Priesthood." *Origins*, September 23, 1983, Vol. 13: No. 15, pp. 257-259.

_____. "Mystery and Worship of the Holy Eucharist." *Origins*, March 27, 1980, Vol. 9: No. 41, pp. 654-665.

_____. "Redemptor Hominis." *Origins*, March 22, 1979, Vol. 8:No. 40, pp. 627-646.

Keefe, Donald, S.J. . "Biblical Symbolism and the Morality of *in vitro* Fertilization." In *Theology Digest*, Winter 1975, pp. 308-323.

_____. *Covenantal Theology: The Eucharistic Order of History*. Lanham, M.D.:University Press of America, 1991.

_____. "A Methodological Critique of von Balthasar's Theological Aesthetics." *Communio*, Spring, 1978, Vol. 5: No. 1, pp. 23-43.

Kepler, Thomas S., ed. *The Table Talk of Martin Luther*. Grand Rapids, MI: Baker Book House, 1952.

Kilmartin, Edward J., S.J. "Apostolic Office: Sacrament of Christ." *Theological Studies*. 1975, Vol. 36, pp. 243-264.

Ladner, Gerhart Burian. *The Idea of Reform*. New York: Harper & Row, Publishers, 1967.

Lehmann, Karl. "The Focus of Discussion Today: Luther and the Unity of the Churches." *Communio*, Fall 1984, pp. 196-209.

Lindbeck, George A. "Lutheran Doctrine of Ministry." *Theological Studies*, December 1969, Vol. 30, No. 4, pp. 508-512.

Lortz, Joseph. *The Reformation in Germany*. Vol. I & II. Translated by Ronald Walls. New York: Herder and Herder, 1968.

_____. *The Reformation: A Problem for Today*. Translated by John C. Dwyer, S.J. Westminster, MD: The Newman Press, 1964.

Lowith, Karl. *Meaning in History*. Chicago: The University of Chicago Press, 1970.

Lutheran-Catholic Dialogue Group. "Catholic-Lutheran Agreed Statement on the Eucharist." *Origins*, January 11, 1979, Vol. 8: No. 30, pp. 465-480.

Markus, R.A. *Saeculum: History and Society in the Theology of Augustine*. New York: Columbia University Press, 1970.

Mascall, E.L. *Corpus Christi: Essays on the Church and Eucharist*. London: Longmans, Green and Co., 1955.

McIntire, C.T. *God, History and Historians: An Anthology of Modern Christian Views of History*. New York: Oxford University Press, 1977.

McKenzie, John L. "Aspects of Old Testament Thought." In *Jerome Biblical Commentary*. Edited by Raymond E. Brown, SS., Joseph A. Fitzmeyer, S.J. and Roland E. Murphy O. Carm. New Jersey: Prentice-Hall, Inc., 1968.

Milburn, Robert L.P. *Early Christian Interpretations of History*. New York: Harper & Row, Publishers, 1954.

Mowinkel, Sigmond. *Religion and Cult*. Translated by John F. X. Sheehan., S.J. Milwaukee: Marquette University Press, 1981.

Neuhaus, Richard John. "Ecumenism and Authentic Renewel: A Response to Paul Johnson on Papal Strategy." *Catholicism in Crisis*. December 1984, pp. 9-11.

Niebuhr, Reinhold. *Faith and History*. New York: Charles Scribner's Sons, 1949.

Nisbet, Robert. *History and the Idea of Progress*. New York: Basic Books, Inc., Publishers, 1980.

O'Collins, Gerald G., S. J. "Reality as Language: Ernst Fuchs's Theology of Revelation." *Theological Studies*. 1967, Vol. 28, pp. 76-93.

O'Malley, John W., S.J. "Reform, Historical Consciousness, and Vatican II's Aggiornamento." *Theological Studies*. December 1971, Vol. 32: No. 4, pp. 574-600.

304

Origen. *On First Principles*. Translated with introduction by G.W. Butterworth. With an introduction to the Torchbook edition by Henri de Lubac. New York: Harper & Row, Publishers, 1966.

Osborn, Robert T. "A New Hermeneutic?" *Interpretation*, October 1966, Vol. 20, pp. 400-411.

Pelikan, Jaroslav. "The Emergence of the Catholic Tradition (100-600)." Vol. I. *The Christian Tradition: A History of the Development of Doctrine*. Chicago: The University of Chicago Press, 1971.

_____. *Historical Theology*. New York: Corpus, 1971.

_____. *The Vindication of Tradition*. New Haven: Yale University Press, 1984.

Penaskovic, Richard. "Roman Catholic Recognition of the Augsburg Confession." *Theological Studies*, June 1980, Vol. 41, No. 2, pp. 303-321.

Perrin, Norman. *The Promise of Bultmann*. Philadelphia: Fortress Press, 1969.

von Rad, Gerhard. *God at Work in Israel*. Translated by John H.Marks. Nashville: Abingdon Press, 1974.

_____. *Old Testament Theology*. Translated by D.M.G. Stalker. New York: Harper & Row, Publishers, 1965.

Rahner, Karl. *The Celebration of the Eucharist*. Translated by John O'Hara. New York: Herder and Herder, 1968.

_____. *The Church and the Sacraments*. Translated by John O'Hara. New York: Herder and Herder, 1965.

Ratzinger, Joseph. "The Pastoral Implications of Episcopal Collegiality." *Concilium*. January 1965, Vol. 1: No. 1, pp. 20-33.

_____. *The Ratzinger Report: An Exclusive Interview on the State of the Church*. Translated by Salvator Attanasio and Graham Harrison. San Francisco: Ignatius Press, 1985

Riga, Peter. *Catholic Thought in Crisis*. Milwaukee: Bruce Publishing Company, 1963.

Robinson, James M. and John B. Cobb, Jr., eds. *The New Hermeneutics*. New York: Harper & Row, Publishers, 1964.

_____. *Theology as History*. New York: Harper & Row, Publishers, 1967.

Sasse, Herman. *This is My Body: Luther's Contention for the Real Presence in the Sacrament of the Altar*. Minneapolis: Augsburg Publishing House, 1959.

Schillebeeckx, Edward. *Interim Report on the Books Jesus and Christ*. New York: Crossroads Publishing Co., 1981.

_____. *Jesus: An Experiment in Christology*. Translated by Hubert Hostens. New York: Seabury Press, 1979.

Schleiermacher, Friedrich. *On Religion*. Introduction by Rudolf Otto. New York: Harper & Row, Publishers, 1958.

Schoonenberg, Piet, S. J. *Covenant and Creation*. Notre Dame: University of Notre Dame Press, 1968.

van Seters, John. *In Search of History : Historiography in the Ancient World and the Origins of Biblical History*. New Haven: Yale University Press, 1983.

Swidler, Leonard, ed. *The Eucharist in Ecumenical Dialogue*. Preface by William W. Cardinal Baum. New York: Paulist Press, 1976.

Tylenda, Joseph N., S.J. "Eucharistic Sacrifice in Calvin." *Theological Studies* September 1976, Vol. 37: No. 3, pp. 456-466.

U.S.A. National Committee of the Lutheran World Federation and the Bishop's Committee for Ecumenical and Interreligious Affairs. *Lutherans and Catholics in Dialogue: IV Eucharist and Ministry*. Washington, D.C.: United States Catholic Conference, 1970.

Voegelin, Eric. *Order and History*. Vols. I-II. Chicago: University of Chicago Press, 1956.

Vorgimler, Herbert ed. *Commentary on the Documents of Vatican II*. New York: Herder and Herder, 1967.

Wach, Joachim. *The Comparative Study of Religions*. Edited with introduction by Joseph M. Kitagawa. New York: Columbia University Press, 1958.

Weber, Joseph C. "Language-event and Christian Faith." *Theology Today*, 1965, Vol. 21: No. 1, pp. 448-457.

Wicks, Jared, S.J. "Abuses under Indictment at the Diet of Augsburg 1530." *Theological Studies*, June 1980, Vol. 41: No. 2, pp. 253-302.

_____. "Justification and Faith in Luther's Theology." *Theological Studies*, March 1983, Vol. 44: No. 1, pp. 3-29.

_____. "Luther on the Person Before God." Theological Studies, June 1969, Vol. 30: No. 2, pp. 289-311.

Wood, Susan, S.C.L. *The Church as the Social Embodiment of Grace in the Ecclesiology of Henri de Lubac*. Ann Arbor, MI: U.M.I. Dissertation Information Service, 1986. Unpublished dissertation. Marquette University, 1986.

Young, Norman. *History and Existentialist Theology*. Philadelphia: Westminster Press, 1969.

Zeeden, Ernst Walter. *The Legacy of Luther*. Westminster, MD: Newman Press, 1954.

Index

historicization, 70
marian character, 283
praxis
active suffering, 99
relevance and identity, 105
Roman Catholic understanding, 166
simul justice et peccator, 64
struggle in history, 109
unique claims, 153
Fallen creation
simul justice et peccator, 23, 164

—H—

hermeneutics
Christ as hermeneutical principle, 93
hermeneutics of a crucified God, 94
historicism, 23, 95
historicity
and the sacraments, 132
historical continuity, 33, 41, 63, 84,
    114, 271
historical continuity and the sacraments,
    121
historicity of faith and the Eucharist, 141
historicity of the faith, 3, 4, 6, 7, 8, 15,
    16, 17, 24, 32, 39, 42, 43, 54, 57, 61,
    65, 82, 137, 193, 225, 236, 240, 258,
    284
and eucharistic presence, 133, 271
and non-historical religions, 143
and the Christ-event, 158
and the Church. See Church:historicity
    of the faith
and the eschaton, 91
and the Eucharist, 141
and the New Covenant, 232
and the sacramental mediation of Christ,
    82, 121
and theo-drama, 144, 195
and worship, 145, 287
as covenantal, 230, 260
based on individual act of faith, 62

based on individual decisions for faith,
    39, 67, 220
Catholic difficulties, 292
liturgy of the word, 61
problem of fallen creation, 35, 113, 165
Roman Catholic, 221, 290
temporal existence as redemptive, 149
the problem today, 197, 287, 294
the Protestant dilemma, 289
history
and the fall, 148, 260
as interpretation, 84
as proclamation, 54, 60
as promise, 58, 64
as religious interpretation of time, 147
as sacramental time, 237
as salvation history, 239
as the self-communication of God, 208
only in Christ, 157
salvation history and secular history, 239

—I—

Incarnation
and the end of history, 213
and the historicity of the Church, 276
as language-event, 28, 49
as sacramental, 171

—L—

liberation theologies, 11
liturgy
and revelation, 237
and sacrifice, 179
as sacramental action, 180
liturgy as sacramental action, 271
liturgy of the sacrament, 7, 8, 9, 121,
    126, 127, 141, 145, 163, 172, 173,
    197, 199, 242, 253
liturgy of the word, 7, 8, 9, 11, 16, 31,
    38, 44, 45, 47, 51, 64, 77, 96, 97,
    101, 114, 117, 131
and the problem of history, 288
and the sacraments, 51

as promise, 39
relationship of word and sacrament, 173
Luther, 18, 19, 27, 31, 51, 78, 165, 216, 294

—M—

Mary
Bride of Christ, 189
paradigm of the Church, 187
Moltmann
apporaches to worship, 98
faith and history, 109
Mystical Body, 268

—N—

nature and grace, 160
new covenant
as marital, 138
Christ as the new covenant, 138
new hermeneutics, 11, 12, 32, 65

—P—

proclamation, 15, 18, 20, 24, 25, 30, 31, 32, 33, 34, 35, 36, 47, 49, 50, 52, 53, 54, 63, 98, 175, 288
and the cross of Christ, 107
and the crucified God, 96
and the future, 57, 112
and the sacraments, 176
as a time of love, 58
as language-event, 27
as promise, 57, 113
in the Church, 198
primary mediation of Christ-event, 22
sacramental function, 247
simul justice et peccator, 96
Eucharist, 97
Protestant Theology
problem of faith and history, 11, 117
problem with Catholics on the sacraments, 164
Protestantism

and the sacramental nature of the faith, 118

—R—

revelation, 22, 24, 32, 33, 34, 47, 48, 49, 50, 51, 194, 257, 266
and creation, 209
and fallen creation, 58
and historical religions, 144
and proclamation, 96
and salvation history, 209
and secular history, 71, 87
and the Church, 6, 176, 221
and the Word of God, 175
as act, 145, 226, 256
as historical, 146
as language, 19, 48
as salvation history, 68, 206, 209
as the norm for faith, 192
as theo-drama, 145
as word-event, 29
God's actions, 146
trinitarian revelation in Christ, 110
word-event as action, 74
Revelation as word-event, 26
Roman Catholic, 18
and the liturgy of the sacrament, 119, 199
on Protestant ecclesiology, 215
the historicity of the faith, 119
Roman Catholic worship, 98

—S—

Sacrament
and salvation history, 200
sacramental presence as miracles, 80
sacramental nature of creation
theo-drama, 169
sacramental realism
ex opere operato, 20, 199
sacraments
and salvation history, 77
and the Church, 246